# LETTERS TO HIS WIFE

Da Capo Press Music Reprint Series

GENERAL EDITOR

ROLAND JACKSON

# FERRUCCIO BUSONI

———

# LETTERS TO HIS WIFE

*Translated by*

ROSAMOND LEY

DA CAPO PRESS • NEW YORK • 1975

Library of Congress Cataloging in Publication Data

Busoni, Ferruccio Benvenuto, 1866-1924.
Letters to his wife.

(Da Capo Press music reprint series)
Translation of Busoni: Briefe an seine Frau.
Reprint of the 1938 ed. published by E. Arnold,
London.
Includes index.
1. Busoni, Ferruccio Benvenuto, 1866-1924.
2. Busoni, Gerda (Sjöstrand) 3. Composers—Corre-
spondence, reminiscences, etc. I. Busoni, Gerda
(Sjöstrand)
ML410.B98A33    1975        780'.92'4 [B]        74-34378
ISBN 0-306-70732-2

# BUSONI

*Letters to His Wife*

BUSONI, 1922

# FERRUCCIO BUSONI

## LETTERS TO HIS WIFE

*Translated by*
### ROSAMOND LEY

**LONDON**
EDWARD ARNOLD & CO.

PRINTED IN GREAT BRITAIN BY
BUTLER AND TANNER LTD., FROME AND LONDON

# LIST OF PLATES

(In the text are reproduced some of the drawings with which Busoni used to illustrate his letters.)

# TRANSLATOR'S NOTE

Ferruccio Busoni wrote more than 800 letters to his wife, Gerda. The comprehensive selection from them translated here was published in Switzerland in 1935. The series begins at 1895, since the earlier letters were all of a private character.

The start and finish of the letters have usually been omitted and the method of dating has been standardized. Any other omissions (mostly of personal matters) are marked by three dots.

Occasional footnotes have been added, and in the index short descriptions are given of some of the less well-known people mentioned in the text. References to Busoni's own compositions and writings are collected in the index under his name. The letters are addressed to Berlin unless otherwise specified.

R. L.

# THE LETTERS

# 1895

Moscow, 27 *January* 1895.

DEAREST GERDA,

As all the other hotels are over-full on account of a Congress, I am living in a new and small hôtel garni, where I have a small entrance hall, a small salon, and a small bedroom, everything in miniature, but quite nice. My windows, which are at the back of the house, overlook the beautiful church with the five golden domes. To-day, the combination of sun, hoar-frost, snow, and lustre of gold is most unusual, almost fairylike.

Yesterday evening had a magical beauty too (there was a full moon) especially by the town hall and the Kremlin. Truly an heroic romanticism reigns here—even the " Symbolists " could not wish for anything better. The feeling I had as I wandered through the town was like drifting on a lake ; I felt such a stranger, without foothold anywhere. I was so conscious, too, of being unable to make any communication with words. Even in a case of necessity ! . . .

My hotel is close to the School of Music. The new house is to be built on the site of the former School of Music ; so the Institute has taken rooms here temporarily.

I made my call on Safonoff, who was having a rehearsal. He received me in the most affectionate manner, kissed me and bade me most heartily welcome.

The journey was miserable. We almost stuck in the snow as I feared, but still all went well in the end.

Some sad news. Lesko [1] had a stroke and died four weeks ago ! Quite quietly. They thought he was asleep, called him, he didn't answer, shook him, he did not stir—he was dead.

Papst seems to have had a tremendous affection for him, and cared for him well. They say he cried at his death. . . .

[1] Busoni's Newfoundland dog.

II

I miss you very much and want to share the beautiful impressions with you. I think of you always and love and admire you continually, as you are, so simple and right. . . .

They only speak Russian in my hotel. Altogether what a difference here compared with Petersburg ! . . .

MILAN, 5 *December* 1895.

This feeling of being known and yet a stranger, which I encounter in Italy, and this character of the country and the people which I find partly attractive and partly repulsive, is so strange that it is quite indescribable.

The journey was very tiring ; we only reached the Italian frontier after 24 hours.

The route was monotonous, and there were only two hours of beautiful scenery in the Tyrol. It is a remarkable sensation, travelling through a narrow valley, dark with shadows. It all looks so cold, lonely and comfortless in the valley ; while a snow peak, standing up behind another mountain, looks quite warm and yellow in the sunshine. It makes one think that everything must be beautiful and pleasant on that peak, compared with the place where one is oneself. At night, too, with moonlight and slight fog, it was remarkably beautiful.

I had to stop three hours in Verona. It was midnight. A guide took me to a fourth-class Italian inn. I had bad roast meat and grand wine. Cattle-dealers from the neighbourhood came in, types in blue cycling capes lined with red, with " Calabreser " hats. It was like the second act from *Carmen*—without Carmen—and not very comfortable.

In spite of the late hour and fatigue and fog, I went through the town with the guide. It has a Roman amphitheatre, something like the Colosseum, which is very imposing ; (it holds seventy thousand people). The houses, the tombs of Romeo and Juliet, all the best Renaissance style. . . .

The Board of the society for which I am playing is very highly esteemed. The Directors are very conscientious (so they say), and permit no transcriptions in their programme. I was obliged, therefore, to withdraw the Tannhäuser Overture. But when I said that the Bach organ fugue was also a transcription they said it would be better not to mention that in the programme . . . What do you think of all this, dear wife ? ! !

One seems to avoid ordinary expressions here altogether. I was not a little astonished when I saw put up on the closet door in my hotel : " Jardin "—A garden where only cactus bloom ! ... It is strange what a childish pleasure it gives me to speak Italian ; to be a foreigner and yet not one.

MILAN, 7 *December* 1895.

A thousand thanks for your dear letters, they are a comfort to me in the dejected mood in which I drag myself round here in spite of my efforts to overcome it.

I sit in the hotel at a miserable upright piano, with a bad cigar in my mouth, in an unheated room. The cool, almost hostile—at least mistrustful—way in which they have received me here, has disappointed me very much. It took the whole strength of my ability and will-power to win the public yesterday evening. I succeeded in the end, and to-day the papers, with one accord, are full of enthusiasm. I believe that the Società del Quartetto feared I might be the cause of making them look ridiculous. You will get an idea of the efficiency of the orchestra and the conductor if I say that, compared with them, the Gewandhaus in Reinecke's time would pass as an ideal of perfection and importance. The conditions are hopeless at present. Just to raise the country to the level of attainment in knowledge and belief reached long ago by Germany, would be an immense piece of work. And by the time this was achieved the other countries would again be ahead.

From a literary standpoint things do not look any better ; with the exception of the philosophical dramas of Bovio (a Tolstoi without the Russian's ease and clarity) nothing of importance has appeared in ten years.

I shall get away and thank God I shall soon be with you again.

PARMA, 9 *December* 1895.

The little town of Parma (home of the well-known Parmesan cheese, as well as that of the painter Correggio ; Paganini's tomb is here too) is genuinely Italian, which Milan is *not*, and it has pleased me best. Here one sees abbés, asses and other features of local colour in Italy.

The wine is unrivalled, the population ignorant, the place old and unprogressive. The audience was enthusiastic, unprejudiced, uncritical and unselfconscious, different from Milan, where they are much more rigid in their ideas than true Germanic people ever could be. . . .

Do you know that Paganini's son still lives here ? I will tell you more when we meet . . . I feel very far from you and deplore not having you with me. We must come to Italy as " tourists " and enjoy the old things, the food and the wine. Everything else is worthless.

And even that, without you, is only worth half as much.

# 1896

In Copenhagen, with a heavy heart, I was obliged to make up my mind to an *immediate* continuation of the journey. I did it with a heavy heart, because the weather in Copenhagen was brilliant, like late summer ; we have had nothing like it for months ! I might have been setting out on a holiday in the spring, as far as weather was concerned.

The stretch between Copenhagen and Helsingborg I really enjoyed ; the landscape (especially between Hilleröd and Helsingör) is glorious.

What trees ! And what autumn colours !

At Helsingör we quite overlooked the fantastic Kronborg castle in best Renaissance style during our unfortunate journey on the ice ! . . .

I was *obliged* to take a *sleeping berth*, the last night, in order not to arrive in pieces. (*These* pieces I should not have been able to play) . . .

I see there is an exhibition here by Walter Crane advertised in the " Kunstforeningen." Of course I shall go in the afternoon.

Nansen, Nansen, and Nansen !

Nansen—ties
   ,,   —cigars
   ,,   —hats
   ,,   —boots
   ,,   —stockings
   ,,   —lectures
   ,,   —" Fram " besög
Na'n seh'n Se mal. . . .

I rejoice like a child at the thought of the Tauenzien-str.[1] . . .

[1] Number 10 ; Busoni's flat in Berlin at that time.

Tschi, tschi moi ! . . . Have read that a certain Fernicio Bussoni is going to play here ! Who is that ?

GÖTTINGEN, 6 *November* 1896.
To be in Göttingen even for one evening is annihilating ! Arriving in the evening, there was only a choice between the theatre and the Rathskeller " where the town band played." In order to go *somewhere* I went to the theatre and remained until the end of the last act but one. In the streets it was as still as death, closed shops, closed windows, bolted doors. Not a soul to be seen. Half an hour later the people came out of the theatre. At first in groups, of 3, of 4, in couples ; they soon passed. Then the musicians with their wrapped-up instruments ; last of all two firemen. Then one or two more, then another, then it was all as quiet as a mouse.

Five minutes later an old woman came out of a gateway and smilingly enticed her dog to come in ; shut the door. Renewed stillness.

Now it was all over.

Out of humour I went back to my bad hotel, drank a glass of wine, and now I am writing to you.

The journey from Hanover was beautiful, the weather wonderful, and the landscape glowing with the most magnificent combinations of autumn colours. The sun was setting . . .

The town of Göttingen (so-called town of the Muses) numbers 24,000 inhabitants ; it is quite the smallest town in which I have played during recent years. In the past I could have collected a sackful of such reminiscences. My tour in the Tyrol (when I was from 12-13 years old) still remains in my memory, and during that tour a town like Göttingen would have been a culminating point.

My room is so cold I scarcely dare to go out. . . .

VIENNA, 3 *December* 1896.
Here is a pretty state of things ! Grieg ill, and the viola player in the quartet ill too ! As the Bohemian Quartet cancelled its engagement once on this account, two trios will be played to-morrow (if Nedbal cannot play) and I shall then play a solo

number (Brahms). Hanslick sat at the rehearsal to-day like an Egyptian divinity (he slept once or twice too), was very stiff, ceremonious, but charmed with me. (The comparison with Rubinstein was brought in once more.)

Vienna in sunny weather is always beautiful !

Rehearsed trios yesterday, idem to-day, practise regularly ; am very tired.

Think of you *every moment.* Frau Grieg spoke very beautifully about you yesterday.

VIENNA, 4 *December* 1896.

Your dear lines have done me so much good. A thousand thanks for them ! I have just come back from the concert. Nedbal was well, so we only had Tschaikowsky. *Hanslick* also came to the concert. Great success ! The hall was so full people were sitting on the platform. Great applause after the piano variations in the middle of the piece . . .

AACHEN, 9 *December* 1896.

. . . I read what Hanslick writes about me in the " Presse " to-day, " Busoni, a magnificent, delightful pianist, the only one who reminds one *entirely* of Rubinstein." It has given me much pleasure. . . .

I am living in an hotel which is Empire " through and through " but very fine. All the furniture is genuine " romanesque," made out of red wood with brass ornamentations ; the table with marble top and claw feet. The candlesticks are bronze like doric columns, each armchair like a little throne.

Two very beautiful courtyards, with cement pavement, surrounded by columns and arches, give an air of nobility. The concert hall wonderfully beautiful. The whole arrangement of the concerts here is " strictly according to Gürzernich." . . .

CREFELD, 12 *December* 1896.

There is a concert here in an hour. Yesterday evening out of desperation I played—skittles ! There was nothing else to do.

VIENNA, 20 *December* 1896.

I was able to lie down until 8 o'clock, then I slept again, sitting up, until 12.

On the way I only got a ham roll! In the evening I was feverish, had a headache. My number came at the end of the programme and I was obliged to wait in the artists' room for it until 9.30. At last it was my turn to play. (?) The success was enormous. They say I played exceptionally well. Then supper with Brahms, Leschetizky, Epstein, Door, and the conductor Fuchs . . .

Spoke to Richter to-day. . . . In the afternoon a reception at Gutmann's. Was obliged to play. Mid-day concert (philh) with Gabrilowitsch (he played excellently).

It appears that I am " the fashion " here. But in Vienna that only lasts until the next sensation. To-morrow, visitors again and invitations.

I could scarcely think of getting into a railway carriage again to-day anyhow . . . I am looking forward tremendously to being at home.

# 1897

. . . The rehearsal took place directly after my arrival. I was done up from the 8 hours' travelling, the early rising, and the lack of food during the whole journey. Added to which I played before a *full* house—the solos too.

The next evening (concert) I was quite fresh again. The Wanderer-Fantasy went *very* well ; the success was quite extraordinary, even clamorous. One finds there are always a few important people wherever one goes. The excellent *Herr von Dameck* (formerly in the Petri quartet—we met him in Berlin at the Auer-Tschaikowsky concert) lives in Elberfeld. A man of extraordinarily clear understanding and fine irony, cultured, and a philosopher of the first order. Then the eldest son of Herr von Hase was there, the future head of Breitkopf and Härtel, a perfect replica of his father. . . . The Ibachs live in the neighbouring town of Barmen (it runs into Elberfeld now) and they sent me a big concert grand to the hotel and invited me there.

There was snow, so I was obliged to stop in Elberfeld the whole Sunday unfortunately. One of the Directors gave a big party . . .

Shall meet to-day, here in Verviers, *Prof. Seisz* from Cologne, who is coming for a few days' recreation. A fine, friendly man. Mengelberg's teacher. . . . I shall be with you again soon, at which I rejoice like a child. . . . In Elberfeld I got 100 mk. more than I expected ! Always onwards, always cheerful, etc.

LIÈGE, 24 *February* 1897.

I have a really pleasant impression of my tour. Compared with what I expected Liège is not like the Netherlands, but is more the type of the towns in north Italy. On the whole one is carried back about 25 years. Sometimes I thought I was in *Trieste*, sometimes in a town in the *South Tyrol*. The former can be traced in the look of the theatre and the cafés, and the latter in the appearance of the churches which are very beautiful and interesting. Hills and fortresses surrounding it give charm to the town. The streets are very narrow. It pleased me at first to hear French spoken everywhere . . . One gets some picturesque impressions here. In the corner of an old wall I saw a young Italian woman sitting ; she was selling chestnuts by the light of a dim lamp. That made a pretty picture. The church of St. Jacques is splendid. Chiefly Gothic, the back Norman, and on one side an extremely elegant Renaissance porch. This is not disturbing because it is all genuine.

A nice maidservant stopped me " Pardon m'sieur, est-ce que ce n'est pas après vot'e p'tit chien que vous cherchez ? Parceque il-y-a là un p'tit chien perdu." That is how the p'tite chatte spoke.

We stopped two hours in Cologne. But unfortunately from 9.30 till 11.30. I only saw the Cathedral in silhouette ; Cologne has the narrowest streets I know and the Cathedral looks like Gulliver in Lilliput. I shall have time, on the way back, to study this Bach-like composition in architecture. . . . The journey from Cologne to Liège (in a Paris train) was unbelievable. What dreadful carriages ! What noisy conductors ! What bad discipline ! They raced to and fro, gave the signal for departure two or three times, jumped into the carriage five times.—" Have you any luggage ? Are you going to Paris ? Is it you, sir, that's going to Liège ? " But, worst of all, these old carriages made fifty years ago ! ! ! I didn't arrive until nearly two o'clock and was quite done up. . . .


(*Addressed to Thale*)

BERLIN, 11 *July* 1897.

I had a remarkable experience last night. I sat down about 12 o'clock to write an overture and continued writing until morning. *I began and finished it without a break.* Of course nothing is perfect, and the piece will have to be revised. As it is, it is not bad, very flowing, and almost Mozartian in style . . . This achievement has given me pleasure, and you, too, I know, will be happy about it.

*(Addressed to Thale)*

BERLIN, 19 *July* 1897.

To-day the sun came out at 11 o'clock ! ! !  I could not bear to be in the house and went out into the sunshine.  This, together with your cheerful letters, gave me a happy day.  After a miserable week of rain—sunshine !  It was like a present of which I hope you, in the Harz, have had your share. . . .

I have been thinking about my overture the whole week, and to-morrow I hope to have finished the sketch . . .

Your lines have cheered me *very* much—no melancholy . . . kikili-putschinolli ! ! !

Old Thayer [1] (Beethoven's biographer) is dead.

WIESBADEN, 25 *October* 1897.

. . . The weather is glorious.  Everyone goes about without an overcoat.  One meets friends everywhere . . . Max Reger, the comedian Rosé, Mannstädt and, to my great surprise, amico Stolz, are here.  Happily he is in better circumstances now as director of the chorus and conductor at the Imperial Opera House.  It was pleasant to meet such a true friend. His friendship, I believe, is indestructible and unchangeable ; but it is well known one can be deceived.

I rejoice at the thought of seeing you the day after to-morrow. I have wished a hundred times that you were here.  I shall arrive in Eislaben probably before mid-day.

Was very industrious.  Everything is going well. . . .

LONDON, 31 *October* 1897.

When I arrived after a very good journey, during which I slept almost all the 18 hours in the most varied positions, the morning was foggy which is not unusual.  I was feeling fresh, happy and invigorated ;  with a certain feeling of optimism, ready to take in fresh impressions and to see the favourable side of things.  The sun was red and without rays ; here and there, in the landscape the tops of the trees stood out quite clear and sharp, and the trunks disappeared in a kind of whipped cream, so that it looked like a Chinese picture . . .

I have seldom been on such a calm sea, one could have played

[1] He had been a fatherly friend to the little Busoni.

billiards on the boat ; and it was so quick that we arrived half an hour " before time."

The first impression of London is thoroughly sympathetic, and quite as I expected it to be. It is a really big city, whose size does not lie only in its dimension and population. In every direction the streets are lively, and when one district ends another begins. The omnibus traffic is confusing—the way in which the conductors (without uniform) invite the people to get in is very comical ; they lean out sideways, and beckon with hand and arm, calling out the names of the places on their route at the same time. The hansoms—two-wheeled carriages, open and yet quite sheltered, in which the coachman sits up at the back absolutely invisible to the passenger—are the best cabs in the world ; they even surpass the Russian isvostschiks. The soldiers too, with red jackets, brimless caps worn dashingly on one side, and walking-sticks in their hands, are quite graceful and elegant compared with the Germans with their studied movements. The Scottish Regiments in their well-known national dress are very fine.

The book-shops and antique furniture shops catch the eye at once, because of the good taste and genuineness of the articles exhibited. Beautiful editions, however, are by no means cheap. . . .

In the streets one still sees original characters, figures out of Dickens, which give one pleasure after the average types one sees in Berlin and America.

The piano which Bechstein has allotted to me is excellent and so I hope, for the listener, none of my powers will be lost. I was welcomed by the same young Mr. Bechstein whom once I met in Berlin, and who awakened my sympathy so much. The architecture of Bechstein House is charming, and the whole establishment holds a very important position.

I saw Richter when I was out to-day. Regent Street (which is somewhat similar to 14th Street), Piccadilly (like 23rd) and Oxford Street (corresponding to Sixth Avenue in New York) are all in my neighbourhood, and one comes across friends there as frequently as in the Friedrichstrasse in Berlin, or the Graben in Vienna. I shall be glad when you come . . .

BUSONI, 1897

LONDON, 5 *November* 1897.

Yesterday evening (afternoon !) was a *very good* success, without being a completely enthusiastic one ; and it convinces me that *nothing* can be done in London with one or two recitals, but much can be done, perhaps, with perseverance. They say Paderewski and Sauer began in the same way, that is to say, with empty halls and moderately good criticisms. The latter to-day are full of respect for me . . . they are not abusive but do not praise sky-high. A young pianist, a new pianist, a pianist simply called Busoni, as yet unknown—that is how they all begin.

I must say I was a little depressed to-day with the feeling of always having to begin afresh, a Sisyphus of débuts. At the age of 31 this has not been necessary for other people, like Liszt and Rubinstein.

Certainly, here, I have neither
in society—nor
with the critics—nor
for the public—nor
in the shop windows—nor
in programmes
done anything to make myself popular. The enthusiasm grew after every piece yesterday, there was an encore too. (I played well.) . . .

. . . Oh, the so-called " cheap " books in England ! . . . This sigh comes from my heart : three days ago I saw for the first time a *really worthy* monumental edition of " Don Quixote," 9 thick volumes in *Folio*, in which are all the original etchings, engravings, even drawings and water colours, of artists of all times and countries who have illustrated " Don Quixote " either with separate pictures or in sets. There are even different experiments with the same illustration ; print, paper and binding splendid, price 2400 marks. Well, I shall never possess it. I must resign myself to that ; for if I had as much as 2400 marks to spend on books, I should buy myself a little library with it. . . .

LONDON, 3 *December* 1897.

I had a pang as I saw the train go out, and I have seldom felt so alone as I did when I woke this morning. *Radiant* weather, such as you had no experience of in London unfortunately, was a consolation to me ; really genuine Vienna weather, cold, sunny and clear. Added to this, I found in the " Daily Telegraph " the first really warm and detailed account of the concert. . . .

It was pleasant in the evening at Pagani's. The Koelner quartet was there (I know all the members of it, Willi Hess is the leader) and with them *Popper* and Arbos. The latter has assumed a great friendship for me. In order to profit by being here in London he thinks he wants a friend like me. He said, too, that he *must* make a change in his life now ; things could *not* go on as they are now, and he didn't know which road to take. A No. 1 self-tormenter and worrier. That led to the consideration of the English feeling for art in society. We came to the conclusion that we have to do with a period of culture that is over-refined, sensation-seeking, and shallow. In short, the standard of culture has *fallen*. It is an unhealthy state, chiefly for the artist himself. If one compares the mode of life of a man like Alma Tadema with that of Rembrandt, one can see where the fault lies, and it makes one shake one's head. . . .


LONDON, 4 *December* 1897.

Nothing has happened to-day except that Fuchs gave a very good turn to my portrait. But sitting for it is tedious and takes up too much time. Friedheim came to see me in the afternoon. I played Liszt's (Don Juan) Fantasy to him with which he was delighted. " Liszt himself could not have played it better." I also played Hexameron, Norma, and Stumme. Whilst I played he gave me some suggestions which were very stimulating. He heard Liszt play these pieces, revels in recollections, and in spite of that was, apparently, very surprised with my playing. He paid me the highest compliments. . . .

I am glad that I shall soon have finished here, but I shall do my best at both the recitals which are yet to come.

To-morrow, Sunday, there is no post, so I shall have to wait until Monday to get any news of you.

What a good thing you telegraphed . . .

LONDON, 6 *December* 1897.

. . . The concert went excellently ; the success increases every time.  Gabrilowitsch was there.  Hexameron (with Friedheim's hints) made such an effect that every variation was applauded.  After the theme, great applause.  *That* is how things should go, then one gets a little self-confidence. . . .

Will you not come to Vienna ?  It would be lovely.  Answer at once so that I receive the letter whilst I am still in London. . . .


LONDON, 8 *December* 1897.

. . . The success I have had here has been steady and unusual so that my return for the " season " is very probable.  Then you shall come over when I come and be here the whole time ; it will be lovely . . .  Grieg wrote me a very charming letter. Friedheim is full of admiration for me and agreed at last that even without Liszt I have " arrived." [1] . . .

[1] That is to say, without having been a personal pupil of Liszt's.

# 1898

CASSEL, 22 *January* 1898.

. . . The gallery here is beautiful, but it can add nothing to the impressions I had in Holland and London.

A *Turk* (full length figure) by Rubens here is first-rate, equal to Velasquez' Capitän Borro. Some Rembrandts are incomparable and there is a Guido Reni which has quite reconciled me to this painter.

Yesterday the success was *enthusiastic* (Erlkönig). Of course they said to me " *this will mean a lot with our public.*"

Cassel is very pretty—" *But one day you should come to us in the summer* " is what they say. Now I am going to Solingen. . . .

BUDAPEST, 2 *March* 1898.

At last I am here and know what I am going to play. The dogs never answered yesterday although I enquired by telegram. I sat at home, restless and anxious, and practised 4 things.

I met Rosenthal in the street yesterday; he came up to see me for a quarter of an hour and began to talk about technique at once. In other respects he is just as he used to be; after a lapse of fifteen years I have never found anyone so little changed as he.

The day before yesterday, in the evening at half-past ten, I looked in at *Ronacher's* for a moment.

A lady was singing; it was too serious for a Chansonette and not important enough for anything serious and tragic; but in some ways the performance was talented and refined.

Herr Schnabel is Leschetitzky's youngest hope—a fifteen-year-old pianist. He was standing next to me at Ronacher's, introduced himself, lent me opera glasses and programme, and told me the lady singing was Yvette Guilbert. In this way I

26

saw her without intending to do so and was able to make an estimate of her powers without prejudice.

The first impression of Pest on a beautiful sunny morning is splendid.

Have just arrived, there is a rehearsal in an hour.


(*Addressed to Woltersdorf*)

BERLIN, 16 *July* 1898.

I met an old lame man yesterday, clean-shaven, with long white hair, very poor and in picturesque rags. He had such a good, truly noble expression in his eyes, that he seemed to have sprung out of Hugo's "*Misérables*," one seldom sees such a figure in Berlin. I felt obliged to speak to him, which seemed to please him very much ; he was 77 and had been a gardener. One could imagine Linné looking like him. His mind was still clear and his speech distinct. He gladly accepted sixpence and thanked me with such kindly feeling that I enjoyed the experience for quite a quarter of an hour afterwards.

I found something else too, by Liszt, a *Capriccio alla Turca*, which is the original version of the later *Fantasy on the Ruins of Athens*, a very valuable and effective piece.

Finally : Chorals by J. S. Bach, edited by Philipp Emanuel, original edition, some glorious pieces amongst them, and the models for his Choralvorspielen printed in 1784 . . .

It took me an hour and a half to-day, just to write out the four programmes for Berlin ; with dates, details of the movements, etc., which had to be very exact. They will make a good impression. . . .


(*Addressed to Woltersdorf*)

BERLIN, 20 *July* 1898.

*Rules for practising the pianoforte*

1. Practise the passage with the most difficult fingering ; when you have mastered that, play it with the easiest.

2. If a passage offers some particular technical difficulty, go through all similar passages you can remember in other pieces ; in this way you will bring system into the kind of playing in question.

3. Always join technical practice with the study of the interpretation ; the difficulty, often, does not lie in the notes but in the dynamic shading prescribed.

4. Never be carried away by temperament, for that dissipates strength, and where it occurs there will always be a blemish, like a dirty spot which can never be washed out of a material.

5. Don't set your mind on overcoming the difficulties in pieces which have been unsuccessful because you have previously practised them badly ; it is generally a useless task. But if meanwhile you have quite changed your way of playing, then begin the study of the old piece from the beginning as if you did not know it.

6. Study everything as if there were nothing more difficult ; try to interpret studies for the young from the standpoint of the virtuoso. You will be astonished to find how difficult it is to play a Czerny, or Cramer, or even a Clementi.

7. Bach is the foundation of piano playing. Liszt the summit. The two make Beethoven possible.

8. Take it for granted from the beginning, that everything is possible on the piano, even where it seems impossible to you or really is so.

9. Attend to your technical apparatus so that you are prepared and armed for every possible event ; then when you study a new piece, you can turn all your power on to the intellectual content ; you will not be held up by the technical problems.

10. Never play carelessly, even when there is nobody listening, or the occasion seems unimportant.

11. Never leave a passage which has been unsuccessful, without repeating it ; if you cannot do it in the presence of others then do it subsequently.

12. If possible allow no day to pass without touching your piano.

. . . What do you think of these " maxims for Practice " ? They are formed from my own experience.


BERLIN, 21 *July* 1898.

Safonoff telegraphed yesterday that he would not arrive until Sunday evening. So I have not seen him yet. Because of this the " Fagottoff " (bassoonist) came at half-past one and played me a concerto by Weber. That reminded me of my blessed childhood, when I listened to similar things on the clarinet.

Have practised for six hours. The bell rang twice this afternoon, but I did not permit anyone to disturb me and I played at being a " deaf one " whilst I continued playing " die Stumme " (" the dumb one ").

LONDON, 11 *December* 1898.

. . . The first person I met here was Delius. He was very delighted, and exceedingly warm. Then Pitt, who gave me the idea (a good one, I believe) of repeating the historical concert with Wood. What do you think about it ? I shall come from Manchester on purpose to talk it over with Wood. . . .

I think of you every moment and look forward so much to being at home, to Christmas, and then to the Beethoven concert. . . .

LONDON, 16 *December* 1898.

. . . My sonata had such a success with Dayas and Brodsky that they were moved to tears. Dayas' enthusiasm, especially, passed all bounds and days afterwards, in honour of the event (as he said) he gave a dinner at his house (for he has a comfortable home and has furnished a whole house). Which dinner was given with excellent intentions and an open purse, but without much success. Only the Brodskys and I were invited. Brodsky had had some annoyance in the morning and appeared in a most morose humour. No word, no smile. Frau Brodsky had stomach trouble and ate nothing but came merely on account of " the sympathetic atmosphere " . . .

This London is beautiful. Last Sunday I went into Hyde Park for a quarter of an hour. There were men and women speakers. An old, very ugly, shabby and spectacled auntie, suddenly took up her stand, deposited a little box on the ground, took a bible out of it and began, in a singing, tearful voice, the introduction to a speech. Three people stopped to listen (including myself), then another three, and in the end there were about a dozen. Then she opened the bible and sought for a sign. There were many signs in it. On almost every page. She sought but did not find. She turned the leaves backwards and forwards. I thought to myself, " Now you will lose your dozen listeners." But the public began to be amused and waited with good humour for the moment when the sign should be found. The auntie laid her hand on the open book, and raised her eyes on high ; after a little pause the machine began to be in motion again. But during the pause the twelve people had dispersed ; for the point had passed. That is enough for to-day.

I think of you every hour, especially if I see something beautiful or am with good people. But I shall be at home soon . . .

# 1899

LONDON, 9 *January* 1899.

To-day (Monday) I decided to pass the day in London . . .
It was a brilliantly sunny day, such as one seldom gets here.
And a second sun shone on me, for I went to a splendid Rem-
brandt Exhibition in the morning. What a pity you were not
with me. I met Delius too. But now the toil and trouble begins.
I hope to get some pleasure from Edinburgh . . .

LONDON, 22 *June* 1899.

Yesterday I met Richter in the street and he took me to
a place where all Germans feel comfortable, namely, to
Gambrinus.

" Unfortunately, I was not in Vienna when you played there,
but I have heard that Mahler gave you a lesson in the rehearsal.
That is the limit ! He doesn't like soloists because he has no
routine and cannot conduct at sight. But a conductor must be
able to do that just as well as a pianist, mustn't he ? "

(" Sie, ich wor leiter nöt in Wean wenn S' g'spielt hob'n,
oder ich hob' g'hort, dasz Ihna der Mahler in der Prob' a Stund'
geben hot. Do hört sich do' alles auf ! Der mog kan Solisten
nöt, weil er ka Rutin hot und nöt von Blatt dirigirt, dös musz
ober a Kapellmeister a so guat können als wie on Clavierspieler,
gölt'ns ? ")

And so he went on talking about all that he had at heart . . .

Frau Matesdorf is charming, as naïve and good-natured as a
child, but she has caught me, like a commonplace flounder, for
a Sunday afternoon at home.

Still more about Richter. I said to him, " I congratulate
Vienna on your decision to remain there."

" That isn't decided yet. I must think it over well first. I

don't think I shall be able to stand it." (" Dös is no nöt g'sogt.
I wir mar dö Sach noch *sehr* überleg'n. I glaub', i halt's nöt
aus.")

" But the papers all give the news as a certainty."

" Yes, paper has patience." (" Jo, dös Papier is g'duldig.")
Horribly wet weather.

This evening the soirée, to which I look forward with as
much pleasure as a child to a beating. . . .

LONDON, 23 *June* 1899.

It gave me great pleasure to become better acquainted with
Ysaye ; he played with me yesterday. He is a *great* artist and
an amusing person, rather a mocker, but, as I said, an artist of
the first rank.

Without boasting, I had the greatest success yesterday in spite
of him and Melba ; " it was the success of the evening," someone
said to me.

I shall only stop a few days longer ; if Sunday did not come
between I should come sooner. I have a longing for home
although it is unusually stimulating here . . .

LONDON, 26 *June* 1899.

. . . Have been once or twice with Ysaye whom I like and
yet don't like, but who possesses a remarkable magnetism,
such as Rubinstein had, for instance. So that if he is impolite
or coarse one is not angry but depressed. He laughs exactly
like Rubinstein and is just as bestial, common, and kingly as he
was.

The well-known people I have met are, Carreño, Teresina
Tua, Camilla Landi, Johannes Wolff, Hollmann, and Muck
whom I have met many times at the Matesdorfs. The evening
before last, both the Mucks were there, Arbos and Schultz-
Curtius. I was in a mood for playing so I played a great deal
and played well.

I have invitations and rendez-vous from so many sides that
I cannot travel before Thursday evening. I dare not miss any
good opportunities just for the sake of a few days, however much
I should like to be at home again. I am not in a good mood
because I have done no work at all. . . .

MANCHESTER, 23 *November* 1899.

. . . My recital yesterday went brilliantly.   I played as well as I can play.   Nothing went wrong, and the enthusiastic success and the criticisms which have appeared already to-day, show a big step in the process of taking root in London.   As you see, for the first time, there is no censure, and the " Daily Telegraph " is very detailed.   There will always be a coolness in the tone of the newspaper reviews, for this belongs to a certain kind of distinction in journalism in this country.   I see that, not only in my own criticisms, but in those of other artists who have been well known in England for a long time.


LONDON, 29 *November* 1899.

Now the concerts are coming in rapid succession and the success grows.   The day before yesterday I had enormous success in Manchester ; yesterday in Nottingham.   It was very well arranged there ; only invitations were issued for it, and those were sent to the best public in the old town. . . . I have been to London in between. . . . Always playing a different programme is a great strain, but also stimulating.   Physically I am very tired, but otherwise *well.* . . .


MANCHESTER, 7 *December* 1899.

Yesterday evening Dayas and Brodsky played my sonata excellently. In consequence of the great success I was called on to the platform " to receive the honours."

*Everyone* sends you warmest greetings. . . .


LONDON, 8 *December* 1899.

How beautiful to get a letter and card from you to-day.   Thank you with all my heart !

Now the worst is over.   Until yesterday I worked like a dog. I was obliged to prepare the last programme (106 Beethoven, 4 Ballades Chopin, Polonaise A flat Chopin and " Robert " by Liszt) in a day and a half, but it went well, really excellently. And after this great effort came the evening soirée at the Matesdorfs.   Amongst the interesting people there, I found I was most sympathetically and quickly in touch with Sargent.   On my return from Scotland I shall go and see him ; he was pleased with my love for painting and general outlook on it, and enjoyed my playing very much.   Perhaps he will paint me, which would give me absurd pleasure (and you, too, I am sure) . . .

The 32 C minor Variations were one of the " most genial " (forgive the expression : at the moment I can find no other) of my new achievements.   The 12 Studies by Chopin were, this time, perhaps, more perfect than ever before.   There has been a tremendous amount written about me . . .

To-day I met Grützmacher (son, a member of the Hess quartet) who asked me to play with him in Bonn, the evening *before* Cologne.   Beethoven's birthplace is half an hour from Cologne. I shall do it. . . .


LONDON, 9 *December* 1899.

The " free days " after Scotland were very strenuous and this is how it was ; on the 5th was the concert in Glasgow ; on the 6th I travelled six hours to Manchester, was present at the Brodsky quartet concert and was invited to a late party (at Speelman's).   On the 7th Fuchs with his cello woke me in order to play my suite for cello ; in the afternoon Brodsky played my Sonata and the Brahms Concerto, and in the evening (now comes the best) I decided to give a private recital to Mayer and Dayas, in Mayer's house.   I played :

> Toccata C major.   Bach
> Adagio and Fugue from Sonata Op. 106
> 3 Studies by Chopin
> Norma Fantasy.

I have seldom played so well, and the impression which I saw I had made was a great triumph for *me*, a comfort and a pleasure. After the Adagio nobody could speak a word.   After the Norma Fantasy (during which Dayas' eyes nearly started out of his head) he sprang up and said, " What a pity that the ' Old Man ' [1] did not hear it, he would have given you his sword and died in peace." . . .

[1] That is to say, Liszt, whose pupil Dayas had been.

34

# 1 9 0 0

The following is word for word out of a French Dictionary (Larousse) : *Buson* (diminutif de *buse*) Nom vulgaire (!) d'oiseaux rapaces brésiliens du genre *buse*. Le *Buson* de Dandin est le buteogallus aequinoctialis. Le buson de Spix est une autre éspèce de buse, le spizigeranus meridionalis. Figuratif : Homme stupide (!) What sad notoriety my name has acquired ! So that if one says Quelle éspèce de *buson* que celui-là, it means, What a simpleton he is !

Now about Essen. Newly built and in modern style. The hotel here is magnificent. It belongs (like everything here) to *Krupp*. There are many pretty details, carpets and decorations . . . It was night when I arrived. The town has the peculiarity of look-ing better by night than by day : the darker the better ! (Now it is snowing.)

The manufacturing and resi-dential parts of the town are separated. The well-known church, built in the 9th century (vide Brockhurst) is certainly old, but only a quadrangle with holes remains and through frequent " renovations " is altogether messed up. . . .

There are old houses too, and narrow crooked streets. But

35

what is old and crooked is not always interesting. For example, not in Essen.

Und nun gehe ich in Essen, unter Essen, zum Essen . . .

ESSEN, 14 *January* 1900.

Oh—these provincial places ! I have passed two days of almost physical suffering here. These people, Directors, amateurs, connoisseurs ! This Krupp-worship, and this kind of " court life " carried on at the Krupp residence, which is called " am Hügel." These reminiscences about artists and the way their opinions are quoted ; and everybody's ideas after having read a Lessmann musical paper ! All these things and such a lot of others too ! I am so out of humour that I must give people the impression of being a stupid, sleepy person, for I am quite silent and retire into myself. . . .

COLOGNE, 16 *January* 1900.

Yesterday evening I was in a variety theatre for ¾ of an hour, where there was a new turn which made a certain impression on me. I have always felt drawn to marionettes, especially if they are related to a sense of mystery. This time there was nothing mysterious, but something in the relative perfection of the performance was very remarkable. On the stage there was a theatre in miniature, and in this a whole variety performance was given by mechanical dolls (so far as mimicry is possible without word or song). There was also an orchestra and conductor and boxes filled with the audience. There were *niceties* about this mechanism which were not understood and valued by the public. Niceties of observation and correctness, for the understanding of which an audience with an equally correct power of observation is necessary and this the public does not possess. For instance, the first number was given by a trapeze artist. The movements, the bending of the body, etc. were quite right. At the end, when he sprang down from the trapeze, he made another little spring as he reached the floor, which is what the law of elasticity demands. That is fine.

Then came two so-called music clowns. They had bells on their hands and feet which were made to ring through the shaking of the limbs. There were 8 bells. These were tuned so that a melody could be shaken (not played) on them. That also came off quite correctly. Just the right arm or leg shook at the right time and for the necessary length of time, as required by the melody. Then came the lady on horseback, and at the end 8 Ballet dancers. They were alone at first; then a " Prima Ballerina " came from the back into the middle. Everything very graceful, rhythmic, and with such close observation of life that it made an actually satirical impression. Added to this, the conductor conducted very exactly, according to the rhythm and even according to the character of the piece. And the marionettes' first violin and doublebass players bowed with precision. I was charmed by it. After the applause the curtain went up once more on quite a dark stage, and a " serpentine dancer " appeared, who looked and moved so like a real dancer that she might have been mistaken for one.

This small and illusory world made such an impression of reality that one felt one was living in a true one, and when the lady appeared who directed it all and to whom the whole thing belonged, she seemed to be a fantastic giantess. She was certainly as tall as the theatre.

When I came out of the theatre there was snow on the ground, hard, dry snow. This, combined with the prevailing cold, affected the people on the streets like champagne. First, some boys in a side street began to slide on the slippery ground. Soon a gallery of onlookers formed. Some of them withdrew from it, and began to slide in the main road themselves. The shop-girls on their way home from business were infected. Then it spread still more. Everyone, even men in spectacles, were sliding or trying to slide. They ran into one another, dashed into the one in front, or fell down. If anyone fell the bystanders laughed. Before long the whole street was laughing. There was a sliding, running, pushing, falling and laughing as if everyone were intoxicated.

I have seldom seen such a comical and lively picture . . .


ZÜRICH, 20 *February* 1900.
It feels as if one were in the south; blasts of wind blow the air up from Italy. But it is quiet and boring. It was lovely in Strasburg. I became very friendly with the Blumers. *He* is a splendid man, good-looking, solid, and straightforward;

37

one of the simplest characters I have ever known. *She* is a little philosopher, young and interesting. Both are very good and extremely honest. " As to the wines," they were too seductive. Of an evening we have often been " flûté " as they say there, that is, " addicted to quiet tippling." The concert went brilliantly and made a sensation.

These two weeks in Switzerland will be long ones ! For me there is nothing more agitating than quietness. It makes one want to jump out of one's skin.

Holbein's " The Dead Christ " and " The Woman with Children " are in Basle ! I am glad about that . . .

BASLE, 25 *February* 1900.

. . . My success in Zürich was so great that the Tonhallen-Gesellschaft invited me to give a recital on Thursday evening . . .

Here Holbein and Böcklin *absorbed* me. " The Woman with Children " and " The Dead Christ " by Holbein. There are some incredible drawings too. By Böcklin I will only mention : " Vita somnium breve " (Life is a short dream) in which child-hood, youth, old age and death are united in one picture. (In the foreground, two children play in the grass by a little stream ; in the middle, like a monument, the marble fountain with the spring of life. At the back, left, the youth on horseback goes forth into life, and in the foreground, right, the girl watches him go. Above the fountain sits a broken-down old man, with death behind on the point of taking him). What colours ! ! Then " The Holy Wood " (" Der Heilige Hain "), and his last self-portrait.

A picture with mermaids playing in the water round a rock. And others too.

There is a splendid cathedral here, on the hill, with cloisters and wonderful Gothic sculpture. There is a remarkable view from it down on to the river and the town. It was sunny this morning. Unfortunately the first sunny morning since I came to Switzerland. I am bringing something pretty back with me . . . (I am just expecting Otto Hegner to lunch).

BASLE, 27 *February* 1900.

The concert in Basle took place two days ago and I am still there. The season is fascinating, almost like late spring ; already sunny and warm. It is picturesque and old-world here, at the same time rather lively; like it is in the large provincial towns in Italy. That is why I have preferred to rest here for two days, quite unknown, rather than accept the invitation to Zürich or to Strasburg. The people believe that I have already left. But I must go to Zürich to-day, because of the Zürich recital . . .

General enthusiasm here, especially amongst the young pianists. Lochbrunner came from Zürich. Hegner was quite beside himself. I played the Beethoven concerto (have seldom played it so well) and the Paganini Variations, Brahms. Encore : Polonaise, Chopin.

When I see you I will tell you in detail all about two young sons of Segantini whom I met in Winterthur. They accompanied me to Zürich and will probably come to the recital.

The programme is :

> Bach-Busoni
> Beethoven 106
> Paganini-Brahms
> 2 Legenden (Liszt)
> Mazeppa (Liszt)

The S. with whom I am living are the only people who speak well of F unfortunately . . . That is why one should *never* have anything to do with small towns ! They resemble nice daughters of small bourgeois people who are attractive and agreeable outwardly, but who become small-minded and malicious in the narrow circle of social life.

The hotel in which I am living is large, comfortable, and in its way, beautiful, but it must have been built in the Biedermann (or Biedermeyer) time. The style of this period, or its lack of style, suggested the following reflections. This period must have considered purely *historical kinds of style* (in architecture and in handicraft) very much as we (in dress) think of historical costumes. We find them beautiful, picturesque and becoming ; but we should think it a masquerade if we dressed ourselves in clothes belonging to the Roman, Mediæval, or Rococo style. The roots of our childhood are in the Biedermann period, and in spite of my judgment I still think of a Biedermann room as a room furnished in a solemn, massive style ; and I get no feeling like this from stylised furniture, even if it gives me more artistic

39

pleasure and satisfies me more æsthetically. In my mind, a distinguished old club-house is always furnished in the Biedermeyer style (for example, the Schillerverein in Triest) or perhaps in " Empire " taste ; but never with artistically fanciful furniture . . .

LONDON, 20 *June* 1900.

The Tschaikowsky Concerto is over and went excellently ; but once, and never again. I felt as if I had on a new pair of boots ; they looked elegant but I was glad to take them off. . . .

LONDON, 25 *June* 1900.

I have wished for a long time that someone would write a certain essay and at last I have found it. It is—what do you think ?—an essay on " Mälzel's Chess-Player " and by no worse a writer than Edgar Allan Poe ! This is a masterpiece of logic and advocacy and gives the most incontestable explanation of the swindle. I am surprised that it is not spoken of more frequently. No one but the master of the " The Murders in the Rue Morgue," " The Purloined Letter," and the creator of Ann Dupont, could have arrived at such a solution with calmness, discernment and unanswerable deduction. Besides this, he is Goethe-like in his clarity of style and in his powers of description.

LONDON, 19 *October* 1900.

The 24 hours' journey which followed the concert was hard work after an incomplete night's rest. I was obliged to cancel my rehearsal to-day, I am too done up ! But London is always beautiful and it is a pity I must leave again to-morrow evening. The journey along the Rhine yesterday, from Frankfurt to Cologne, was beautiful too. We passed castles, ruins, vineyards, and steamers all in a beautiful light . . .

AACHEN, 24 *October* 1900.

It is a beautiful, distinguished old town, this Aachen. The people are so kind and refined. In the music shop they were charming and took endless trouble. There is a heap of over

2000 (unbound) volumes lying there in the attic, and amongst them there should be many old ones by Liszt.[1] . . .

This evening and to-morrow evening there is a Symphony Concert with *Marteau* (Sinding Concerto). Have not yet decided whether I shall remain. Perhaps ! Thank God I am free ! Unfortunately my spirits have gone down. . . .

BRUSSELS, 26 *October* 1900.

I remained in Aachen and heard Marteau's excellent performance of Sinding's Violin-Concerto. Of course I was noticed at once. The conductor Schwickerath even greeted me from the platform . . .

To-day I dined with Ysaye who has a beautiful home, beautiful wife, and beautiful children. The composer Fauré, from Paris, was there ; he played his own variations to us. I played Bach's Toccata and the variations by Rubinstein. I was in a good mood for playing, and both the excellent artists were charmed.

The 50th performance of St. Saëns' Samson and Delila will be given to-night. He is here himself, and I shall make his acquaintance, which of course pleases me very much. . . .

They are planning a recital and the promoters of the popular concerts are planning a commemoration for Joseph Dupont at which Ysaye and I are to be invited to play. The harvest of Liszt editions here was plentiful, I bought 36 unbound volumes. The next time you must come with me . . .

BARMEN, 2 *December* 1900.

. . . I was pleased to see the good von Dameck. Next summer he makes his journey to Iceland, where I should very much like to accompany him, for ever since reading Jules Verne in my childhood I have dreamt of seeing this country. Perhaps I shall do it. . . .

GLADBACH, 7 *December* 1900.

Three wet days ! And what rest could I get ? ! After the concert in Cologne I had to go to Mainz at midnight. I arrived

[1] Busoni was a zealous collector of first editions of Liszt's compositions. Of collections of this kind his was the most comprehensive.

41

there at three o'clock and at this hour, in the rain, I had to walk for half-an-hour to the hotel because there was no cab. In the morning I was awakened out of a deep sleep by a messenger from the orchestra, who was in a hurry because the rehearsal had begun already. A *Public rehearsal* ! At first I thought I would not play at all ; but as I was forced to do so, I played *pp* the whole time, so that the audience was hardly able to hear anything. (You have got what you asked for !) Steinbach, the conductor, brother of the great conductor at Meininger, was rather offended because I did this. As for me, by the evening, I was hardly equal to playing at all ; such a thing has never happened before.

And what a place this Gladbach is ! What places all these frontier towns are ! Wesel is still to come, but after that I shall take the first express to Holland !

I already count the days to when I shall be at home again. I have still got important work to do in Holland. In Cologne I had great success . . .

Thank you for your dear, dear letters . . . Write often. Be happy. Think well of me . . .

WESEL, 9 *December* 1900.

After travelling in a slow train for a couple of days, in Düsseldorf to-day at last I caught an express (D-Zug) with a dining car ! This cheered me a little for the time being. But of what use was that ? To counterbalance it I have hit upon an hotel in Wesel which is lit " by candlelight." The rain keeps me in the house at 8 o'clock in the evening and down below the streets look gloomy—gloomy, black and shining like the inside of an enormous eel and just as deserted. . . .

As the town lay on my " triumphal road " I was the guest of X in Neusz to-day. If one has met a young man in a foreign country there is always something strange about getting to know his parents and his parents' house. The analogies between my parents' house and the scenes from " Heimath " (by Sudermann) always return with varying nuances. Papa X is an odd person, weak, obsequious, and confused. He belongs to the category of better people ruined by provincial smallness and family cares . . . He looks rather like " the man with the dog's head " in Barnum's Circus, clasps the above-mentioned dog's head every moment

42

with both hands, as if in despair, saying at the same time in the most imploring and submissive tone, " Oh no, oh yes " or, ' Is that really so ? " Unfortunately the mother is unattractive . . . The sister is very ugly but is unbelievably good, so it seems, and clever too. She looks like quite a different kind of dog, taking more after the shorthaired races, something like an English bulldog crossed with an ape. Oh, a household like this is a misery ! They entertained me with their best and honoured me as if I were a guardian angel. But I was not happy and had to take great pains to suit myself to their intelligence and education. . . .

How glad I am about Lello ! For Benni, perhaps, you should buy the Märchenbuch des Jungbrunnen that is advertised. I think it ought to be good. It is just as important to train the taste and the eye, as to cultivate the heart ; just as important as all dead knowledge is unimportant. My opinions have finally led me to this conclusion. . . .

UTRECHT, 15 *December* 1900.

Yesterday morning was beautiful and sunny in Amsterdam, and I had a free day. I was twenty when I woke up, twenty in feeling, step, and sense of smell. Everything looked new and I made discoveries in details, effects, forms and colours, as one does at the age when one really *sees* things for the first time and imagines one is the discoverer of them all. It was a beautiful feeling, born anew, and I hope it will often come again. . . .

I lunched with Mengelberg. His orchestra is now one of the best in Europe. I expressed the wish to come often. He thought it would always be difficult to combine the 6 towns, so I suggested that on my frequent journeys through to London I should play regularly, but only in Amsterdam. He was very pleased about it . . .

I went to the Reichsmuseum with the Kindler, who was at the concert. For the first time I understood the significance of Rembrandt's third style more clearly and was deeply moved. But how long the road is to everything ! The old Elias too, and the younger van der Helst charmed me afresh. I was surprised at the impression Rembrandt's " Nachtwache " made on me this time. I admired the " Kleine anatomische Lection " (the boldness of which is only now quite obvious to me) and that miracle of colour called " Die Judenbraut." The good mood I am in was a great help . . .


ROTTERDAM, 20 *December* 1900.
With the co-operation of Mengelberg and his orchestra it was quite delightful in Arnhem, Haarlem. I have won the friendship of all these people. Yesterday Mengelberg made a warm speech about the " Great Master." . . .

# 1901

MANCHESTER, 25 *February* 1901.
Your letters have warmed me, cheered me, and made me
happy.  Thank you for them. . . . It is quite settled that I
shall return home on the second.  Until then

### Daily

concerts (as the billposters say in the " Biergarten ").  The
recital in London went very well.  But I am beginning to notice
fatigue.  And when I had given the concert in Brussels I thought
that the principal work for the winter was over !  I have still
about twenty concerts before the first of April, four of which
are in London.  Perhaps you will travel back with me on the
7th.  Everybody wishes you were here and most of all your
liebender herzlichst küssender
Ferro Mann.

LONDON, 28 *March* 1901.
Thank you very much for your dear letter.  Do not be disappointed if, after all, I am not able to be at home by the first of
April ; we will keep my birthday on Easter Sunday, which is
quite in order.  I am so overtired that, to my great regret, I
had to refuse to play at the Philharmonic concert yesterday.
On the journey back from Birmingham I had an attack of fever.
It got so much worse that, after playing at the rehearsal, which
I did with difficulty and from necessity, I was obliged to go
to bed in the afternoon . . .  To-day the fever has gone
and my head is clear ; the doctor says that I am in an
exhausted condition (without being ill), and that I must postpone my journey if I do not wish to experience the same thing
again.

We must thank God that it is not worse and in this way console ourselves for the spoilt birthday celebration, the money lost (for I lose over 2000 marks) and our meeting delayed which, for me, is the hardest of all.

I wonder if it will be possible to console Delius so easily ? I am very unhappy for his sake for I know how much depends on it for him. He should try to get a later date. But if the worst comes to the worst, the *whole thing can stand as it is for next autumn.* I have felt for a long time that something was going to happen but hoped to be able to finish here.

Please greet Delius and give him my apologies.

Give my greetings to all who may come with birthday congratulations on Monday. They will be disappointed, but they are warmly invited for the Monday after next.

I kiss you and greet you with all my heart, my dear wife. . . .

I am enjoying " War and Peace " and I am glad about the boys. . . .

LONDON, 30 *April* 1901.

. . . I slept on the boat as if I had been at home. It was certainly the smoothest channel crossing I have ever had ; incidentally it was my twenty-seventh crossing. Sunday was sad. I could get in nowhere . . . Finally I decided to go to the artists' room at the Queen's Hall and practise on the Erard upright piano. That was all right.

Colonne is quite aged, bent and bald. Was he not fresh and energetic still, with rather a military looking moustache, when we met him in Paris, or am I mistaken ? His whole demeanour is softer and more smiling than it used to be, but that hardly improves him. I felt so fresh and youthful yesterday evening and so full of ideas that it was difficult for me either to remember them or to write them down. The new little orchestral piece is quite finished in my mind, and I have worked at the concerto, also at the Bach edition and I have collected things for the essay. But my strength is not back yet, it only flares up, and after the Liszt concert, which was brilliantly successful, I could not sleep at all.

46

## A SHORT DIARY FROM PARIS

*Wednesday, 1 May 1901.*

Arrived at 7.15 p.m. Charming little private hotel on the Quai Voltaire.

Supper on the Boulevard at 8 o'clock.

To the Folies-Bergères about nine . . .

*Thursday, 2 May.*

On the search for Liszt editions the whole day. Begged for addresses from one place to another, and made some surprising finds.

To Bullier's in the evening about 10 o'clock. It was the opening day of their summer season. In a girl with short hair, hat on one side, pale complexion, and a cigarette in her mouth, recognised and greeted Frl. Teresita Carreño. Accompanied her home to Passy in an open carriage ; wonderful moonlight night, fantastic impressions.

During the day met Mr. and Mrs. Robert Freund at the Louvre. We greeted each other warmly.

*Friday, 3 May.*

Lunched at 12 o'clock with the Freunds in the Hôtel de Londres. Had a pleasant walk and conversation with Robert until 3 o'clock. After that undertook a round of the Latin quarter by myself.

Considered the most beautiful and stimulating part of Paris. Enjoyed it enormously. Looks old-world, picturesque and lively.

Was always on the look-out for Liszt editions . . .

In a secondhand music shop the manager was saying to a customer, " But when I went in for being an artist, I earned much more than any artist ! They couldn't play any of their tricks on me. You see, I have succeeded. And I don't care much one way or the other."

All this was said in a very loud challenging tone of voice. I begged for the address of another secondhand shop. " But, sir, I am the only person in Paris from whom you can get any Liszt ! " " How is that ? " " Well, whenever there is some going I buy it up. So you see ! "

And there was nothing else to be got out of him . . .

GLASGOW, 16 *September* 1901.

Of all English towns Glasgow seems to me to be most like those of Western America. (Chicago type.) As an artist one feels out of place ; what there is to be seen is neither picturesque nor interesting, only bulky and crude. It is too small a place to give a big industrial exhibition, and not artistic enough to collect a *beautiful* one. The present Exhibition is small and ugly (not so big as the one in Berlin). The buildings, the way in which it is laid out, and the people are all ugly. The hall in which I have to play three times is a temporary building. It is bare and insipid, and looks like a circus inside and outside like an overturned punch bowl ; (or a chamber in an unoccupied room in an hotel). I am afraid of these recitals at exhibitions and of the public which, in a sense, is like a Sunday public, amongst whom I don't know a soul and to whom I am an unknown quantity myself. The miseries of a virtuoso's career stand out clearly once more and I realise how much I suffer. . . .

I had the opportunity of practising on a Steinway this afternoon. My fingers never forget this instrument ! . . .


GLASGOW, 17 *September* 1901.

If destiny, through some devil's intrigue, were to force me to live in Glasgow, I should give up music and become an umbrella maker. In the noble heart of Scotland the position of umbrella maker is more profitable, more highly esteemed and, for the people, of palpable utility.

The concert yesterday was very much as I expected. On my arrival in the artists' room I was surprised by the Exhibition Committee's request (hats off !) that I should play the whole programme without interruption. I was glad really, but afterwards it turned out to be a strain. The public was very enthusiastic and numerous . . . Afterwards there were living-pictures, and fireworks in the park. This feeling of being a number in the exhibition is bad for one. Yesterday there must have been about 100,000 people in the exhibition, but what kind of people !

48

*Zur Zer-* **BROCHENEN LYRA**
**F. B.** **BUSONI**

*gewesener grossherz. s. Hofpianist*

**jetzt Regenschirm-FABRIKANT in GLASGOW**
— || —

*empfiehlt sein unerschöpfliches Lager von Regenschützstöcke, auch mit Spielwerk. Abnehmer von 5 Stück Koennen einen Vortrag auf dem Clavier hören. Bei Einkauf von 12 Stück ein ganzes Programm. Die Kunst ist flüchtig, aber meine Schirme halten ewig. — Sturmschirme mit Aeolsharfeneinrichtung. Billig!!*

GLASGOW, 19 *September* 1901.
. . . Yesterday there were about three thousand people at the concert. Great success. It's uncanny.

To-day I am going to the section of the exhibition devoted to art, which is said to be excellent . . .

GLASGOW, 20 *September* 1901.
Your Monday's letter *only arrived yesterday*, and it brought sunshine to my heart . . .

There is sunshine outside to-day ; after a stormy morning

with violent rain, the sky is clear now.   The change was sudden
without transition, and that doubled the effect.   But my confidence in the umbrella business is a little shaken . . .

But, the sun, the sun !   I see " ghosts " !   Visited the gallery
yesterday and sent you a book of illustrations at once.   Rodin's
work makes you feel that he is a citizen of a great city, surrounded by provincial citizens.   For simplicity and greatness
and psychologically too, nothing so important as his " John "
has been created since the work of the great Italians.   " Work,"
a picture by Brown,[1] is quite unusually effective.   Remarkably
well thought out and executed, but perhaps more remarkable
still is the way in which it is painted.   It reminds me most of
Leempoels, but it is gaily coloured and the effect of the sunlight
is thrilling.   It seems to me that this Brown (who is already
dead) must have been a man with very considerable talent, but
too much intelligence.

Yesterday morning I worked well at my concerto.   It really
will be something good I hope . . .

LONDON, 10 *November* 1901.

. . . Up to the present the few days I have been here have
been filled with work.   I only arrived at 2 o'clock on Wednesday,
and was obliged to do a lot of stupid little things ;   look for
somewhere to live, order a piano, buy the music for the Sonata
recital.   Then I wrote to you, and finally I was so done up that
I was obliged to postpone practising my fingers and the Sonatas,
which were half-forgotten, until the following day—the day of
the concert.   My fingers had become quite stiff, for I was frozen
and starving when I arrived.   On Thursday I went through the
things for two hours by myself, then for two hours with Ysaye ;
after that there was scarcely time for me to change before having
to play for another two hours in public.   That made six hours—
and without lunch !   On Friday I had to do a lot of thinking,
making six programmes for Newman, and I prepared for my
recital (at the Crystal Palace on Saturday).   I played well there,
but was quite alone in that miserable place, in front of a strange
and not very musical audience. . . .   One good thing is that
the piano here is first-rate.   Our playing with Ysaye was really

[1] Ford Madox Brown.

50

CARICATURE OF YSAYE, BY BUSONI
(at the bottom are Percy Pitt and Busoni)
(*From the original sketch in the Artists' Room at Pagani's, by kind permission of the Proprietors*)

beautiful, and clean too. The programmes I have drawn up for the Trio evening and both the recitals are splendid. I have put the Dante Sonata into one of them after all. So far I am well. I am only very, very weary and have much to think of. . . . Becker is a good artist, but does not quite fit in with us . . . I have become increasingly friendly with Ysaye. He loves me very much now and the other day was quite moved by the Beethoven Sonata Op. 109. . . .

London, 20 November 1901.

*Tuesday night* [19 *Nov.*]

Yesterday I travelled six hours to Newcastle, played in the evening, and came back the same night. To-day was a day of neutrality. Ysaye in Liverpool ; and I spent part of it in reviewing my life and drawing up the sum total. In doing so I thought of you very much and of all the good things I owe to you ; I thought of the invariable cheerfulness you have shown during all the times of uncertainty we have experienced together ; how you have always encouraged and trusted me and how through your sunshine you have chased away all fogs. I feel obliged to write this to you and to thank you once more.

I shall practise again to-morrow. I have to prepare something entirely new or half new for every concert here ; which gives me a lot to do because of the short intervals between them. I am writing all this on purpose. The distance between us, in time and space, is so great that it is only too easy to be deceived into thinking that our thoughts are far apart too. I wished to show you that it is not so—Goodnight, dear Gerda mia. . . .

*Wednesday morning.*

You will be sure to write something about my programmes. Perhaps you may still make changes in the recital ones. . . . " La vie des abeilles " by Maeterlinck is a book after my own heart. Pure, deep and natural ; fertile in ideas and original. Maeterlinck seems to be soaring still ; his feet scarcely touch the earth. . . .

Now I must study a very naïve (not to say anything worse) Trio by Saint-Saëns, for there is a rehearsal in the afternoon.

In order to refresh my memory I was obliged to buy a copy of the Weber Sonata and I took the Liszt edition " just to see " (as one says in poker). Many of the things that I have arranged and altered, which are almost self-evident, did not occur to Liszt. On the other hand, we have done some things alike. . . .

# 1902

. . . There was a concert in Birmingham yesterday evening,
in Sheffield to-day, and to-morrow in Manchester.

Ysaye was so rude to me yesterday, that I have had enough
of him. It was about the rehearsal for a piece by Saint-Saëns
which I did not know at all, had neither seen nor heard, and
had to *play the same evening.* Ysaye allowed me to wait for
three hours at Bechstein's. I sent a messenger three times and
each time the answer I received was, that he was asleep or lying
down. It was 1 o'clock by then (the train went at 2) and I had
eaten nothing. I went to him and told him that, under these
circumstances, it would be impossible for me to play. He
made such a scene that finally Newman, who was there, told
him that he was being rude and was in the wrong and should
be silent. It agitated me very much (as I was already in a nervous
state) and by the evening I was quite done up. We tried over
the Sonata (that is, we read it at sight) one hour before the
concert, in a shop. I was almost ill, as was inevitable, and we
played like two cobblers.

To make matters worse, the weather has been dreadful, to-day
and yesterday.

O England !

O Tunis !

But I slept for 10 hours last night.

We have not rehearsed for to-night either (a new programme).
But I shall not ask Ysaye to do it. You see how petty one
can become when one has to do with petty people. It is
lamentable.

The next letter will be better. I feel quite well in spite of
the provinces, rain, and cobbling. . . .

MANCHESTER, 6 *February* 1902.

Everything gets worse here unfortunately. I play worse every day, feel more tired, and more melancholy. These things are not for me. Would rather give lessons. I think of you so often and with so much affection. I think of you all. Should like so much to be at home.

If it goes on like this I shall be quite useless for Vienna. I am going to make the programme for Vienna to-day and send it to you for (1) expert opinion, (2) completion, (3) despatch to Gutmann. . . .

LONDON, 10 *February* 1902.

Many thanks for your dear, dear letter which I only got early the next morning in Newcastle. It has eased my mind very much and made me happy. Don't be upset with me for having given up the concert in Aberdeen (Tuesday). It was a *real* necessity. I had such an overwhelming desire for some rest ! I have, therefore, *three ! ! !* free days, which I am enjoying here in London. To-day I have done some real work once more ! . . . Three or four times more, and then 'tis over !

Ideas begin to come almost directly I feel free and that is the only true joy there is in life.

I have thought it out and decided not to use Oehlenschläger's Aladdin for an opera, but to write a composition in which drama, music, dancing and magic are combined—cut down for one evening's performance if possible. It is my old idea of a play with music *where it is necessary*, without hampering the dialogue. As a spectacle and as a deep symbolic work it might be somewhat similar to the Magic Flute ; at the same time it would have a better meaning and an indestructible subject. Besides this, I have planned 6 works for the summer, the principal one being the pianoforte Concerto. How beautiful ! Another thing is the publication of the " Geharnischte " suite.

VIENNA, 4 *April* 1902.

How lovely it was to learn of your safe arrival from your telegram, and at the same time to receive your good wishes !

On the whole it was a sad birthday in spite of the trouble *Gomperz* took to improve it at lunch, by means of a favourite menu, presents and friendly words. The picture of you and Benni stood in front of my plate, with a garland round it. That was dear of you. . . .

I feel very fresh and alive here and I have ideas. Unfortunately it is over now really, for I thought of going to Triest this evening (Thursday). Or shall I put it off for yet another day ? . . . I wrote in detail to Delius. Yesterday evening I saw d'Annunzio's Francesca with Duse in it. In order to complete my impressions of present-day Italy, I was anxious not to miss it. It is, I think, a superficial work. It seemed to me that there was not a single word worth remembering. Many words, sometimes beautiful and sounding well, but no thoughts. The people rather like dolls and costume dummies and the action twined laboriously round a small kernel taken from Galeotto's book. Beautiful, picturesque pictures but not by him. Transcribed, rather, from Burne-Jones and similar painters and by mistake painting and literature often change places. The success was entirely due to Duse ; she stood and sat like a beautiful picture, but is somewhat mannered. . . .

TRIEST, 6 *April* 1902.

Last night (Friday-Saturday) in Triest I had the following dream. I saw a new species (whether animal or human it was impossible to decide) ; they were small, not bigger than squirrels. They had lizards' bodies, with tails like foxes, only twice the length. I can't remember anything distinctive about their heads, except that their faces had a wise and human expression. There was a big hall. Big enough for them to move about in, and drive in carriages as if they were out of doors. The carriages were very elegant, kind of state carriages, and were driven one after another as in a corso or a procession. A great festivity was taking place. It was easy to see that they belonged to a great and ancient civilisation, by the way in which the ceremony was conducted and by their behaviour. I spoke to one of them and asked why I was seeing them for the first time, and why I had never heard them mentioned ? I was told that only those who had become pure in heart could see them. Therefore the faithful and naïve people of the Middle Ages had known them well and had had intercourse with them. (It occurred to me then, how much had been talked about hobgoblins, spirits of

55

the elements, etc. during the Middle Ages.) The refined
XVIIIth century had disowned them and consequently not been
able to see them any more. " But," I said, " how is it that
S. Francis of Assisi knew nothing of them, he must certainly
have had a pure heart ? " The answer was, S. Francis of Assisi
was certainly pure in heart, but he thought the vision was a
temptation of the devil and denied the reality of it.

That was the dream. . . .

LONDON, 4 *May* 1902.

To-day, Sunday, I wanted to go to Paris in the evening
because Ysaye and Pugno are going to play my Sonata to-morrow
afternoon, but I noticed that I haven't got enough ready money
and it is impossible to get any to-day. Ysaye says that Pugno
is in a blue funk and that if I come I ought to telegraph in good
time. To appear unannounced would be running the risk of
Pugno playing me a nasty trick and calling me out of the audience
to play my Sonata myself. . . .

We met Saint-Saëns who is as cheerful, sociable and lively
as a child, in spite of being nearly seventy. We have got to
know more of each other. He conducted his Prélude des
Barbares which I liked better this time.

Elgar promised me the first performance of the Overture and
Finale of his Gerontius for my concerts in Berlin.[1]

I met Nikisch just for a moment in the Hotel. He had had
an extraordinary success the evening before.

I played well myself (without a rehearsal) and was recalled
five times. It was the greatest success I have ever had with
Beethoven's E flat Concerto. Weingartner was very friendly ;
he was very much applauded too. Altogether the feeling in the
audience was very warm during the whole festival. Of all the
six concerts the one at which I played had the biggest audience.

My Sonata has also been played in Amsterdam (by Wijsman
and Spoor). . . . That my Violin Sonata should have so many
performances in such a short time is very stimulating. From
next autumn onwards, I am determined to be equally zealous as
a composer as I have been as a pianist.

[1] The orchestral Concerts (of new and seldom performed compositions) with the Philharmonic Orchestra in Berlin, which Busoni organized
from 1902 till 1909.

This summer promises to be very fruitful ; I am feverish for work. At present there is nothing settled here but it is almost certain that I shall be obliged to come again at the end of May or the beginning of June. . . .


(*Addressed to Stockholm*)

BERLIN, 11 *July* 1902.

. . . I have been extremely busy and find complete satisfaction in my work. Only the meals are melancholy. Nikisch remains with the Philharmonic (I thought as much) and I am to play at the first concert. Perhaps Saint-Saëns . . . Delius wrote a card—his score is being printed. Fernow is full of anxiety because he is afraid my concerto may harm the Philharmonic Concerts. I was obliged to talk to him for a long time before I could get this perfectly senseless idea of competition out of his head.

I must stop for the present because I am immersed in the Tarantelle which ought to be complete in its first rough form to-day. I am deep in it. Swim in a sea of triplets, beat the tambourine, stand on one leg (but not because the room is not big enough). This Tarantelle, following the Adagio, is like going into a thickly populated street on coming out of the Forum, or like a national festival in full swing in front of the Pantheon. The lovely song " e si, e si, e si che la porteremo, la piuma sul capello, davanti al colonello, giuriam la fedeltà " comes in very well here.

Well, much happiness both to you and to me (Lello is well and charming. . . .


(*Addressed to Stockholm*)

BERLIN, 17 *July* 1902.

. . . The end of my concerto has now turned out just as I wished. I have almost finished the slow movement. Both the " gay " ones are sketched out too. If only it will go on like this. . . . It is raining horribly now . . . The pieces which Remy brought are just like the weather to-day. He—Remy—has the defect common to all Frenchmen, of being patriotic. He likes to find fault with what is German and to praise what is French, although he tries to be just. But in this respect he is not altogether successful, for his Latin superficiality and impetuosity stand in his way. His judgment is always formed too quickly, and is clever at the expense of truth. . . .


(*Addressed to Stockholm*)

BERLIN, 21 *and* 22 *July* 1902.

. . . Life here takes its regular course. . . . Lello wakes me every morning—which is very charming and reminds me a little of Lesko. For three consecutive evenings I was in Anzoletti's company. I am very, very fond of him . . .

This drawing enclosed is crude and clumsy, but not ridiculous. I have a little weakness for it. It is the idea of my piano Concerto in one picture and it is represented by architecture, landscape, and symbolism.[1] The three buildings are the first, third and fifth movements. In between come the two " lively " ones ; Scherzo and Tarantelle ; the first represented by a miraculous flower and bird, freaks of nature ; the second by Vesuvius and cypress trees. The sun rises over the *entrance* ; a seal is fastened to the door of the end building. The winged being quite at the end is taken from Oehlenschläger's chorus and represents mysticism in nature . . .

(*Tuesday*) I have opened the letter again in order to tell you of my grief at the collapse of the Tower of St. Mark. When such giants come to an end it means that in everyone something comes to an end too. . . .


(*Addressed to Stockholm*)

BERLIN, 22 *July* 1902.

. . . There is a night of love, with a Serenade, in the Tarantelle, and a Vesuvius eruption too. It is getting on well . . .


(*Addressed to Stockholm*)

BERLIN, 28 *July* 1902.

. . . The Tarantelle will fulfil our hopes ; it will be very important. I have played some fragments from the Concerto to Anzoletti. He was visibly moved and could scarcely

[1] Later Busoni's drawing was used by Heinrich Vogeler for the title-page of the Concerto.

speak. That was a great, pure, and well-earned happiness for me . . .


(*Addressed to Stockholm*)

BERLIN, 1 *August ! !* 1902.
The Tarantelle will be Naples itself ; only the score will be rather cleaner, nevertheless not so clean as the other movements. At the moment it still contains *too much*, and must be cleared up again. But the conception of the whole thing is there. . . .


WIESBADEN, 21 *October* 1902.
Arriving in unusually beautiful weather in Mainz, early in the morning, gave me a feeling of liberation—the colours in the landscape, the Rhine and the wide perspective, the existence of which one forgets in Berlin, all did me a great deal of good. The Cathedral was an immense surprise, for no one had told me about it, and it is one of the best romanesque buildings in Germany. I sent a photograph of it to you immediately, so you will realise that I thought of you although I did not write. I was too tired to write. The night journey had fatigued me although I had slept. In addition to this, I rehearsed, practised, and gave a recital in Mainz and to-day I decided I would do *absolutely nothing*, which I hope you will not think wrong.

It was a great success, I played very well.

Little houses are built up all round the Cathedral, so that one can only see as much of it as is to be seen on the photograph. . . . Besides this, the town has some old things which are pretty, and it lies amidst glorious scenery, and the wine here is of the best. Wiesbaden, which is a mixture of a small town and a watering place, seems absolutely boring to me to-day.

The Kaiser was here until yesterday, and to-day there are half-dismantled triumphal arches to be seen, and heaps of flags and garlands lying on the pavement. The occasion was the unveiling of a monument to the *Kaiser Friedrich*, which is so miserable, paltry and conventional, that if it were to be taken down again there ought to be a splendid festivity to celebrate the event. . . .

# 1903

TEPLITZ, 9 *February* 1903.
Teplitz—Rain—Tiredness. To-morrow
I must go to London at 5 a.m. A good
Bösendorfer and old Bartusch (tuner
from Vienna) are my one little bit of
consolation.

I send you my heartfelt greetings.
Please write to London . . .

LONDON, 22 *February* 1903.
. . . Now I am looking forward to my last recital here.

6 Chopin Studies.
César Franck
6 Liszt Studies.

. . . A great change is taking place here (through my work)
in the feeling about Liszt. One paper wrote that they would
like to hear me give a *whole Liszt recital* (extraordinary for England)! Another wrote, that it was a pity I only played 6 Studies
by Liszt instead of the twelve, " the whole set which had recently
made a sensational success in Berlin."

LONDON, 24 *February* 1903.
. . . I am so looking forward to being in the south ! ! ! Even
though I am very tired (I have just come back from Harley) I
enjoy the thought of leaving an island which is an " island " in
every way . . .
I have made the acquaintance here of a young musician called
Percy Grainger, an Australian. A charming fellow, highly gifted

60

and a thinker. He became attached to me from the moment we met. He played me a very good Toccata by Debussy . . .


LYON, 12 March 1903.

My train only leaves this evening and I shall be obliged to travel to Fiume without a stop if I wish to arrive at all punctually ! Probably Carl XII never came out of Turkey because he suffered, as I do, from " Reisefieber " ! [1] and I understand and love him for it.

I have finished my Tarantelle in my head, and it is very good.

I like Lyon very much, the weather has been incomparable. The recital—so-so ; rather funny, they gave me a miserable Erard, which was put up on an amateurish platform. It seems that the people were " dumbfounded " ; they had never dreamt of such piano-playing. The tone of the place altogether here is very pleasant and serious. The town very lively, scenery very beautiful, parts of the architecture very good ; besides this it has half a million inhabitants (âmes).

Thank you for your dear company in Switzerland. I was very happy there. Auf wiedersehen. . . . Kiss the children . . .


VENICE, 14 March 1903.

Yesterday I travelled through the widest part of Italy, from west to east. It was strange to wake up and suddenly see nothing but Italians and only hear Italian spoken. Venice is sad, or it seems so to me. The sun has been true to me since you left, but there always seems to be something tragic about the sun in Italy—it shines on so many ruins ! . . .


FIUME, 15 March 1903.

. . . Italy went by like a cinematograph, but to make up for it we took 11 hours to travel from Venice to Fiume yesterday ; a German express would have done it in 3–4 hours. Arriving dead tired, at 1 o'clock in the morning I got a room " with a bit of a stink " in a mediocre hotel. Old Bartusch, whom I call Bartbusch, is my one happiness. And to-morrow I must start at

---

[1] Anxiety caused by the details connected with travelling.

five in the morning for Triest, where I have a difficult programme to play in the evening. It is not a pleasant prospect. Fiume is exactly like a little Triest. They are as alike as two boxes of bricks, one costing one mark and the other two marks fifty. I have never met such a similar similarity. Harbour with pier. Corso, and the mountain town, old and poor, with some romanesque remains, behind the Town Hall. The same box of bricks only with a smaller box and fewer bricks.

To-day, Sunday, military music in the market-place. A lot of hat raising on the part of the men, and affectedly genteel nods on the part of the women. Pretty " milliners," elegant, and without hats. But the confusion of tongues surpasses Triest. They speak *four* here and not one is pure. Italian, German, Hungarian, Slav.

Little steamers go to neighbouring places. They are ready to start. Smiling anxiously, elegant provincial ladies cross the landing bridges, loaded peasant women and family parties of the townspeople going for the " trip." The sun shines, inflexible and strong, almost threateningly. Abbazia, the artificial Nice, is very near, a quarter of an hour. They expect people to come to the concert from there. That, at all events, is an audience from a great and important city. On the journey from Venice to Fiume I had a sympathetic travelling companion, an old Hungarian painter ; fellow-student of Böcklin, Lenbach, Leibl, Defregger. A genuine, knightly old Hungarian, half-aristocrat, half-artist, with excellent artistic judgment. . . .

MUNICH, 31 *March* 1903.
The concert yesterday went very well. Weingartner was very pleasant. . . . It rained horribly. It is cold. My train to Salzburg goes at 8 o'clock. *Perhaps after all you will decide to come there !* I shall be 37 years old to-morrow ! And of these years I have passed 14 beautiful ones with you . . .

STRASBURG, 2 *April* 1903.
The way in which you have thought of me for my birthday was really infinitely good and dear of you. I thank you *so* much and should like you to know how I have thanked you for it in my thoughts every moment since yesterday. . . .

*(Addressed to Alt-Aussee)*

BERLIN, 12 *July* 1903.

. . . I miss you here and have devoted myself to work immediately. From the station I went home and at once settled down, mystically comfortable, in the *small* room where I make daily progress with the big sketch for the Concerto. And to make it perfect, I also work at the details every day. In this way, as far as is humanly possible, I hope to produce a perfect work. . . .


*(Addressed to Alt-Aussee)*

BERLIN, 15 *July* 1903.

. . . I shall go to England to-morrow. It has been a difficult decision to make. I have had " Reisefieber " for three days and all thought came to a standstill.

The Concerto is rounded off to my complete satisfaction, I have " dotted all the i's." . . .


*(Addressed to Alt-Aussee)*

BERLIN, 16 *July* 1903.

You must forgive me for what I did to-day. I cancelled both concerts in London on the 17th and 21st. That sounds short and dry but, I went through several bad days before things reached this pass. I have never noticed this kind of nervousness in me before. What I was most concerned about was the interruption whilst I am writing down the concerto. I felt that it would never be completed if once I were interrupted ; (nobody could understand the sketch made in pencil) and I thought, too, that the distraction would make me forget all the important details not yet written down. . . . Finally, I decided that I *really* ran the risk of not finishing the Concerto if I don't work at the sketch again until the end of July. Owing to this excitement (and having to practise the piano again) I have lost four days. . . . When once I have the Concerto clear and settled in front of me, I shall treat myself to a little journey. . . .

Please, dear Gerda, write that you agree and are not angry. I feel so free and am so happy otherwise. *I only wait to hear from you* in order to be quite joyful . . . Perhaps a little telegram, just to oblige ? would be very hurrah-ed . . .

*(Addressed to Alt-Aussee)*

BERLIN, 19 *July* 1903.

How good and dear your telegram is, how grateful I am to you for it ! I write just to tell you that with my whole heart !

Since deciding not to travel I have worked magnificently ; *I have written out the first movement in detail in three days !* I mean to make up for my little recklessness by work. . . . The piano, too, gets practised daily. To-morrow I shall begin to work on my orchestral concerts. . . .

*(Addressed to Alt-Aussee)*

BERLIN, 23 *July* 1903.

Work proceeds with colossal regularity, à la Zola. I enjoy it extraordinarily.

Your letters, when they come in the morning, illumine the whole day for me. I am quietly cheerful and have been feeling a little satisfied inwardly for quite a long time now. I shall have to start for England on August 25th. . . .

Hansom cabs have been introduced in Berlin ; rather broader and lower than the London ones ; they look very well . . .

The great Whistler is dead . . .

*(Addressed to Alt-Aussee)*

BERLIN, 25 *July* 1903.

I am in a good mood but rather tired for I have just finished writing down the 2nd movement : two movements (over 50 pages) in 10 days ; that is quite respectable. I play the piano every day. The work connected with the programmes for the orchestral concerts has begun too. Letters from composers begin to come in, or rather to stream in. . . . Forgive me for being short (not indifferent) but my head is like a barrel with Diogenes inside, without a lantern. . . .

*(Addressed to Alt-Aussee)*

BERLIN, 29 *July* 1903.

I am deep in work ; the working out of the Adagio goes smoothly ; but the Tarantelle will still give me many a nut to " crack " . . .

What I hear about Lello gives me the greatest paternal joy ;
but what is the son-and-heir doing ?

I enclose a portrait of Rampolla, this pontifical Bismarck ; a
wicked, great and unforgettable face. . . .


(*Addressed to Alt-Aussee*)

BERLIN, 3 *August* 1903.

. . . My thoughts are chiefly occupied with the concerto which
becomes more perfect and compact as I write it down. I took
in hand two little operations to the Tarantelle which make it
bloom still more . . . The big sketch is going more slowly than
it did, and that will make it easier for me to make the score
afterwards.

The weather here is cold and rainy like November. I long
for the sun as one longs for something unattainable.


(*Addressed to Alt-Aussee*)

BERLIN, 6 *August* 1903.

It is very important for me to get to the end of the third movement, and I hope I shall do so to-day. I have gone ahead again
and the nuts I was afraid of in the Tarantelle have been successfully cracked ; (without nutcrackers—with my own teeth ;
nothing but the nuts broken). Everything seems to be succeeding
and you will be pleased. . . .


(*Addressed to Stockholm*)

BERLIN, 11 *September* 1903.

When no telegram came from you on Wednesday, either in
the evening or late at night, I was seriously anxious. I read the
paper eagerly the following morning to see if there were any
mention of storms, delays or anything else in Sweden ; as I found
nothing I felt re-assured, and finally the telegram appeared in
the afternoon. I worked industriously. I have begun the
instrumentation and it should be worthy of the work. I practise
very industriously and do my correspondence. I hope with all
my heart that you feel well and that you are happy yourself, and
that your presence gives happiness to your family. I am with
you all in thought to-day. I hope it will be a beautiful day for
you all. Unfortunately I have been unable to get anything for

Pappus,[1] and have only sent a telegram ; but he will feel that the good wishes come from my heart . . .

(*Addressed to Stockholm*)
BERLIN, 12 *September* 1903.

What great happiness your dear letter gave me to-day ; I felt as if I were with you all and in feeling I took part in the re-union of your family.

And your beautiful dream ! It is almost Flaubert's St. Antoine. I shall keep the letter for it is not at all an ordinary one and not " miserable " as you think. Yes, I have faith in the concerto and, almost to my own surprise !, it becomes perfect in form only in the full score. It is going to sound well . . .

STRASBURG, 21 *October* 1903.

How life slips by one ! Days are like eels ; you seize them by the head, and they slither out of your hand by the tail just as you think you hold them tightly. I played the St. Saëns Concerto *after all*, for St. Saëns will be here in a few days and I did not want him to hear anything stupid . . .

The Concerto had a greater success here than elsewhere, for they do everything that is possible to please the French.

CHESTER, 9 *November* 1903.
6.30 p.m.

Just arrived in old Chester, cheesetown, the English Parma. Have still got an hour before I need make a leisurely change into shirt and dress clothes and take advantage of it (tea is ordered) to let you know a little about myself. The crossing was very good ; no sign of sea-sickness, everything went well and I slept quite tolerably on a bed which (to judge by its hardness) might have come from a penitentiary—a bed for sinners . . .

I found Draber in the Café Royal. He tells me he carries on a friendly correspondence with Mahler and will write to him about his fifth Symphony for my orchestral concert. That would be very nice. Mahler could then conduct both the Liszt piano pieces. . . .

[1] Busoni's father-in-law, Carl Sjostrand, celebrated his 75th birthday.

66

GERDA BUSONI AND HER TWO CHILDREN, BENNI AND LELLO, 1902

. . . Mahler has promised at once to come without a fee; but it will be difficult to agree about the programme. The 5th Symphony is not yet finished and the third, which he would like to do, requires women's and boys' choir, alto solo and the passengers from Noah's ark. As I have neither alto, tenor, nor bass Hippopotamus, nor chromatic snakes, nor pedal-birds of Paradise at my disposal—! Well, we must wait and see. . . .

It has annoyed me to learn that I could have played here in the Richter concert instead of being obliged to go sailing and tossing over to Ireland. . . . The critics in Berlin are very much on my side this time. New things that are good will never be recognised immediately, but this time my principle has been appreciated . . .

I undertook a big feat which has left its traces in limbs and nerves. Arriving here in the morning from Ireland, after two night-journeys there and back, I was met by Schulz-Curtius who asked me if I would play at the Richter concert the same evening for Hess, who had been taken ill. It was a Brahms evening, and there was no choice; the D minor concerto was the only possibility. So I sat down immediately for three hours, in order to get the thing into my memory and fingers.

There was a rehearsal with the Manchester orchestra in the afternoon: in the evening the Concerto went brilliantly and with great success. Both physically and mentally this was one of the most fatiguing performances I have had and it was very much appreciated (by Richter too). In spite of being nearly done for, I was obliged to go to Cambridge the next day for a recital. My playing there, too, was very good and fresh, but to-day I have reached the boundary line. I begged Marga to go to Cambridge with me. After the concert we were invited by Mr. Dent, who speaks Italian so well, to a little supper in his small, very tasteful bachelor quarters (in the University buildings) . . .

Dear Gerda, I hope you will sympathise a little with me over the exertion I have been through. I am glad I was able to do it. Mr. Dent's cheerful zeal to show hospitality and his naïve, agreeable modesty were quite touching . . .

There is a recital here on Saturday afternoon (Chopin), Tuesday, Liverpool ; Scotland begins on Thursday with Dundee. I
wrote in detail to Mahler and hope for an answer to-morrow.
Except for the Richter concert I have really had no artistic
pleasure here ; Chester, Crystal Palace and Dublin were almost
disheartening. The distinguished university audience in Cambridge and the undergraduates sitting on the platform revived
me again, and, as I said, had a considerable effect on my playing.
For 1½ hours I felt no fatigue . . .

PARIS, 8 *December* 1903.
. . . The crossing by day was so horrible that even to-day I
am seriously ill. The picture I saw when I arrived in Dover
was horrifying. The sea was quite dirty and frightfully stormy,
loathsome. The boat rocked uncannily even in the harbour.
One felt as if one were going straight into the throat of an angry
monster. I considered quickly whether I would postpone the
journey again for it looked as if one were going to meet death,
or at least a spectre-like uncertainty. But England, unfortunately, is an island, and one has to make this crossing *sometime* ;
I had no time to wait for good weather ; a decision had to be
made. I was on this terrible boat and the bridge was pulled
away behind me. We took 2½ hours and from beginning to end
and for three hours afterwards I was extremely ill and suffered
horribly. I shall certainly never go to Corsica [1] now ; I can't
run the risk of such an experience again !
In the evening in order to get some air I went to the Boulevard
and at the first corner I met both the Deliuses. They send you
many greetings. . . . Forgive me, I think I am not clear in the
head and write confusedly. What will happen to the piano-
playing to-day nobody knows . . .

PARIS, 9 *December* 1903.
As I have already telegraphed, I had an unexpectedly big
success yesterday evening. " Since Rubinstein we have not
heard such a fine pianist "—that was the general verdict. I was
and am very happy about it. I continued being sea-sick until

[1] It was Busoni's constant wish to visit Corsica.

68

three o'clock and was on the point of cancelling the concert—
and then I collected all my energy and practised for three hours.
In the evening I was fresh and played well; the piano was
miserable, mis-er-able, and it took a great deal of skill to make
it sound a little like my playing . . .

# 1904

On the journey from New York to Boston,
3 *March* 1904.

I am writing to you on the way to Boston so that you may have
the threads in your hands immediately on your arrival. Unfortunately they seem to have been cut for quite ten whole days
(perhaps more !). Parting from you was harder for me than I
showed and I shall never forget the feeling which came over me
as I waded through the ugliness of Hoboken in order to reach
that everlasting ferry. It was like a relapse in an illness which
one thought had been overcome ; for on the *Moltke* I almost felt
" European " and my spirits began to go up again.

It worried me too, that you had not yet started and that I had
no exact information about your departure. I begged Clark to
write at once and tell me what time the boat started. We had
barely time to pack and have some breakfast ; with both of
which Mr. Clark " helped " me with equal pleasure and taci-
turnity. Only once he broke out into a short but enthusiastic
hymn about you : " if he married it would have to be a woman
like you " (but there is no second you) . . .

In the train I fell into a deep sleep which lasted for three
hours. Then I ordered tea ; now I am smoking and writing,
and expect to reach Boston in an hour. I must ask you to forgive me for having given you some sad moments here, but I
could do nothing to prevent it and it was with difficulty that I
suppressed half my bitter mood ; you were always so good and
I thank you. . . .

BOSTON, 4 *March* 1904.

. . . Yesterday I led the ideal American life the whole day.
I waited till late in the evening for " ferries," " cars," " trains,"
etc. Finally I was quite weary.

Mrs. Gardner fetched me from the morning rehearsal and took me to her house which is indescribably beautiful, valuable and tasteful. It contains an *ideal* concert hall. All the beauty that I saw there was very uplifting : Venetian, Gothic, Titian, Velasquez, and a wonderful bronze bust by Benvenuto Cellini spoke a language to me which one does not hear in this country. The sun penetrates into every room in the house ; the big court is heated by it and this gives an impression of Italy ; it really was Italy itself. The programme I am sending contains the whole of my Boston history. Also that of the " Todtentanz " (by Liszt), (which was drawn up in 1839 and first performed in 1864. You see : " What is good matures slowly.") . . .

BOSTON, 5 *March* 1904.
The day was over-full yesterday. In the morning—rehearsal, then Mrs. Gardner, then lunch in the Botolph Club ; public rehearsal, wrote some letters and received visitors, finally in the evening at Gericke's until midnight . . .

Mrs. Gardner had paid over 500,000 Dollars duty on condition that she made a present of her house to the town. When that was all put in order, they found that she would *not have the right to live in the house which she had given away*. But as she went on living there they forced her to pay an additional 200,000 Dollars within 3 days. The woman is now almost poor. What she has collected there represents an enormous sum (there are so many rare books that they are hardly noticeable ; amongst them an old Dante edition which alone cost 2500 Dollars). She has one of the most beautiful Titians I have ever seen : " The Rape of Europa." All the columns, arches, doors and windows are *genuine* ; Roman, romanesque and Venetian.

Dear Gerda, I am writing to you for the *third time* to-day ; but I am so accustomed to telling you about everything I see and experience that it has become a necessity . . .

(To-day I'm off to Chicago—oh !)

On the journey from New York to Chicago,
6 *March* 1904.
Yesterday's concert was very nice, great success, two laurel-wreaths ; I played my best. But they don't understand it, and

it is almost useless playing to them; with the exception of Löffler, Stasny, Grünberg and Gericke.

Hale only speaks of technical wonders, but I have built up the Todtentanz from loose stones really.

The " Wüstensatz " in the Saint-Saëns was only sound and poetry (everything came off particularly well yesterday) and when writing about this he still talks of technique and nothing else ! Artists are only there for artists ; everything to do with audience, critics, schools and teachers is stupid and dangerous rubbish . . .

Löffler made me a present of a beautiful book by Whistler [1] (a rarity).

Mrs. Gardner was at both the rehearsals and at the concert ; I believe I have a good friend in her.

We had quite a festive evening. *Everybody* regretted your absence . . .

The Strauss concert in N.Y. must have been sad, the hall was almost empty and Don Quixote went so imperfectly that he had to break off in the middle and begin it again . . .


DETROIT, 8 *March* 1904.

. . . If there is a bookshop here they are so ashamed of it that it is hidden away somewhere. I travelled 28 hours yesterday (the train was late as usual, but only 2 hours this time) Boston–Chicago, arrived 2 o'clock in the afternoon, played at 8 o'clock in the evening (without rehearsal, it went well) and at midnight went on to Detroit . . .

In Chicago I shall only have a relative amount of rest ; I have to play, practise, finish the Mephisto Waltz, and invitations are pouring in with such importunity . . .

Whistler provided me with excellent company on the journey. How unjustly he has been treated and in what a coarse way ! And how rightly he feels as an artist !

I wonder every moment what it is like on the boat. I hope things are not very bad ; it is not much better for me . . .

[1] " The Gentle Art of Making Enemies."

. . . I am dropping with fatigue, *literally*, and must soon dress for the concert !

Beginning with the day you sailed, I have written to you every day ; one letter has gone already to-day. In thought I send you a greeting from my heart. Probably you think of me too. You see, Marconi did not discover wireless telegraphy.


CHICAGO, 12 *March* 1904.

Now to-day, Saturday, the 12th, you will soon " see land ! !" Daily and hourly I hope that the journey will be as endurable as possible for you—I wonder whether I shall get a telegram to-morrow ?

As I shut up my volume of Molière yesterday evening, before going to bed, I said to myself : I ought to be really grateful to Molière for having helped me over an hour. But the thought was scarcely formed when I felt ashamed and annoyed with myself for having had it. What ? Did I consider my life of so little value that I wished to get over an hour as quickly and unnoticeably as possible ? Is not that exactly the reverse of what I wish ? An hour ! Every minute can contain a special happiness—and the hours of my thirty-eighth year are—taken literally—*counted* ; I know that they can never come again and yet I thank this old French jester for having stolen one of them from me ! .But I must tell you about my dream last night ! I was in an old town (N.B. which I have seen 2–3 times already, in dreams, but which I have never seen in reality) and, from the top of a gothic tower, I was obliged to go down an *outside* winding staircase. I stepped through a window into the inside and came straight into a chapel where a service was being held. (I think it was " Catholic ".) Then—at a sign from the priest—a piano was brought in like lightning, half through the air, by three men and three demons. And that was "le piano du diable" (I know I thought in French). Then I had to play at the church ceremony all the most godless stuff that I could remember. I know that, amongst other things, I played the Kaspar-Lied from Freischütz and the Mephistofeles-Serenade by Berlioz. If the passages were difficult, then the thing played by itself. Like lightning it was carried away again. I cried out : "Stop, I must still play something *religious*," but it was too late. This

73

is all the fault of the Mephisto Waltz at which I am working industriously and which will be masterly.

At the Symphony concert in Boston I had two scores in my hands, the " Elijah " by Mendelssohn and " L'Enfance du Christ " by Berlioz. There are such amazing moments in the second less well-known one, that (in spite of being an old expert) I gaped and was almost left with my mouth permanently open.

Yesterday I went to the class held by Mr. S. It was a repetition of what happened at the Conservatorium at Helsingfors. A

MAP
of the
BUSU
of the
UNITED
STATES
showing the
long and
dolorous Tour,
the anti-
sentimental
journey of
F.B. 1904 Chicago
MICHIGAN
→ Boston
Buff'd
Cincinnati

youth and two silly geese of girls played—the master made a slightly embarrassed, half-humorous speech, and finally seated himself at the piano. The poor fellow could do nothing. But the geese gobbled delightedly, the master made a few ironical remarks about himself, renewed delight, oh ! oh !, but to me he complained that he was not in practice whereupon I said I had noticed nothing.

The day before yesterday I spent the evening at Consul Graf Roswadowsky's. *Excellent* people ; they both possess the noblest simplicity. Wonderful Italian food. With Ganz I played les Préludes and Mazeppa on 2 pianos. . . .

I have booked a cabin on the *Blücher* already.   Joyful, most joyful meeting. . . .

CHICAGO, 15 *March* 1904.
. . . Yesterday I went to the Walküre . . .   But what a disappointment it was, after many years, for me to hear this work again.   How poor and empty it seemed and how cheap !   (There are only about four motives in the whole piece and three effective endings to acts.   Possibly this discouraging impression makes me exaggerate, but to me it seems to be " ageing " rapidly. When I think of Don Giovanni, which is 115 years old, there is no comparison.   The performance was weak in spite of such artists as Burgstaller, van Rooy, and Ternina all taking part. How seldom can an artist do what he is capable of doing at a given moment, and this time they were all tired and had colds. Result :   I was in the dumps about everything connected with the stage.   Mottl, who conducted and held *everything* together (I admired him very much this time) warned me seriously not to come.   And he was right. . . .

CINCINNATI, 17 *March* 1904.
Here I am at Cincinnati !   Last concert but one the day after to-morrow.   I was very satisfied in Chicago ; they fully appreciated me.   Both the Roswadowskys are charming.   He is not deep or intellectual, but in goodness, noblesse and simplicity a genuine nobleman . . .

CINCINNATI, 18 *March* 1904.
What a metropolis Cincinnati is compared with Indianapolis ! But how differently I *see* everything from 10 years ago.   How slowly one learns " to see."   How few learn it completely. I was told that in Indianapolis a lot of the niggers mix with the Indian women and this produces a type like Satan incarnate.

The last day in Chicago, I over-tired myself by playing Norma, Sonnambula, Variations by Rubinstein and the Mephisto Waltz twice, to Ganz and Schiller, and it was on the same day that I *wrote for six hours at the transcription.*   Well, it serves me right.

75

Just think I have only 5 more days here ! ! ! ! !

May our next meeting be as soon and as joyful as possible . . . Tschi-pu-li-ki ! ! (which in Japanese means : Dein sehr liebender).

FERROMANN.

ROCHESTER, 21 March 1904.

Although the last concert takes place here to-day I feel quite " awfully unwell." What can one do, or even *think*, in such a barbaric hole ? The hotels are the most entertaining places. This Auditorium Hotel provides for all tastes ; it has a theatre, concert, restaurant with elegant women, bars, newspapers, cigars. . . . To me the chief difference between Englishmen and Americans seems to be : that the first are always silent and the others always babble. This is most noticeable when travelling. I was looking at a magazine to-day with portraits of prominent Englishmen who lived in the 'forties. These types of " faces " are very different.

There is an essay on Strauss in the same magazine, by a man called Huneker, and what he says about Wagner is very good. He says that Wagner was complete in himself, but Liszt " was the torchbearer " for progress ; also that Wagner's importance lies in his *music* and not in his reforms.

What Whistler says is very good too ; he says that the artist has to *choose* ; that there is *everything* in nature and only the artist's *choice* can make a *picture* out of it ; just as the keyboard contains all tones and they only become music when they are grouped together.

To-day I write the word finis under America. With how much greater pleasure shall I place the word under my concerto ! I plan to do Aladdin, Ahasuerus and the second part of the Wohltemperierte Clavier.

It is unnecessary to say how much I look forward to everything at home. Sad, that I hear nothing from you, whilst you will have my news up to the day of my arrival . . .

Not quite a day-book and not quite a night-book : Sketches on board the *Blücher* during the crossing from New-York to Cuxhaven : 24 March to 3 April 1904. Ferruccio Busoni.

Although the weather was more or less unfavourable as long as I was in America, I awoke on the morning of my departure with the most brilliant day before my eyes. Everything was sunshine and brightness, the air warm yet crisp, the town appeared to be renewed. This, and the thought of departure, put me into one of those infinitely rare, almost unreal, conditions of the soul which makes every detail seem delightful and interesting.

This condition makes one see many things as if for the first time in life, and that lends one a deceptive feeling of youth. My carriage drove through a quiet and distinguished quarter of Hoboken, which pleased me so much that for a moment I almost felt a desire to stay. Animated life on board, farewell scenes, both melancholy and joyful, and both suffused with this sun, enlivening everything and giving rather an air of festivity to the whole scene. As the steamer began to move, the band played an old German song very full of feeling, and below, hundreds of people close together, all waving handkerchiefs, were apparently receding from us, but we steamed quietly past the highest buildings of New York, the Statue of Liberty and imposing steamers. Everything was enveloped in the sunshine and transfigured by it. Then I cried, seized by a melancholy happiness ; in a way exalted and yet so very sensible of all human weaknesses and the timidity of most when a big decision has to be made and the distance to be traversed is great. I felt that I was turning my back on a period of my life, on a big country, on a world complete in itself, too unceremoniously perhaps, and without giving it its due importance. I was excited by the prospect of the long wished for opportunity now perceptibly nearer, of again meeting everything dear to me ; by the responsibility of the new duties waiting for me, undertaken voluntarily or imposed upon me by circumstances ; by the fact that the next few days will complete a year of my life ; and I had an involuntary inclination to draw up a balance between what is done and what has to be done. I am always more vividly occupied with what has to be done rather than with what has been done, even if the latter is much the more difficult of the two. This is a source of perpetual restlessness in me.

I felt satisfied, this time, with the amount I have done. I have accomplished *two-thirds* of what I proposed doing this year (a rare percentage) and yet I tremble before the one-third which remains to be done, more than I am able to feel a sense of rest about the two-thirds which have been done . . .

Two days of the voyage were lovely ; sunny and quiet. On Friday afternoon for half an hour I had the enjoyment of *complete* rest ; I sat in the sunshine and enjoyed this unusual moment. But I was soon impatient again ; this intolerable passivity. One counts the quarters of an hour. And to-day, Sunday, suddenly fog—the whistle sounds and counts the quarters too. On board everything is crumpled together. If only I could do something in which I am interested ! I have had one great pleasure. I have read Stevenson. He is *great* : a storyteller, a thinker, a realist, a visionary, poet, philosopher, simple and complicated ; he has the grip of a master when he begins and his hold never slackens. He is new, original, but of the type that could just as well have been born 300 years earlier or later. He is deep without being heavy ; he is a moralist and above all a *writer*. For there are two important points : the artist must, before everything, be quite *professional* ; and far-seeing, too, beyond momentary considerations of time and space. Artists with these qualities are the ones who *remain* . . .

I have the score of R. Strauss' " Sinfonia Domestica " with me on board. Strauss is a person of decided talent and has rich gifts. Polyphony and movement are necessary elements in him. In this piece, the musical illustration misses fire (I have only read it) for the child's cry is the only thing not to be misunderstood, provided one knows the title beforehand. It is a long work consisting of small movements, and the movements of small motives. He uses much material from his earlier compositions. Like a family picture, it is very joyless, irritable, excited, restless. The score looks like the streets in New York. Its name is the only effective thing about the Oboe d'Amore, that old instrument, the deeper oboe ; but who hears the name when it is played ? The frequent use of a complete clarinet family, as in chamber music, must make a pretty colour effect (a family within the family).

A masterly fugue.

A Scherzo ; a cradle-song ; both according to recipe, without surprises. A couple of well-known climaxes, which come from Tristan. It breaks off frequently and begins again. Contains lyrical and popular trivialities (the latter by polka rhythms, as

78

used previously in Till Eulenspiegel, in Don Quixote, and Feuers-not). An admirable facility for making things complicated and spreading out what is small. Strauss seems to write out both the principal voices, then the principal middle voice, and afterwards cram in everything there is still room for in between. One can go on and on with that, but he does not stop in time. He does not understand the *mastery of the unfinished*. On the whole, a work for which one has the greatest respect, from which one gets much amusement, and in which there are many quotations (especially technical ones). This is as far as the first impression goes.

*Monday* 28.

Have read Stevenson with increasing admiration. *He does not repeat himself.* A bazaar of ideas and scenes ! He possesses the key to the problems of fiction like no one else.

I have read some short stories about Spain, France and Ireland ; also a psychological and a philosophical one. All through them there is colour, character and thrilling plastic art ; humour, seriousness, poetry of nature and human observation. And— above all—the *art of the writer*.

There is a beautiful Steinway grand on board. I dare not open it. I can never overcome this scrupulous feeling about half-publicity. (I should have a great desire to play—if only I were alone !) Besides, the company on board is unsympathetic and does not hang together. They all look at each other in a stiff, almost hostile, way. I have only spoken to one of them, an American sculptor, Niehaus, (a child of 58, but honest and an artist).

The fog has vanished quickly. The beautiful weather continues.

### ATTEMPT AT A CRITICAL ANALYSIS

In his novel " The Strange Case of Dr. Jekyll and Mr. Hyde " Stevenson has undertaken to embody (the word is to be taken realistically) an abstract moral idea : he begins his work with one of those master touches of fiction, which immediately sub-jugates the soul of the reader to the author. Through a long series of situations and mysteries, continually accumulating, he is not allowed to recover consciousness ; this is done first by the solution which tears asunder the knots of the secret, and—because it brings on to the scene *as a living person an idea which cannot be embodied*—assumes such a violent and grotesque form, that it would have brought an author of less authority and inferior skill to disaster.

The idea which gives Stevenson the motive for his work, and which is *nowhere expressed*, is as follows.

Every person originates from both the elements, *good* and *evil*. But if anyone wished to try and divide his individuality according to both these elements, *he could not succeed*.

Man can give way to his *bad instincts completely*, but not altogether free his good impulses from the bad. Thus the *better* person (if we now suppose two separated, distinct existences of the same one) will preserve his innate wicked inclinations, and cherish the longing to give way to these every now and then. This extract of the bad will produce an individual, who at the beginning must be *smaller*, *weaker* and *younger* than the original individual. Smaller and weaker, because the evil is only a part of the whole, and younger because this part has been put into action less, has been less used, than the person as a whole. But, whilst the person as a whole has the propensity to put his devilish side into practice, the bad, and in one way more perfect part of that person, has no impulse to do good because it knows nothing about that. But after each new trial, the pleasure taken by the primitive man in exhausting his passion becomes stronger and the desire to do so more frequent ; and the small, weak, and younger second person begins to grow, to become stronger and older and gradually obtains control over the first, against his will and to his despair, until at last he is overcome.

The form in which Stevenson clothes this deep idea I would rather keep secret here, in order not to destroy the surprise effected by the author on the reader at the end.

The German, E. T. Hoffmann, had the glimmer of a similar idea when he planned the figure of the goldsmith in " Fräulein von Scuderi " : but the problem was not so clear to him and he did not carry it to its final conclusion. Hoffmann's feeling for the fantastic and Poe's strength are united in this book ; the development of the action is romantically tense and borders on the sensational. On the whole, it would be difficult to meet with a more remarkable type of novel.

*Tuesday* 29.

Did not get up till 12 o'clock to-day. The boat has " rolled " worse and worse ever since yesterday afternoon. When it began I was sea-sick for 5 minutes but *not longer*. I seem to have learnt this art too. I may still find it very useful. Finally a " poker party " took place. This is a really good pastime here, as I don't excite myself over it.

*Wednesday* 30.

And now we have fallen in with a so-called " ground swell " and the boat either tosses or " rolls " horribly. I am not sea-sick but " hard at the limit "—my stomach has become suspiciously " dainty." The nights are very distressing, I get up from my bed every day, as if from an illness. And yet people always say that a sea voyage like this is a recreation.

It appears that nearly all the passengers here know me. And, of course, I shall be pressed, more or less clearly, for " a little piece."

When will one be left alone for once ?

I have never looked forward to anything so much as to the completion of my concerto and to the rehearsals and the performances of my orchestral concerts ; to my well-earned distraction. How many beautiful things there are still in my life.

This is the last voyage I can endure for the present ; my energy in this respect is exhausted and I have lost my patience.

I feel that my nerves exist, and like children they grow too much for me and could soon tyrannize over me. But neither children nor nerves shall ever do that.

How young our European music is, still only a few hundred years, and our culture numbers many thousand. There must be a reason why music develops so late. Perhaps, because it does not find its models ready-made in nature as the other arts do, and the first impulse—to imitate—cannot arise.

It should not surprise us, therefore, if the Americans still possess no art of their own in music.

The very lively sense that Americans have for reality makes them excellent painters.

I feel that music is nearest to the *abstract* sense ; in which the

Americans are still children and amateurs. Above everything music is *most nearly* related to nature ; *not to its forms, but to its being*.

31 March.

To-day I am already thinking about " to-morrow " which is the day we arrive in England. How clumsy such a great boat is ! It only reaches Cuxhaven three days later. I could not decide for a long time whether to travel overland to Berlin from *Cherbourg* ; everything considered it is more practical to travel further by water—if fog does not intervene. I am suffering from the effects of reaction now, both physically and mentally, and I feel more tired every day.

1 April.

I staged quite a good April hoax. At the Captain's dinner last evening it was officially announced that I was going to give a recital at 11 o'clock this morning. All the people, who only get up at this hour, were already on their legs at 9. *I was the only one who remained in bed.* I sent word that I was not well— unfortunately I really am not well. The food here is most pernicious. In addition to this a cold, exhaustion, nerves——
How could I have played ?
Have not touched the keys since the 21st. Now I am 38 and at 40 " the mountain is climbed." Which is worse ? The laborious ascent, or to have arrived at the top ? query. But I am not dissatisfied. If things go on as they are going at present and no worse !
It is the *land* which gives beauty to the sea ; it is only when the coast comes into sight that the sea acquires drawing and colour and seems bigger, too, by comparison.
I noticed this again as we approached Plymouth ; it was an extraordinarily rich picture.

Plymouth.

The letter from Gerda has quite transformed me—dear of her and charming—as always. Europe is beautiful and I belong to it once more—but its pettinesses are extraordinarily trouble-some, especially when one comes back from another con-tinent. The English papers give the music programmes for the week.

In London the Messiah and the Pathétique are to be performed . . . One might just as well be reading the papers for the previous years. In Berlin the Pathétique is being played and the vicious circle continues. And in New York there was a big fire again.


2 April 1904.

We arrived so late in Cherbourg (why ? There is no explana-tion) that we were only able to unload the passengers for Paris on the following morning—at 5 a.m., it is true. At 6 o'clock we started for Cuxhaven, so if nothing intervenes we ought to be there to-morrow the 3rd, at 12 o'clock mid-day. The weather is glorious, clear, calm and fresh.

Yesterday evening I turned over the leaves of R. Strauss' score again. It gains nothing from renewed acquaintance.

His orchestration—in spite of unusual virtuosity—is not " sonorous " because his style of composing is opposed to his orchestral writing. It branches out too much. I believe he has made a mistake in some of the proportions again. He has said himself, " Wagner makes everything sound but I am often unable to achieve this." That is because Wagner concentrates every-thing on the principal idea. Strauss really has 12 subordinate ideas and they are in confusion ; the chief idea lies more in the atmosphere than in the motive, but it is easily effaced by over-loading.

But I must hear the work. Music is there to be heard.

Half the passengers have landed. It feels very solitary on board. One gets accustomed to everything and certain faces belonged to this voyage ; they are now missing.

I was unwell yesterday evening and this morning early and the condition of exhaustion, which is familiar to me now, was not far off. Now, after lunch, I feel better—I hope to evade the crisis this time . . .

This is the last evening on board and I close this ragout, which one cannot call a " Daybook ". At most a twilight book—for thoughts dawn in it ; they half sleep. But there is an evening and a morning twilight ; I hope it is morning twilight and that a more beautiful, newer and clearer day will follow.

The evening of the 2nd April 1904 on board the *Blücher*.

FERRUCCIO BUSONI.

LONDON, 20 *November* 1904.

All my ideas of a Sunday afternoon in London were surpassed to-day. It would be impossible to imagine anything so empty, gloomy, lonely, dead and paralysing as the reality.

" Florian Geyer " was a good travelling companion. The language astonished me at first ; it is ancient, rich and strong (for the first time I met with many unintelligible expressions), but the incessant jargon, which is forceful and Luther-like, is very fatiguing. All the more so because all the people, without distinction of character, make use of the same forms of expression. During the whole piece, the ideas exchanged are only about past or expected occurrences ; one never sees the events about which citizens, peasants, warriors and knights speak most excitedly. Lastly, only men speak, and what men they are ! Of a mediæval type, violent, devout, and superstitious ; as they still were at the time of the Reformation. Wonderfully portrayed and vivid too, but to me strange and repulsive. It is a dramatized chronicle of the peasants' war, like Gobineau's of the Renaissance ; whether the difference in the enjoyment lies in the subject or in the artistic treatment of it, I cannot say with certainty . . .

This journey in the Irish fog has something so sad about it ! Besides, I am battered from the journey. I will try to work a little . . .

LONDON, 22 *November* 1904.

" To-night will be the third night I have not stretched my legs on an honest bed : " they would have been able to report in " Florian Geyer." (A book that grows very much towards the end.) , . .

The arrival in Ireland was very beautiful ; it almost reconciled me to the senseless toil of the journey . . .

84

To Mrs. Busoni, in Berlin, beloved consort, twofold mother, and Court pianist's wife.
From F. B., traveller in highly fragile toneware. Otherwise sound.

. . . At this moment I am preparing to travel to Manchester. " no day without a journey " this time, and of course I am not in the best humour. An hour ago I had Schultz-Curtius and Frau Matesdorf to lunch with me at Monico's. It was quite nice but not particularly " youthful." As a human being and an artist I prefer to look forward rather than backward, and my preference for the company of younger people is connected with this fact. And I hope it will be like this until the end ; for when that ceases, it is depressing—as your father said whilst he stood on his hands and planted his legs against the wall. . . .

MANCHESTER, 24 *November* 1904.
Darkness and frost prevail here, as in a refinely contrived department of Dante's Inferno, where travelling Virtuosi, who threw away the best part of life because they were covetous for fame and money, grind their teeth . . .
Richter was particularly pleased with the Henselt Concerto (at the rehearsal). How great are the differences in people and musicians ! . . .

CREFELD, 28 *December* 1904.
I had a little misfortune on this unimportant journey ; for, first of all, *whilst sleeping I passed* Crefeld and went on ; woke up at a little station almost in Holland and was obliged to wait nearly an hour for a train back ; nobody collected the tickets, which was extraordinary, and I got boldly into a first-class back to Crefeld (without ticket) so that I travelled two hours for nothing (but uselessly).
Secondly, I had notified no hotel and hit on a deplorable one at first and was obliged to find something better.
The third, and worst thing was that I had quite forgotten that I have to play Beethoven's Choral Fantasy—was neither prepared nor had I brought a piano part with me. As if that were not

enough—the weather is still cold and rainy which makes this ugly town still uglier ! It is built in a square, that is to say, it is surrounded by a north, south, east and west Boulevard, so that I have a suspicion that it was originally called Carré-feld. And here I have to stop for two days ! Basta ! . . .

# 1905

I was very, very disappointed to-day when instead of you, yourself, your telegram arrived . . . The only consolation is that you have escaped a horrible crossing . . .

I have discussed a project for a new grand with Caufall. It is a question of adding and introducing two manuals to the " modern " piano, the register of the " Clavicembalo " and a " coupling " stop. If that succeeded, there would be a new epoch for piano-playing. The present state of things is hopeless, and the development of the pianola and similar inventions are not to be underrated . . .

(*Addressed to Godinne, Belgium*)

BERLIN, 12 *July* 1905.

. . . Yesterday (Wednesday) Mengelberg came just as I had begun my lunch and he joined me. The food was good, the meeting comfortable (and friendly) . . . The " Chianti Busoni " [1] was sampled—it was quite excellent. A new invitation to America (the third) has come to-day . . .

The first act of Turandot is finished and the first piece of the " Suite " from it is planned.

(*Addressed to Godinne*)

BERLIN, 14 *July* 1905.

To-day 50 pages of the Turandot score are finished (still not quite half). The pleasure and ease continue.

[1] From the vineyards of an uncle.

*(Addressed to Godinne)*

BERLIN, 15 *July* 1905.

. . . I am indoors even more than usual, always occupied with something, and am at home before midnight always ; I sleep like a child, am called at 9 o'clock, and begin at 10 regularly : " the charming Chinese tyrant " is attired, and will soon have on her wedding veil and have laid aside her cruelty. There is still a choice to be made of materials, colours, and jewels, and they must be arranged in a way to make them really shine and please.

. . . What Schopenhauer says about music is magnificent. " By virtue of the inexpressible intimacy of all music, it passes in front of us like a quite familiar and yet eternally remote Paradise. It is completely intelligible and yet inexplicable, which is to be explained by the fact that it reflects all the emotions but none of the actualities of our being and is *far removed from its torment.*"

This eternal pessimist is right once more, however. If he speaks he knows why and how.

I am writing everything as it occurs to me ; just as when you are at home, I show you this or that as the occasion arises.

The weather is lovely now towards evening—but the courtyard in front of this quiet flat is sad.[1] I have such mixed feelings of hopes and reminiscences that I do not know if I am a greybeard or a youth. Perhaps for the first time I am sensible of my real age to-day. For :

> At forty you have climbed the mountain
> And you stand still and look back.


*(Addressed to Godinne)*

BERLIN, 22 *July* 1905.

. . . Yesterday I was overtired because I had been creating with such rapidity, and the first of the well-known walls got up in front of me ; not so high, however, but that a little skilful climb will get me over it.

" I can climb " ! but if one gets weary, the climb is harder. To-day I am almost over the wall . . .

It would be best if Ysaye were at the opening [2] concert and

---

[1] Augsburgerstrasse No. 55, Gartenhaus.
[2] The orchestral concerts arranged by Busoni.

more convenient for him too, I think . . . He should also conduct.

I shall make the orchestral part of the programme French and the solos classical. Kreisler proposed Bach's Double Concerto and Mozart's Violin and Viola Concerto. Besides that, Ysaye ought to conduct the Second Symphony by d'Indy. In between the two solos should come César Franck, scored by Pierné, and at the beginning an Overture either classical or French or Belgian . . .


(*Addressed to Godinne*)

BERLIN, 24 *July* 1905.

. . . Turandot will appear on the stage to-morrow. Even to-day, cruel, proud sounds announce her approach. But one must not forget that she is beautiful . . .


(*Addressed to Godinne*)

BERLIN, 25 *July* 1905.

. . . I still sit at home all the time, have worked splendidly, *she* has appeared ! . . . The march of the heroine has improved as I wrote it—do you remember a type (female) that you noticed in Madrid and I sketched on the spot ? (it's a fact). Even more has come out of that . . .


(*Addressed to Godinne*)

BERLIN, 26 *July* 1905.

. . . Turandot has reached the 72nd page. I gave it a rest this afternoon. I took your warning to heart, but the thing goes by itself almost.

There is enough material for *two* orchestral suites. I have been working at Turandot's march and I have made it like a portrait of her. In my mind I have thought of it as four character pictures : cruelty—passion—the veiled beauty and the unveiled beauty.


(*Addressed to Godinne*)

BERLIN, 30 *July* 1905.

. . . The " Philharmonic orchestra " sent word that for the

first concert only two rehearsals were possible,[1] and they hope I will agree to this.  I wrote a letter back which ought to be printed !

1. That I had engaged them in good time ; and that all later engagements which might interfere with mine are of secondary importance.

2. That if they did not keep the conditions and the evening was spoilt thereby, they would be obliged to pay " a fine," as I should have to do in a similar case.  But as it would mean that the whole series would be spoilt, they would have to pay a three-fold fine.

3. That they ought to be ashamed of having so little ambition as to put on one side an important, difficult and *new* programme.

4. That I demand the 3 rehearsals and, moreover, that nobody must fail to come and there must be no substitutes allowed.

5. That the rehearsals must be arranged as favourably as possible for the performances and so on.

(A reply came on the same day, saying that my wishes will be carried out.)

My parents, instead of regretting that I had difficulties, send reproaches to-day.  Patience ! . . .

Work goes forward and the scene will change again soon.  It (the work) is bigger and more important than I thought it would be.  I have made the sketches with extraordinary rapidity and they contain far more than I thought they would at first . . .


(*Addressed to Godinne*)

BERLIN, 31 *July* 1905.

To-day I have quite finished the Turandot march (84 pages) ; it is a very effective and rather imposing piece of music.  I am looking forward to beginning something with new sounds and new atmosphere to-morrow . . .


(*Addressed to Paris*)

BERLIN, 2 *August* 1905.

I think you are now in the enigmatical, incomparable, in-

[1] This refers to the " orchestral concerts with new and seldom performed works," arranged by Busoni.

exhaustible town of Louis XI and XIV and of the memorable year 1793. No town has so many points of contact with humanity as this cruel, fascinating monster . . . Meanwhile I have three riddles to solve ; and I have to get rid of the people in the second act. I began practising industriously again yesterday, some new things too . . .

*(Addressed to Godinne)*

BERLIN, 6 *August* 1905.

. . . I am so full of my work that I can think of nothing else. When I have visitors, and even whilst I am playing to people, in my mind I steal away into my little room again quite unconsciously. I often interrupt my meal, and in this way it has reached the 100th page, which is only the end of the second act.

The Concertstück by Egon is very good ; a little too much head and purpose but a good step further on. We have undertaken some cuts and changes which will improve it still more. What a long road the road to mastery is, even for someone who is very gifted—and often still further for him, because he sets himself bigger problems ! The unbelievable clarity and the ease of execution in these last compositions of mine satisfy me very much . . .

LEIPZIG, 4 *September* 1905.

The weather is so uncertain that one can get no enjoyment out of life. But anyhow, the " Fair " is going on . . .

In thought I went through my bundle of work from the beginning, through all its different stages. I remember that I went through a horrible time whilst I was writing the " Second Quartet." [1] The first movement lay unfinished for over a year, and I had no courage or inspiration to continue it . . . The task was too big for me ; and it was only after two years that I had developed enough to tackle it again and with great will power was able to finish it : I was at a very uncertain stage too, when I wrote the Symphonic poem !

No, my existence as a composer really begins with the second violin sonata.

I am resting here a little and feel comfortably bored.

[1] Begun when he was 20.

. . . I stayed up very late with Egon in the Hotel . . . I read my " libretto "[1] He found it very convincing, new and strange but yet, he felt, it could not be otherwise. It has an unusually firm and clear form, and Egon brought to my notice what charm lies in the fact that " nothing spoken about is brought to any conclusion . . ."


BIRMINGHAM, 29 *November* 1905.
The rainy weather continues—it is not cheerful.

Caufall's behaviour towards me is touching. He appeared in my room at 2.30 to-day, with a menu : " I think it must not always be piano-playing ; you must have a little to eat too." . . .

I have been obliged to read the short story by Gobineau through once more and was struck by the success of my first throw at adapting it for the stage. The point now is whether it will flatten with further work . . .

A good part of the dialogue can simply be translated from the original, throughout, it is short and dramatic and his expressions pregnant. As soon as the text is ready I shall divide the thing into " pieces of music " in my head, it is so simple ! . . .

[1] " Der mächtige Zauberer," Opera text after Gobineau.

# 1906

(*Addressed to Stockholm*)

BERLIN, 17 *February* 1906.

I must thank you again so very much for your great restraint on Thursday.[1]

Many people sent letters and flowers after the concert. I am writing to the Russian consulate for a visa for the passport . . .

Yesterday I was almost more exhausted than I have ever been. Was obliged to rehearse, practise and play. A concert without you was, for me, and even for the others, strange and empty . . . I am quite down. The journey will be still more difficult under these circumstances . . .

(*Addressed to Stockholm*)

KARLSRUHE, 19 *February* 1906.

I am writing on the chance of its reaching you, to tell you how deeply I feel for you. These days have given me a shock ; I notice it physically too. This suffering takes me further along the road of life. Is it to a higher level ? This will come to light when the clouds have disappeared again.

The libretto [2] is completely edited . . . In the middle of everything else the music has occupied me too.

I left the house with a heavier heart than usual yester-day ; I have felt your absence—in addition to everything else—oppressively . . .

BASLE, 25 *February* 1906.

The description of Pappus' beauty in death moves me so much every time I read it. And I had to read it three times. How

[1] The news of the fatal illness of his father-in-law, Carl Sjöstrand.
[2] To the " Brautwahl."

relieved I am to know that you will have no painful impression to remember . . .

TRIEST, 2 March 1906.

Yesterday I played in Graz ; from there, on the same evening, I took the train to Triest. First I supped with Mr. and Mrs. Kienzl. The arrival here to-day was particularly charming ; the view of the sea by Nabresina is always a surprise, although one knows what is coming. It is a radiant day, the air clear and mild. Triest looks like the priestess of the sea. In the customs, bearing and looks of the people I am struck by a resemblance to Madrid. The women often have the same expression ; the culture is very similar. I went to the hotel and it was three hours before I could decide to drag myself to the " Via dei Fabbri." [1] It is not cheerful at home and it is very wearisome. Mama is certainly very alive still and Papa does not look so bad as he does in the picture, but I can scarcely bear to be in this atmosphere. It was infinitely beautiful to see you in Vienna. You were in such a soft and tender humour . . .

TRIEST, 4 March 1906.

. . . My windows overlook the harbour. The beauty of the morning to-day is incomparable. The sun seems to penetrate everywhere ; the only shadow which I see is that of my house on the ground, in front of me. The sea is smooth, with unbroken lines, like a tightly stretched piece of delicate blue satin, with a strong dark blue at the extreme edge. On the right, the Karst Mountains, a reddish grey, and against the slope the houses looking like little white dice, thickly sown ; it gets misty in the direction of Miramar. Everything white stands out sharply. Sailing boats and little steamers with red, blue and black funnels are the only mobile things in the rigid picture. It must be magnificent to see the town from the sea, climbing up white and semi-circular, and on the top, at S. Giusto, there must be a prevailing sense of peace made by the sun and walls which must make an almost holy and heroic feeling. When I see all that again, it always makes me think of Triest in Napoleonic times. The town was rich then, and respectable merchants, dignified and calm, with high cravats, carried on trade between the gay-

[1] Busoni's parents lived in the Via dei Fabbri.

BUSONI, AGED 12

coloured east and stiff, grey Hamburg. A little current from the air of that time was still blowing during my childhood, and Triest steered a middle course between the irregularity and cunning of the orientals and the strict correctness of the Hamburg patricians.

At that time the " new " town arose, the empire-town, outside the old and closed in hill-town, which even to-day is extremely remarkable . . .

And with the removal of the Free Harbour, which was pain and grief to my grandfather, Triest lost its importance and sank down into its present characterless state. But just as people one loves and has known for a long time always look the same to one, I always see the Triest of my childhood. In the same way I have seen no change in my mother for 30 years, but in reality it cannot be so. In the same way I see my present face in the child's portrait which I send you ; and which, in expression, seems to me to be out of the ordinary. From the name of the place at which the photograph was taken I must have been about 12 years old.

There is nothing worse than looking back ; or than places, people, and facts that lead one to do so. I seldom do it and should like never to do it, but here I cannot help it. Therefore I feel uncomfortable and as if in the night I had been shunted off my track on the main line to a side-station where there is no train traffic. It is an interruption in the life of my true self, the self who, in the world, is famous, active and who looks forward. Whilst here a child, who has grown up, is forced back about 25 years into the unchanged surroundings of his childhood ! Away with it ! And live once more ! Something cries out in me, and with that I think about the idyllic ending of the Adagio in the concerto and the Tarantella which follows.

But after the end of the Tarantella ? The air here is almost like that of Rome, and hypnotizes one and pulls one with soft arms towards the south and Italy's quiet enjoyment of life. Will that be the end ?

Don't let us think of that yet. . . .


LONDON, 14 *June* 1906.
I worked hard at the libretto yesterday, partly in the train and partly here, and it is finished up to the last scene with the three caskets. Much will be altered, meanwhile all kinds of musical

ideas occur to me (still visionary) so that I have successfully planned the introduction to the third act. But nothing will have any form until I am at my writing table and can see the notes on the manuscript paper. I have great hopes for this piece, which is a continuous creative pleasure and scarcely gives any trouble.

Thank God, the Patti-concert is over. Yet why do I thank Him, if it was His will that it should take place?

I was the only normal person on the platform!

The others were:

| | |
|---|---|
| Patti . . . . . | 63 years old |
| Santley . . . . | 72 ,, ,, |
| A girl violinist . . . | 11 ,, ,, |
| Ben Davies . . . | Weight 100 Kilo. |

And this Albert Hall. Good for bull-fights, maybe! but for piano-playing? And the programme—and the Music! . . .


LONDON, 17 *June* 1906.

. . . Yesterday I heard part of M. Hamburg's concert and then went for a moment to Pachmann's. He had just finished the " Invitation to the Dance." As the public applauded, he showed with his hands that he wished to speak. " Mr. Godowsky "—he said—" has made an arrangement of this piece— *very* difficult !—he can't play it himself—he-he. I—he-he don't play it yet before—the public—must be careful—careful—careful—he-he-he "—and went off laughing and shrugging his shoulders.

The " Brautwahl " goes on by itself and takes me with it. The prelude to Act I is almost there, the whole of the first scene in a general way.

The verse for the last scene is also coming—I feel very happy about it—but really only *about it* ; in other respects my mood is not good, but thank God I'm well . . .


(*Addressed to Schloss Habrovan in Mähren*) [1]

BERLIN, 14 *July* 1906.

I received your beautiful letter soon after mine was on the way and it made me quite joyful !

[1] Castle of the famous singer Caroline Gomperz-Bettelheim.

If you are concerning yourself there with details from my childhood, remind Frau Caroline that I received the " Hoffmann " out of her library and I have had these volumes with me during childhood, youth and manhood, and in different ways they have always given me stimulation.

I read something in Hoffmann's biography which I must write out for you. It is as follows.

In the spring of the year 1820 Hoffmann experienced a great pleasure. A traveller brought him a very cordial letter from Beethoven. Beethoven wrote :

" Through Herr N. I avail myself of the opportunity of addressing you, a man whose genius I appreciate. As you have written about my humble self, I must believe you take some interest in me. May I be allowed to say, that, coming from a man like yourself, gifted with so many excellent qualities, this has gratified me very much."

From Von Oehlenschläger, too, there is a letter to Hoffmann, signed : " Adam Oehlenschläger, Serapionsbruder." All this has given me pleasure and the Brautwahl does not stand still . . .


(*Addressed to Schloss Habrovan*)

BERLIN, 16 *July* 1906.

. . . I am getting on with the opera—the purely lyrical does not come so easily. But Manasse's curse and Thusmann's story already sound in my ears. There is invention in every bar and it shall be so up to the end . . .


(*Addressed to Schloss Habrovan*)

BERLIN, 17 *July* 1906.

The song has gone *well*. It constitutes the kernel of the " Zelte " scene (Act I).

Yesterday I was at Bartolini's for a moment. The young men (C and L) have gone suddenly, without paying, and owing many hundreds, have left him in a bad dilemma.

He was magnificent. " Look "—he said to me—" I am good and if necessary would let my shirt be taken off my back. Amongst men one can come to an understanding. They should have spoken to me frankly. I am good " (here he began to get rather strange in his manner) " and my sole religion is : Do unto nobody what you would not wish them to do unto you. I act on that basis. But let someone try to do me an *injustice* !" (and here his fierceness grew visibly) : " I once travelled over the ocean from S. America, leaving all my business in the lurch. I travelled to Italy *in order to cut a man in pieces*."

" But what did you do to him ? " I asked, really scared ; he made my blood run cold. " You can rest assured *that* man will wrong nobody any more." This is in true Renaissance style.

This is my travelling plan : One night through to Munich, then on to Innsbruck, and if I don't like it well enough there I shall go on to Bozen and Trient.

I am so impatient. I am only taking the libretto and manuscript paper, no books and also no dumb piano !¹ I am in a wonderfully good mood with the exception of a little " Reisefieber " ; it is excellent. Your dear news and the remembrance of the last weeks at home are the cause of that . . .


(*Addressed to Schloss Habrovan*)

MUNICH, 19 *July* 1906.

I have brought with me your very dear first letter, in which you suggested I should make this journey. To-morrow I shall go on to Innsbruck . . .

The weather is glorious but scorchingly hot. You should see me in a silk coat !

I have done much more work. The " Zelte " scene is finished . . .


(*Addressed to Schloss Habrovan*)

MUNICH, 20 *July* 1906.

. . . My impression of Munich is not a very pleasant one. There is going to be a shooting competition one day soon and from the shooting ground men with thick beards, woollen jerkins, rucksacks, and cotillion favours, walk about proudly and happily masculine . . .

At 11 o'clock in the morning the restaurants are already full of people eager for luncheon, and the park seats are occupied the whole day. It is so cheap here that in order not to be looked upon with suspicion one dares not give more than a 10 Pfg. tip.

¹ Busoni never possessed a dumb piano.

The institution of waitresses is a pleasant arrangement for mankind, or rather for menkind. Friendly counsel over the bill of fare gives an agreeable introduction to the meal here. I have not looked at any pictures, for my brain is already worried more than enough with the opera. I think I shall go straight on to Trient this evening ; I have had enough of green clothes, goats' beards and bare knees.

From my recollections of Trient, I believe I shall like it there. I was there when I was thirteen, when we left Vienna, and went about from place to place like a caravan belonging to the annual fair. I have vivid recollections of a count and abbé with an unusually clever and distinguished face. I remember, too, that it was winter and we froze in the houses. In the stone hall of a Palazzo Salvotti, which the baron and master of the house had most kindly given up to us, I played with fingers stiff with cold. There were rows of people in overcoats and turned-up collars. I believe it was in the hotel there that I was conscious of my first male emotion, for I kissed a chambermaid with very red hair and quite black eyes, whereupon my mother said " non é bello," and it was precisely these words that produced the consciousness.

Bozen is very near to Trient and I shall choose between the two. The food in the Italian Tyrol is very good, the climate divine, the wine genuine and I will gladly continue taking the baths for 14 days.

I am happy that you have felt so well at Habrovan. The whole family has always been so good to me and to the end of my life they will have my gratitude and love . . .


(*Addressed to Vienna*)

TRIENT, 21 *July* 1906.

With the thermometer at thirty—between 2 and 3 (" dalle due alle tre ") [1] I paid a visit to a Capuchin monastery. I had to see it ; and I wanted the atmosphere too for my church vision. The road up to it was nothing but walls and sun. The " Superior " received me with some reserve, and was rather mistrustful at first. One could hear the brothers chanting their litanies inside. That suited me very well. A cool courtyard, with a fountain in the middle, welcomed me refreshingly. The Superior was a little surer about me when I introduced myself as an artist, a

[1] Quotation from *Falstaff*.

99

friend of the religious orders, and (God forgive me the lie !) as a pupil of the famous Liszt, (but the Superior was quite uninformed about Liszt) so I hastened to add that Liszt had been a priest himself, and a friend of Pio Nono's. The name of Pio Nono put the Superior on firm ground, and he now bade me welcome. He led me to the church, where he made the pre-scribed reverence in front of the high altar (I crossed myself, am still good at it !) and then through the very modest rooms of the monastery. I dared not go into the garden on account of the heat. He told me, too, that it was necessary to arm oneself with a stick as there were snakes in it. The library, he said, must have been valuable at one time, but during Napoleon's reign (always Napoleon !) it had been plundered. Organ they had none. He bade me come back, in a friendly way, and took leave of me with a modest : Keep a happy memory of the Capuchins ! When I asked him whether he had been here for long, he nodded his head and seemed to go quickly through many recollections : " 35 years he supposed." He did not say this with despair or content, but there was a sound of trained resigna-tion in the words. . . .

Now I have settled here, unpacked the manuscript and have a little piano in the room. Unfortunately my creative vein, which was flowing beautifully, dried up suddenly when I left home. Even an hour *before* leaving I was obliged to take out some manu-script paper in order to put down a good idea. Since then everything has stopped.

Yesterday I went quickly to Bozen, in order to decide where to stay. There is no comparison !

Bozen, the German bourgeois town (in the style of Moritz von Schwind, but not so good), and Trient, the Italian Renaissance aristocratic town, like Ferrara, Parma and the like.

Surely it is unique for two such distinct types of towns to lie only an hour apart. . . .


(*Addressed to Alt-Aussee*)

TRIENT, 25 *July* 1906.

. . . One could not be lonelier than I am, even on Mont Blanc. I know no one and speak to nobody, with the exception of the hall-porter and the waiters.

For the nerves it may be very good ; but the effect on my

imagination is just negative.  The landscape is wide and the day
before yesterday I climbed a hill in order to see the whole picture.
Trient's appearance from a bird's-eye point of view reminds one
of Bologna : austere, gloomy and compact, with grey walls and
tiled roofs ; but the landscape here is much grander, it is really
heroic in style.  One is reminded of it, too, by the formation of
the clouds which is like it is in mountainous districts, often
thundery, but with surprising lights from the sun on isolated
parts, whilst other parts lie entirely in cold shadow.  The
perspective at the end of the valley awakens a feeling of longing
and seen in the morning, or even at sunset, it makes a great
impression on the emotions.  I believe, if it is properly absorbed
by the soul it should be productive to the creative flow (later
on) . . .

I am waiting for the next post before closing my letter.

Meanwhile I have made a clean copy of my libretto and, for
diversion, made a pretty drawing for the title-page . . .


(*Addressed to Alt-Aussee*)

TRIENT, 26 *July* 1906.

. . . They have become so accustomed to me here that I no
longer cause any sensation.  I am already counted as one of the
people of Trient, and shall soon be nominated an honourable
citizen.

Oh, why do the girls always walk in profile ?  You cannot
believe how sad the people look here.  They live in a hopeless
town, and every new day is to be feared, for there is nothing
but emptiness and a lack of point in each one, and in the course
of time one gives up expecting surprises !  The worst of it is,
they are conscious of the situation and I noticed the same feeling
of resignation and negation in them and in their expressions,
gestures, and speech, as I did in the Capuchin Prior.

" But what can you expect, here in Trient ! "

It seems to me that the girls give expression to their *need* for
emotion in a mania for quarrelling.  The smallest pretext will
produce an explosion in the already over-laden atmosphere.  An
elderly daughter, accompanied by her parents, on finding her
usual seat on the promenade already occupied, made a scene
about it to the old people for quite half-an-hour.  She spoilt the

beautiful evening for herself and for them. It was not rage over the seat ! but over the uneventfulness, captivity and hopelessness, which had been accumulating—daily ! ! !—for 30 years.

Thank God that the seat was there to make some outlet for the rage !

Compared with Trient, for example, *Empoli* could be called " American " . . .

I am reading some intimate letters by Giusti, full of wit and grace . . .


*(Addressed to Alt-Aussee)*

TRIENT, 28 *July* 1906.

. . . I have bought Verdi's " Ballo in Maschera " here, in order to have some company for a couple of hours. . . .

It is a strong work, brutal, but has great power and is plastic. Some moments in it belong to Verdi's best, it seems to me ; I did not know it, but I found that much of it had been sounding in my ears since my childhood. But the libretto ! And the lyrics ! It is the story of Gustav the Third, transplanted to Boston from political considerations.

One finds in it : " Odo l'orma dei passi spietati."

" I hear the footmarks of the merciless steps "—is such a thing possible ? . . .

This Tagliapietra is a fine, clever young man, an idealist, and he adores me. (He accompanied me to the station, no one else came.) It is psychologically interesting that my father, from jealousy, wanted to frighten him away from me ; so he ran me down when speaking of me. He began, " But you do not know my son ! " then came the list of my failings. Just think, my father, who would not tolerate anyone mentioning the slightest weakness in me, does it himself in order to prevent someone from getting to know me !

Forgive this letter being rather confused, but I have written it in three pieces . . .


*(Addressed to Alt-Aussee)*

TRIENT, 30 *July* 1906.

. . . There is a poem or speech in this little Giusti book, which was written when Napoleon was proclaimed *King of Italy*.

I have sent the book to Papa, because it says so much about places and times which he knew quite well in his youth. He was very pleased with it.

I have read many details here about the poor von Saar ; it has impressed me very much. There was a time when I loved him very much . . .

It takes 10 hours to reach Madonna di Campiglio from here, and even then it is only possible with carriage and horses. Yesterday I tried to climb up the vertical Sahara in the hope of an oasis ; and travelled 1½ hours on a branch line to Lévico, a spa in the mountains, where there are iron baths and many foreigners, so they say. It was a fiasco, for the journey was extremely hot ; on the top nobody was to be seen until 8 o'clock in the evening ; a boring, expensive hotel that I disliked intensely.

I stepped into a little inn : on an old piano lay *Sinding's Frühlingsrauschen* and *Puccini's Bohème*. An oleograph hung on the wall, a copy of one of Sichel's portraits, of a woman. In the street a peasant boy with a squint was whistling the Faust waltz. This shows what is really popular and well-circulated in present-day art ! And yet one speaks of " living " works of art ! ? What peasant boy whistles Don Giovanni, and where can one find the piano score of it in a mountain inn ? . . .


(*Addressed to Alt-Aussee*)

TRIENT, 3 *August* 1906.

. . . I am always *quite*, quite alone, with the exception of the letters and my dear acquaintances Thusmann, Leonhard, the Commissionsrath and even the unbearable Manasse—interesting people—and then, too, Verdi and Berlioz, certainly men of the first order, and finally myself, also endurable.

For an opera composer the only way out of the difficulty is to write his text himself . . . Wonderful, how during the composition one can strike out, add and change, according to the musical requirements.

A composer is circumscribed by another poet's libretto, in the same way that an architect is hampered by the given ground, the reason for, and the money allowed for a building which he designs.

The last three days, I have done Manasse's proposal, and following it, the reconciliation of both the old friends. From the words, " Everything is as it was before," the reconciliation works up to a joyful ending. The way in which they embrace, after coming to a mutual understanding, is very comical . . .


*(Addressed to Alt-Aussee)*

BERLIN, 9 *August* 1906.
. . . I read Tirso de Molina's " Don Juan Tenorio " to the end with great pleasure. It is powerful, has great freshness and facility, is big, and at the same time naïve. The creative artist will never reach this point again. The time for unaffectedness is past. We reckon with too large a public, that knows too much about the variety of things.

It is so difficult for anyone to create just for his own pleasure and for that of his nearest friends ; as Tirso did in the small province and for (probably, towards him) the friendly court and as Goethe did in Weimar. (But his *naïveté* disappeared as his world-wide reputation grew.) If a great and naïve genius were to appear now, it would be a hundred times more valuable than it was 3–400 years ago, because the feeling of responsibility, the competition with a mass of master works, constantly accumulating, and the increased technical demands, make it much more difficult to be a genius of this kind now. In any case Molina's " Don Juan " is a rare type of this vanished art (Holberg is another one) and I not only have a great desire to introduce the piece to Reinhardt, but I should also like to write the necessary music for it which, perhaps, is a little impudent of me. It would consist of some serenades which should be sung, and a couple of invisible choruses which should accompany the apparition of the statue. The stone guest comes, of course, at Don Juan's invitation ; it does not end here, however, but he invites Don Juan, and even asks him " to the Chapel." Don Juan promises. He is to be entertained with a meal, which one gets for nothing in the " Cabaret de la Mort." There must be some uncanny music, which must be played during the meal.

A chorus of spirits sings :

> " Denket alle, die ihr fürchtet
> Gottes unermeszne Strafen,
> Wie so bald die Zeit verronnen—
> Wie man jede Schuld musz zahlen."
> *(Leporello :* " Diesen Vers hab' ich verstanden—
> Er bezieht sich klar auf uns.")

That is a dramatic situation of the very first order !

There will be no lack of engagements this year ; and for that reason, I am still keeping away from too serious work this month ; they keep on coming in.

I am *immensely* pleased at your return . . .

This old man you describe might well have been created by Hoffmann. Something clever and inscrutable, and quite different from anything in daily life, is hidden by a certain bitter-sweetness and obligingness in the character. Councillor Krespel, God-father Drosselmeier, and similar " abnormal " people are like this, as he says himself through the mouth of one of the Serapion brothers.

AMSTERDAM, 4 *October* 1906.

. . . I feel battered to-day and have, with a Napoleonic gesture, *cancelled* a concert in " Enschede "—a factory village !

The second concert is not until Saturday, so that to-day (Thursday) I can live entirely according to my inclination. To this belongs, at the moment, the adaptation of " Aladdin." And yesterday I wrote *two scenes straight down*. I must, of course, write out every word—which makes the task much greater—for I have to change a good deal and to condense and to express some things better . . .

AMSTERDAM, 7 *October* 1906.

Yesterday I gave the second concert and finished the 1st Act of Aladdin. The concert was one of those rarely fortunate ones, when every bar is successful in the way one wishes, new ideas come as one plays and immediately sound right, and the instrument is obedient. I may be deceived, but from beginning to end it seemed to me perfect and effortless in technique, at the same time free and full of swing. Old Daniel de Lange, when he spoke of the transition to the fugue (in the 106) [1] cried and kissed me vehemently. J., on the contrary, said it was a matter of taste and that " his " interpretation was different.

I answered rather violently that it was out of place to speak of a matter of taste in connection with such a mature performance. It should be listened to only.

[1] Sonata Op. 106 by Beethoven.

105

As far as the Aladdin work is concerned, I am contented with it. There is a great unity now in the first act. It runs on a straight line and does not venture on " cross and crooked ways "— the simplicity of the ascending line will make one hold one's breath.

Oehlenschläger's book, under such close scrutiny, suffers from a womanly talkativeness ; and, what I had already noticed, from a lack of mastery of the German language, and finally from too many details.

The homely details take up too much space, almost as they do in old Dutch art. The Mother is decidedly an old Danish woman. With the adaptation I dare let *no word* go by unexamined. I have only been able to keep a few lines exactly as they are in the original. Nevertheless the plan of the book is big and genial and worth the trouble. . . .

LONDON, 2 *December* 1906.

What a distance there is between the Adriatic coast and the English Channel ! I have never observed such an enormous difference before. Here, fog, storm, cold—all the wintry devils together, and only the day before yesterday this summer sunset in Triest ! I have such a horror of the crossing to Ireland—but Schultz-Curtius is immovable . . .

MANCHESTER, 4 *December* 1906.

. . . The whole character of the Harrison tour is disgraceful this time. Compared with this one, my tour with Ysaye was very good. Here in Manchester it is a little better, they know me, love me, and receive me well. Yet it is grand, always to have my *own* thoughts with me and to know that this year, and probably from now onwards, if I concentrate, I can accomplish something every minute. My mind is always active. But my body demands a little repose, for latterly everything has gone at a gallop.

I have such a longing for your letters, dear, dear Gerda ; perhaps never before have I felt so happy and so together with you as now. And that will change no more ; I feel so sure in everything now. In creation, too, I see straight on to the end of the " Zauberer ; " *then*, probably, the famous " third " period will begin for me too, and I hope I shall be able to finish some of the work already begun.

106

I wonder what Bösendorfer said ?

I am very much in favour of the Vienna [1] idea now ; it might give me *a kind of* freedom for three years. For the next *ten* I certainly ought to be able to be rich ! But it is good enough as it is too.

How beautiful it is that you take part in it all . . .

EDINBURGH, 9 *December* 1906.

To-day was the first time that I have practised properly since— I don't know when—and after such a long pianistic pause the 24 Pieludes by Chopin had quite a special interest. Yesterday the concert was at 3, and so it was also the first free evening I had had for a long time ; in fact it was the first time that I had been out at all in the streets. In Manchester, Liverpool, Sheffield, Newcastle, Birmingham, I did not stick my nose out of the hotel. Finally your second letter came here, so that from every point of view I could see a piece of blue sky . . .

I am so beautifully alone here. Sarasate is in another hotel, some of the " Party " departed during Sunday. The town is always remarkable. Clouds are always moving behind the immovable silhouette of the old hill. Divisions of Scottish soldiers in red jackets, plaids and kilts, white gaiters which leave the hairy knee free, march past with bold step. The castle looks down on buildings belonging to 6 different centuries. Sunday is most holy here. This is like *the other end* of the Triest impressions . . .

EDINBURGH, 10 *December* 1906.

. . . Sarasate is a brainless man and without temperament too. But through others he has experienced an enormous amount, and he has been on terms of intimacy with the greatest artists. That gives him a certain historical varnish.

He told me how he and Rubinstein sat at " Whist " in the hotel in Leipzig, on the evening of Gewandhaus-concert. A new symphony was to be played for the first time—by whom is forgotten—which Rubinstein did not wish to hear. About 10 o'clock people came from the concert into the hotel. " Well,

[1] Appointment as professor of the " Meisterklasse " at the Vienna School of Music.

107

what was the Symphony like ? " Rubinstein called out to the
first visitor. " Oh, very musical." " It's damned then,"
blustered Rubinstein and banged his fist on the table. " When
Germans say a work is ' musical,' it is certain to be boring."

. . . I have practised so much, that I feel it in my back. The
24 Preludes are not easy, but I am glad about this new number
which is *good* . . .

ABERDEEN, 11 *December* 1906.
. . . The 24 by Chopin have given me very much to do. They
do not sound so difficult, but they are not any easier than the
Paganini-Variations. And they are so very varied in technique.
One has to be able to spring about ! But they will be an excellent
addition. I am looking forward to the 21st in Berlin very
much . . .

Still three Harrison tour evenings !

And then Adieu, for ever, to this gentleman ! . . .

GLASGOW, 12 *December* 1906.
Always between a journey and a concert. I am sending you
the criticism from Aberdeen, because it is the best which has
been written about me in English. It is remarkable that, up
there, in this small Scottish town, where I was playing for the
first time, I was understood almost completely . . .

The Chopin Preludes have cost me round about 12 hours'
study in four days. Glasgow always reminds me of Chicago—
*so much so*, that to-day I wanted to look for a cigar shop which,
as I quickly remembered, is in America.

Sarasate said of César Franck—" He was a bad accompanist ;
he accompanied very badly. And they have made a god of
him " . . .

BRADFORD, 13 *December* 1906.
What beautiful letters you write ; what a lot of good they all
have done me ! . . .

I had a remarkable conversation with Sarasate to-day about
music, which shows me clearly, that my essay has come *too soon*
for most people. He is, it is true, 62 years old and was never

a revolutionary, but he has been in the midst of good things all his life, and he might have absorbed them more like a sponge. He has some of Brodsky's Olympic obstinacy and also some of my father's way of dismissing things without any judgment : that is the Latin in him . . .

God be praised, at 10 o'clock to-day this tour is done with, and the company !

I shall come into my own waters again.

If one does something against one's conviction, it only half succeeds, or does not succeed at all . . .

# 1 9 0 7

. . . Once more I have come to the end of an almost unbearable week and I regard these days (8–15 March) as thrown to
the winds entirely. Marseilles is a town which has similarities
with, but holds a subordinate position between, Madrid, Naples
and Triest.   With Triest the similarity lies in the position of the
harbour in connection with the town and another one is the
*Mistral* which is very much the same as the *Bora*.   This dreadful
wind visits the town every 2 months for 3–4 days and I had just
the bad luck to meet it.   Architecturally the town is hopeless.
With regard to the landscape, in good weather it probably offers
much that I did not see, because I was only able to hold on my
hat and wipe my eyes continually . . .

Musically, they are ignorant there as they are in Naples, and
they use the slogans from Paris.   Pleasant atmosphere !   The
train back to Geneva got into Lyons precisely at the time when
it should have arrived in Geneva, that is to say, $3\frac{1}{2}$ hours late.
Impatiently I got out at Lyons.   The colour of my first impression
of the town was completely changed, for there was *frost !* wind
and—consequently—empty streets.   The next day I stopped in
Geneva, after having taken $6\frac{1}{2}$ hours from Lyons to get there.
From Geneva to Freiburg required another $8\frac{1}{2}$ hours.   So there
were three long journeys and deserts in between.   Never again
will I give concerts in exotic places !   It was almost an improve-
ment to-day, in this modest little town, to meet with a well-
organized orchestra and to find a reasonable, if only an average,
amount of understanding for my work . . .

MUNICH, 17 *March* 1907.

Yesterday, the 16th, I had a very strenuous day again ; in
Freiburg.   The *Mignon* invited me to play once more.   I had

to practise well before I could do it and not till then! Well, I was in the factory from 12 till 8.30 and played Norma, Don Juan, Polonaise, Ruinen von Athen, and some small pieces, at one sitting. I was offered friendly and excellent hospitality before and after. Then I took the night train to Munich. . . .

(*Addressed to Drottningholm, near Stockholm*)

BERLIN, 7 *July* 1907.

. . . In a voice shaking with excitement, a young student spoke to me in the street, in order to tell me about the great impression which my little book had made on him. It was very gratifying to see this susceptibility, devoted, and uncritical amongst the more intelligent kind of youth . . .

(*Addressed to Drottningholm*)

BERLIN, 13 *July* 1907.

. . . I am just completing one part of the Brautwahl. It was a bigger task than I thought it would be, and I could not master it more quickly because I have an invincible feeling that every bar must say something . . .

(*Addressed to Drottningholm*)

BERLIN, 14 *July* 1907.

. . . I shall enjoy no peace until some sections of my work have been cleared away. I shall go to Weimar about the edition of Liszt, at the end of July or beginning of August. That falls together very inopportunely with Norderney . . .

. . . Everything is going well—thank God—regularly and without disappointments or surprises. One cannot expect more in this life. . . .

My head is full of ideas. But there is always room for thoughts about Gerda. I am looking forward to the " holidays later on " too—and shall welcome you in triumph.

I have been reading Béranger and have studied Part Two of the Trojans (by Berlioz). Both excellent.

BERLIN, 17 *July* 1907.

I have just finished the last note of my act; now, at half-past-five. I am very happy, for it has gone just as I wished. Although it is raining I am going to fly out. To-morrow I shall make a survey of what I have to do and then decide on a plan . . . Now I must rest! I believe this Act is still better! . . .

(*Addressed to Drottningholm*)

BERLIN, 21 *July* 1907.

It is so cold and grey to-day one could think it was early November. But it is the 21 July; unfortunately a Sunday. For three days there has been no " rumbling " in my head but, as I expected, it has given up work.

To-day an amusing *consent* to come to Norderney has arrived from Egon, and Wolff has sent a list of my dates. The big groups, England, Switzerland and Holland, give the list a good shape. Italy is planned for April, then Paris, and in between, six times in Berlin . . .

As regards my plans now, I think I shall make use of the time next week by stopping here, because, 1st, I must make myself fresh again for Norderney as a pianist; 2nd, I must make a fair copy of the second Act of the Brautwahl.

Then come the journeys to *Weimar* and *Norderney*. Besides this, I decided the day before yesterday that from now on until it is finished I would concentrate my whole attention on the Brautwahl *only*, and this is very important.

I have not yet drawn up a list of the other things I have to do, for I have really taken a holiday the last three days. (I sleep like a child!) But I know that I must be in Vienna at the beginning of September (flat, and examinations) and on the 22 I must go to England. Thank God, that the pulse of life beats so fast; it spurs me on more than peace. I am healthy and contented, without being in very high spirits. Is the period of ripe maturity appearing at last? But a little bit of childishness remains in me which will not be " overawed ! " . . .

*(Addressed to Drottningholm)*

BERLIN, 23 *July* 1907.

. . . A trial, which came to an end this evening, has interested me so much that yesterday evening, partly for practice and partly out of opposition, I tried to find another explanation. I have really thought about it and written down my thoughts. . . .

Why has one not got a head like Edgar Poe ? ! I have been almost worried by this thought the last few days, even though I may be a better musician and just as good an artist as he. Of course a good deal of it is due to practice.

Poe followed a similar crime *step for step* in his " The Mystery of Marie Roget " which, many years later, was completely verified. This man Hau's behaviour in the court of justice was admirably cool and consistent ; he was much stronger than his judge. Another trial is bound to follow.

Now I am going to my work ; the second Act (Part I) is a success . . .


*(Addressed to Drottningholm)*

BERLIN, 26 *July* 1907.

. . . It is still undecided about the journey to Weimar. How much I should like to have these four scanty days quite uncurtailed !

I count on every single day now, and with astonishment and almost fright I see the evening throwing out its shadows in advance, and swallowing the day. Life is not long enough and whizzes past, like the landscape seen through the window of a railway-carriage. Things which one has just seen go by lie far behind the next moment. And the distant horizon is reached just as quickly. Sometimes I have the feeling I will leave everything (all my occupations) in order not to feel this eternal " beginning afresh " any more. But a void is still worse. Better a long and laborious road than no road at all, as in sand or ice deserts.

I have had some small pleasures, as for example, the bookbindings which are a success ; and I read a very original story by Clemens Brentano (" Die mehreren Wehmüller oder die ungarischen Nationalgeschichter ") ; then Herkomer, who was passing through, brought me greetings from his friend Widemann (Widemann is the old sculptor at Bartolini's). . . .

F.B.                              113                              H

Bartolini told us about a very adventurous experience he had had in S. America. He promised a Jewish woman to accompany her back to her home, and he literally undertook the journey from Brazil far into Russia, and carried it through with false passports, in the depths of winter, and finally, on the way back, he got stuck in Berlin. He would have been a good man for Napoleon . . .

(*Addressed to Drottningholm*)

BERLIN, 28 *July* 1907.

It is an effort for me to practise the piano, yet one cannot leave it! It is like an animal, whose head always grows again, however much one cuts off. Composing, by comparison, is like going along a road which is more difficult but beautiful and changeable. One is always folding up long stretches of it, reaching stages further on and leaving them behind, and its final goal is unknown and unattainable.

I am glad that you find beauties in Hebbel. He always ponders over things and searches for them, but he seems to me to be one of the very best! . . .

(*Addressed to Drottningholm*)

BERLIN, 30 *July* 1907.

On the days when I get no letters from you I read the last one through again—and *the* last, for which I thanked you immediately, one can still read many times! Imagine, to-day I found a kind of " History of Berlin " which actually contains a picture, after an old engraving, of the " Execution des berüch-tigten Hof-und Münzjuden Leuppoldt," as well as a portrait of a " Leonhardt Thurneisser," goldsmith from Thurn, in his 45th year (a beautiful face). The Jew's portrait, too, is inserted in the picture of the execution; it shows a very clever head, sharp features, and almost Arabic character. They tortured him dreadfully and, unfortunately, after he had borne so many cruelties there could be no doubt about his death. As artists I love both these figures very much and, whilst I work, I am constantly adding little characteristic traits. I feel almost certain now that the Brautwahl will be effective. I am quite impatient, for instance, to show you " des geheimen Kanzleise-

kretär's Thusmann unwahrscheinlichen Bericht " now it is
finished.

Now this is done the form of the introduction to Act 2 is
sketched out and, without further preliminaries, it starts off
*ff* with the waltz " Allegro vertiginoso." On the whole I am
well on with the piece. The libretto is dated as far back as
June 1906. . . .

(*Addressed to Drottningholm*)

NORDERNEY, 1 *August* 1907.

. . . It gives me a strange feeling being obliged to play in
public again, after an interval of three months. I feel " shame "
in doing it, more than ever.

I have a book with me, which promises very well. De
Quincey's " Murder Considered as one of the Fine Arts," and
others by him. It must belong to the Poe-Baudelaire family.
It was De Quincey who wrote the " Opium-Eater."

I hope for a letter from you here. Your last, the golden one,
I have got in my pocket-book.

(*Addressed to Drottningholm*)

NORDERNEY, 2 *August* 1907.

It is the morning after the concert. It went *well*. (Beethoven
C Minor Concerto, Liszt's Héroïde élégiaque and Rakoczy-
March, new) . . .

When I arrived here, the state of the atmosphere was just as
it is at the beginning of the Flying Dutchman. I thought to
myself : " It is not necessary to play the overture here. Nature
plays it herself."

I thought this as I went to the Kurhaus for the rehearsal and
—the first sounds which I heard were those of the Flying Dutchman ; the Orchestra was really playing it. And I was forced
to admit that it was : " A good picture, a work of art, quite true
to life." [1]

What a pity, that in order to reach Weimar in time, I must
leave at the *very latest to-morrow* . . .

The Fürstin Bülow, who remembers having seen me at Wertheimstein (she had to admit to the 24 years which have elapsed,

[1] Quotation from Busoni's Brautwahl.

whether she wanted to or not), has Sapellnikoff here every summer as guest. . . . They were both sweetness itself to me, in that masterly way understood by Southern Italians and Russians and with shamelessly exaggerated diplomacy.

The reading of the very original and witty de Quincey has continued through all these small happenings, like a thread joining many patches . . .

During the summer I examined my development and found that my progress has been great. As you know, I got beyond Schumann and Mendelssohn first of all, in my musical taste. Liszt I misunderstood at first, then I adored him, and then quietly admired him. I was antagonistic to Wagner, then astonished by him, and then the Latin in me turned against him again. Berlioz amazed me ; and I learnt to distinguish between good and bad Beethoven—which was one of the most difficult things to do. I discovered the newest French composers for myself and dropped them when they became popular too quickly. Finally my soul felt drawn towards the old Italian opera writers.

Those are the changes which have taken place over a period of 20 years, and all through those twenty years the score of Figaro has remained unchanged in my estimation, like a lighthouse in surging seas.

But when I looked at it again, a week ago, I discovered human weaknesses in it for the first time ; and my soul flew for joy when I realized that I am not so far behind it as I thought, in spite of this discovery being a real loss, and pointing to the lack of durability in all human activities ; (and how much more in my own !) . . .


(*Addressed to Drottningholm*)

WEIMAR, 5 *August* 1907.

I arrived here on the morning of the 4th, and had a good five hours' work with Obrist and von Hase. . . .

Yesterday we went through *every single Liszt volume*, not to mention sketches, manuscripts and every possible fragment, some very interesting ones among them. They were both rather surprised at my professional knowledge about it all. There is a whole big symphonic Fantasy on themes by Berlioz for piano and orchestra, unprinted. I knew about it once, had looked for it, and then given it up.

The new theatre, from outside, is almost finished. The good old Grand Duke stands in front of the " Russische Hof Hotel "—on horseback!—and dressed in military clothes. It is made in absolutely new bronze which looks quite impossible. All is silent in the Tempelherrenhaus.[1] It is so quiet altogether here that one is almost afraid of meeting a carriage !

The publication of Liszt's collected works seems " fairly " determined on ; but things still get hitched up here and there. Hase was very confidential with me and is more on my side than on that of the Commission.

I will write more soon.

Your last letter bestowed peace and brought happy news. I am really grateful to you, and quiet and happy. *In myself*, I believe I have never in my life been so unified, clear and conscious. All this added together is almost more than anyone has a right to lay claim to, compared with other people ! And yet that is how it is, thank God. . . .

*(Addressed to Drottningholm)*

WEIMAR, 6 *August* 1907.

When I am in Berlin I know what to do with every hour, here there is nothing to do but to " look at the clock." In addition to this the food is bad, drink below the ordinary, and consequently sleep not reposeful . . .

I brought no work with me (on purpose) but the result has not been good. *My* recreation lies in work and being at home. And I must follow this urge (I say this without any impetuosity). In September I have to begin travelling round again, and that lasts until the end of April at least. That is eight months. Wagner wrote once, " One morning without work is hell "— how much more so a week, or more. One cannot stop thought and it only makes one more restless, to think in the abstract. Writing it down makes an end of the whole trouble. . . .

Egon was very " impressed " and in some ways touched by the Brautwahl. That made me *very happy*. Altogether you must not think that I am not happy ; I repeat, that, during the whole of my life, I have never been in such a satisfactory

[1] By the wish of the Grand Duke Carl Alexander (d. 1901), Busoni had held a master class for pianoforte-playing there in the months of August and September 1900 and 1901.

state.  My happiness almost overflows. . . .  When Egon went over the German frontier, he had the Beethoven sonatas in his box, which were fished out at the customs.

"What is that ? " said the customs officer.  " That is music, the Beethoven sonatas."—" Ah, *those* are the Beethoven sonatas," said the customs officer and turned over the leaves.  " As regards the interpretation," he continued (as he gave back the volume), " there is nothing harder to play ; and," he added, (for he took Egon for an Englishman) " a foreigner cannot manage it ; only a German can do it."  Is that not fit for Simplicissimus ? !

I have read de Quincey's " Murder as one of the Fine Arts " with increasing pleasure up to the end.  It consists of three long essays, which were written over the space of 27 years !  In the last one there are two of the most dramatic and clever descriptions of crimes that I have ever read.  He starts from the supposition that a murder has *taken place* ; and when the first impressions of confusion, shock, and sympathy are over, the public, as an amateur, reviews it with admiration and criticism.  That is right . . .

He writes something like this, " The power that a person possesses is wonderful if he can pass lightly over scruples and fear and hold a nation in his hands."  That is right also. . . .

The third essay is serious and inquisitorial, but the two first have a devilish wit. . . .

*N.B.*  I am very glad about the Liszt-edition, which will be a little masterwork.  It has been arranged for my notes to be at the beginning and at the end.

BATH, 26 *September* 1907.
. . . The whole of musical England was assembled in Cardiff.  Amongst those whom you know, for example, Cowen, Hervey, Dr. Elgar, and the dried-up Stock, whose Euterpe swings over Britannia and who begins to show some buds. . . .

Old Bösendorfer, who is even a little younger than before, is building a grand for me with 8 octaves, and with a special damping adjustment.  He is still an admirable, worthy old gentleman.

My classroom in Vienna overlooks the Karls-Kirche, which has always been the most beautiful picture in my recollection . . .
Still more pupils have come.  I wonder if they are *good* ? . . .

I regret that I have no work with me, and on the other hand it is a good thing, perhaps. This trotting round the provinces is not very edifying. Moreover, I am losing many days . . . I see there are going to be nine performances of my compositions this winter. I am glad about it. But first of all I rejoice in my home! Dear Gerda, to-morrow is our wedding day. Thank you for everything good and beautiful that you have given me, and together we must thank the destiny which brought us together and has kept us together till now. I sincerely regret that we shall not be able to pass the day together, but many happy ones will follow.

BOWDON, 30 *September* 1907.
. . . I was very warmly welcomed here and feel that I am amongst really understanding friends,[1] but my longing for home will not be quieted . . . It was very stupid of me to bring no work for I should be glad just to turn it over in my mind. In labore requies—Repose in work—was Liszt's motto, but only work which is of interest . . .

BARROW-IN-FURNESS, 3 *October* 1907.
This time I have traversed a somewhat more friendly part of England. Bath makes a pretty impression, with the beautiful distant hills all round it as background, and its crooked ancient nooks, its tasteful Empire buildings, little surprises everywhere; old bookshops and a magnificent hotel of an exceptionally English brand. The town offered me a pleasant forenoon (the morning after the concert). In Bristol my hotel was in a magnificent position for viewing the country. There is a suspension bridge (in Clifton), built in heroic style over a deep abyss; it is very high and from it one can see far into the valley of the river on both sides. Here too, in Barrow, it is almost rural; the last hour of the journey by the edge of the shore was quite romantic.
On the way, in driving past, I noticed a sheep dog guiding a flock, which was divided into two groups. The animals had eaten their fill, and now had to be driven home. The dog had much to do, for scarcely had he incited the foremost group to go in the required direction, when he was obliged to think of the

---

[1] Egon Petri and his wife.

119

other group, run back, and begin again from the last row.  He
did it with so much cleverness and good humour.  It made me
think of the Berlin policemen, but the comparison was very much
to the latter's disadvantage.


VIENNA, 16 *October* 1907.

 . . . The level [of my class] is about as high (" high " is good)
as my future class in Moscow.  There is scarcely one with whom
I can converse about a picture, a book, or any human question.
If one draws a comparison from psychology, æsthetics, or from
nature, it meets with no understanding.  All I can teach here is
fingering, pedalling, piano and forte and rhythm.  The little,
ugly Russian, who came and cried the last time in Berlin, is
quite a cultivated person compared with the rest !  . . .


VIENNA, 17 *October* 1907.

 . . . My little room in the school building has become quite
cosy.

I have hopes of finding a flat in the Schotten Hof Hotel . . .

The " Schótten Hof " is that big, formal building which
overlooks an open space and is very close to the " Schotten-
kirche " . . . as a child I played to Liszt in this house ;  he
lived there with a cousin.


VIENNA, 19 *October* 1907.

To-day is the most beautiful day there has been this year,
and, thank God, I am free ;  I will enjoy it to the full.  But first
I must write a greeting and some thoughts to you ;  then I shall
wander to the Conservatorium and attend to some small business
matters and (if nothing keeps me) I shall walk round afterwards
with the excuse of looking for a flat, and, finally, have lunch in
*this* !! weather in the Volksgarten restaurant.  Every morning,
at breakfast, I get the " Neue freie Presse." . . .

I have discovered that the ruin of the Viennese (as regards their
relation to art) has its roots in the " Feuilletons "—This system-
atic, *daily* reading of witty, superficial and *short* discussions on
art, sharpened to a point by current catchwords, which has been
going on for half a century, has amongst the Viennese destroyed

their own power of seeing and hearing, of comparison and thinking, and every kind of thoroughness. There is something of the Parisian in these little Viennese, in their pleasure-seeking, and their " superiority," and in their hunt for sensation ; and, as with the Parisians, it is often the cause of their coming to grief. The women, too, remind one of the women of Paris rather than those of London or Berlin ; there are so many who are " pure animals of luxury " amongst them ; you know what I mean. One sees many of the " belle-femme " type here too. Such women as those in the Gomperz family are really an exception ! . . . An air of old-fashioned distinction, which has come down from the salons of 1830, is very characteristic of this place.

Nowhere does one see so many " carriages " in one small place, and the cabs play at being private carriages. They swing along with an air of festive ceremony : one always has the feeling of being driven to a court soirée. This snobbish trampling of horses is only to be heard in Vienna, and it is a significant fact that every house, every courtyard, every pavement, is arranged to allow for a carriage entrance. . . .

Your letter yesterday did me so much good—and a new one has *just* come. What a good thing I had not gone out. Unfortunately, it is very short (and it looked so fat !) . . .

VIENNA, 21 *October* 1907.
. . . The Conservatorium air penetrates through the cracks of the door into my class-room ; I wrote this to Mama some days ago. Her answer was astonishingly sensible, and affectionate.

I have visited *nobody* yet. I had *one* pleasant evening on Saturday ; at the opening of a new cabaret, fitted up by the best painters, architects, and decorators of this country. I sat at the same table with some of these young artists, who were very intelligent and fearfully zealous. Klimt belongs to them too . . .

I thought of writing aphorisms about piano-playing . . . The first thing that occurred to me is :

Before everything there must be technique. It must help to *hide* the difficulties. The difficulties must be hidden, in order that the musical thread, of which the player holds one end and the listener the other, may remain taut. The inserted Cadenza should sound like a parenthesis after which the music takes up its course on the same note on which it was left . . .

VIENNA, 22 *October* 1907.

. . . Yesterday evening, after the lesson, I took three of the men students with me to supper, in order to form some kind of contact with them. It was nice . . . I see nobody, even in the Conservatorium. The people will be very hurt, but they must get used to it. Yesterday the class was *some*what better (the sixth lesson) : the people begin to have an inkling of the standard required. The worst pupils are these little Viennese girls (I have known them from my childhood, the type is still the same) . . . who play *everything*, no matter what, and because it goes half-way, as they have it in their ears more or less, they think that they can play it. This is the reason why that kind of piano talent is so inexpert, for they have no system.

They say Beethoven is *difficult* to play and Liszt only virtuosity. But, " believe just the contrary." [1] For one can always *recognize* a piece by Beethoven ; but you should hear what a Sonnet, or even a study by Liszt sounds like ! It is impossible to understand what is happening when they play anything like that here . . .


VIENNA, 24 *November* 1907.

I have just finished " Turandot's Frauengemach," now only the " Erscheinung " has to be done . . . On the 8th Sauret plays here (my concerto). Shall I stop on this account ?

In the train between Wiesbaden and Vienna I read " The Devil's Disciple." [2] The impression was very mixed, but yet arresting. The first act is absolutely " Dickens." The conversation with a general, from the gallows, seems very improbable. It has everything of the novel about it. But in such stirring times——!


VIENNA, 1st *December* 1907.

I am writing a few lines to you quickly in order to tell you that I have just (7.30—Sunday) finished the 5 Piano pieces.[3] Only a clean copy has to be made now. The last one, " Erscheinung," is certainly the most remarkable.

---

[1] Standing phrase of his Russian pupil, Gregor Beklemischeff.
[2] By Bernard Shaw.
[3] The " Elegies."

122

VIENNA, 3 *December* 1907.

. . . As regards Galston's playing of Liszt, I am glad of his success. If one has penetrated into Liszt's style, his work always sounds better for the instrument than that of any other composer . . . One does not abuse Berlin. Who and what has not got faults? One ought to judge things and people according to their *good* characteristics. . . . The Viennese cannot get away from comparing everything with the past.

The so-called " Wiener Werkstätte " for applied arts is a progressive circle. I have got to know Klimt, an extremely simple, very clever-looking man, almost like a peasant. . . .

VIENNA, 16 *December* 1907.

To-day I shall have finished the Sonnet.[1] When this is done I have decided, for many reasons, to leave the rest of them alone.

First : both the others are so alike—the same key, the same arpeggio accompaniment—that having done the first I consider that the problem of the three is solved. It is also the biggest and richest in variety. I believe it will sound well and be very effective.

Secondly : I can do no more : I must have a rest or the next three months will kill me . . .

I hope you are convinced and that you agree . . .

Yesterday evening (in order to know !) I decided I would hear Madame Butterfly. It began at seven o'clock. The ticket cost 14 Kronen ; at 20 minutes past seven exactly I was out again. I went for a walk, had something to eat and went back again for the last act. *It is indecent.*

I shall never learn to understand the public. It will swallow boredom, monotony, and unreality as if they were liquid pearls.

There was no applause at the end, certainly, but the theatre was sold out. And rich, self-satisfied, smiling Jews came back to the Bristol, charmed.

The people are taken in by the Japanese decorations and the naval officer in modern uniform . . .

[1] Liszt's Petrarca-Sonnet, " Pace non trovo," orchestrated by Busoni.

123

VIENNA, 17 *December* 1907.

It is a good thing that, *for the present*, I have wound up my work with the Sonnet, which I have sent off to you to-day, finished in manuscript. I am almost painfully fatigued, but very contented with the result of this blessed year 1907. . . .

# 1908

I am writing to you, just in order to be with you for a moment ; to say that there's nothing—nothing to tell you. Here everything goes round in the well-known circle . . . It is just as if one were living in the year 1884, which was when I first tasted all these joys, only then the Hanslick Feuilleton came out once a week, on a certain day, like market day in little towns, and Rubinstein was playing.

Ibsen has given me the greatest pleasure—John Gabriel Borkman seems to be simply unsurpassable and perhaps his greatest book. The only part of " Klein Eyolf " that pleased *me—now*, is the end : the rest of it distressed me. I say *me* and *now*. For I see more and more clearly that there is *no absolute* greatness and value : everything is as it appears to one at the moment. And it is only by the impressions which change least with time that one can have any judgment as to what is great or less great . . .


VIENNA, 16 *January* 1908.

The first successful attempt to fly (Flugversuch) has been made : not accidentally ; without a balloon ; with mechanism only.

This, first of all, is a definite answer to Leonardo's question, and it answers too the questions and expectations of the whole world. This seems to be a more suitable and worthy theme with which to open my letter, rather than with that of the also not unsuccessful attempt to play the piano (" *Flügelversuch* ") which I made yesterday evening in the big Musikverein Hall of the " Kaiserstadt."

Every day I regret that you are not with me ; the Bösendorfer was brilliant ; *Göllerich* found the Todtentanz perfect. After the concert, at the Green Anchor, there was pleasant company : Schalk, Botstiber, Dr. Schenker, Galston, and the best pupils, who adore me (I only say it from pleasure) . . .

Really it was a Début again ! Nobody knew how I played and the directors of the conservatorium were quite nervous as to what impression " their professor " would make. The recital will certainly put the " dots on the i's " . . .

I am well—only tired and with a little too much in my head.

I have been very much stimulated by Ibsen. With him the women are always the spokesmen. The men corroborate them with a miserable echo. Hedda Gabler is now perfectly clear to me and could not be otherwise than she is.

I shall be glad when I can freely follow my own thoughts again : I believe much that is good is still to come . . .

If only it were May again ! . . .

The Wiener Tageblatt brought out a splendid article about Gerhardt Hauptmann's newest work. I took the liberty of sending it to him, with a few words on my own account.


LONDON, 3 *March* 1908.

The enclosed letter [1] went to Vienna to-day. Have two copies made, and send one to Bösendorfer and one to the " Neue Freie Presse " and keep the original.

DEAR SIRS,

You have, without any attempt to come to an understanding, hurled a " dismissal " at me, completely out of the blue.

Without taking into any account the possibility of a reply from my side, you have made public a one-sided, and for me, almost slanderous representation of the affair which is still not fought out. You have gone still further by announcing my successor—also publicly.

Herr Director Bopp—instead of referring to me—has examined and chosen my pupils for a public performance, completely ignoring my proposals and opinions, which alone are decisive here.

In addition to this I wish to make the following remarks :

I believe, if your displeasure really arose out of interest for

[1] To the Directors of the Conservatorium.

126

BUSONI, 1908

the master class, that you would have shown a practical proof of this, if you had paved the way to an understanding with me before having recourse to a drastic resolution.

You should have expressed a wish or even made a demand for the modification of the plan made by me.

This would have been the first step towards promoting the welfare of the institution. And you would have found me ready to do my utmost to agree to such an understanding, because the artistic success of my pupils lies near to my wishes and to neglect the duties I have undertaken lies absolutely far from them.

I still adhere to my opinion that it is out of the question to break a contract before the end of the school year—(I was and am absolutely resolved to make good the complete number of lessons and to be responsible for the artistic result)—and a friendly word of reconciliation from you would have been able, too, to check the irregularities which happened against my wish.

This would have been—I repeat—the most practical, most human, and most correct procedure for the welfare of the master class this year. The *announcement in the press* of your thoroughly immature decision, however, did not correspond to those attributes ; apart from misrepresentation of facts, which came about through dealing with them publicly, and against which, here in a distant country, I could not defend myself.

In view of all these considerations the announcement of a successor was tactless.

For that reason I declare that I am the one who has suffered injustice and I protest against it openly.

In spite of this I am trying once more—because of the deep interest I feel for my pupils, who have become very dear to me, and for the preservation of my honour—to propose a settlement to you in a friendly form, which is that you will allow me to continue and finish this school year.

I am convinced that this is the only way in which to protect your own interests and the welfare of the pupils, and in part to remove an injustice which has been done to me.

If you agreed to this I should arrive in Vienna on the 14th of March and be there for a week, and after that devote myself without interruption to my office, from the 21st April until the end of the school year.

May I ask you to telegraph to me here on the 6th or 7th of the month.

Yours truly,

VIENNA, 15 *April* 1908.

It is already past *three* and I am not out of the house yet ; I have been working so eagerly. A happy week ! . . .

There is an unusual, delightful young man here, hardly 20, the son of the great artist-photographer Hanfstaengl in Munich. He has such a genuine, pure nature, and is simple, witty and intelligent. His taste in art, especially, is astonishingly developed. Benni should get to know *him*—he would be an excellent friend for him.

These Hanfstaengls still stick close to all the painters (from Lenbach onwards) . . .

VIENNA, 27 *April* 1908.

As the train approached Vienna early this morning, I had a feeling of youth and of everything just beginning. It was like a reminiscence of that journey, 25 years ago, when I came as a guest to Döbling.

My flat here is behind the Wallfischgasse and is roomy and agreeably habitable . . . There were wonderful pots of flowers set out to welcome me. Frau Pollhammer, my landlady, is a very respectable and good woman, rather more distinguished than Liszt's " Baulline," but very like her and although she is very friendly she is rather managing . . .

*Everybody in Vienna knows that I am here.* The story, even if a nasty one, is of no importance. Do not take everything so hard, dear Gerda, the world *is* like this and it is a great honour (?) if one is talked about at all, even in a bad way.

Egon's letter about it was most refreshing, like an answer of protest . . .

VIENNA, 30 *April* 1908.

. . . The old friends Thusmann and Leonhard Turnhäuser awake from their winter sleep, shake themselves, yawn, and turn around once more, before they get up . . .

128

Then between whiles I think of my adopted child, the *Liszt* edition and a preface for it . . .

How do you like this sentence (about Liszt) ?

"—his change from demon to angel—from the first Bravour-Fantasy ' Sur la Clochette,' (a devilish suggestion of Paganini's) up to the childlike mysticism of the ' Weihnachtsbaum,' in *which that final naïveté, which is the fruit of all experience* floats over, strangely, to a ' better land ' " . . .

In Italy by chance I bought a book " Quanto mi pare " by a Guiseppe Brunati. " Selon mon caprice " would have been a better title for it. It really means despotism. It is a good book, the language excellent, lively in thought and unusual in material.

The hero is the last of a race of magnificent and horrible little tyrants in the time of the Renaissance. The sharp mind, cruelty and despotism of the Borgia type still bloom in his degenerate body and constitute a remarkable contrast to the new Italy.

Fragments from his family chronicle are recounted, and show up what was monumental, even if barbaric, in the old oppressors, in contrast to the colourless mass of present-day democracy. " The genius of rulers " is praised ; a race which has died out. A subject like that suits me *now*.

The type of the ruling Genius seems to have changed and to have passed over to the American industrial kings. *Their* people are the harassed workers, their conquests great speculations, which can often save or ruin a whole country.

I have betaken myself to a voluntary " exile," I see that now——

If only I can get into the right " mood."

Teaching has the relative advantage of keeping my piano-playing fresh . . .

VIENNA, 4 *May* 1908.
. . . A monument to Brahms is to be unveiled on the 7th, to which ceremony I am invited. Italian opera is to be given too, only 4 performances, amongst them Rigoletto and Don Giovanni. I think I shall go—that is exactly the kind of food I require, and perhaps it will make the Brautwahl flow again. *It has not exactly stuck*, but I have to push it, and it is only quite right when one is pushed by it.

F.B.                    129                    I

. . . Thusmann is already wailing cat's music to the frog spawn. Yesterday (Monday) there were lessons. You see, I try to get something done . . .

VIENNA, 8 *May* 1908.

. . . Nothing could have less atmosphere than the " unveiling " [of the Brahms monument]. Some very dry " cappella-chöre " by the master were sung . . . A forest of black umbrellas which intercepted a colourless speech.

Brahms sits comfortably and thoughtfully—it's very like him —on a pedestal which looks like cement but is really cheap marble. Below, on the left, lies (! ! !) a Muse with a common cabaret face, who plucks at a lyre which also is lying on the steps—an unsuccessful figure . . .

Amongst other things, Freund writes to me : " The reason why your work is more difficult to understand is that your harmony is much richer than that of Debussy ; for instance, once one finds out the latter's peculiar tonality everything is extremely simple ; but in your work, the harmony is the outcome of the melody, or rather, of the musical thought."

VIENNA, 9 *May* 1908.

. . . I was at work, have composed 7 pages without a break, it went excellently. Everything thought out yesterday in the street. Hope to be able to tell more to you soon . . .

VIENNA, 17 *May* 1908.

Rigoletto ! I only heard the opera once before, in my earliest childhood, perhaps when I was about nine. I can still remember my Mother relating the story to me (adapted for the young), one evening, in the via Geppa, at Triest. The impressions made by the first Festmusik, the whispered Raub-Chor (Entführung) and the wind in the storm, which is made by men's voices behind the stage, were unforgettable and remained with me until I reached manhood. It was not many years ago—perhaps four— that I saw the piano score for the first time. I still had the Festmusik and the whispered chorus firmly in my memory.

. . . The Brautwahl has progressed still further, I have never worked so easily. I have written and written, in order to *hold on to it* ; and shall then revise the whole. I found Rigoletto yesterday without atmosphere ; it was much too much " sung " ; for example, the duet with Sparafucile (called Saltabadil by Victor Hugo) which is like an etching between a row of coloured pictures, did not produce a " shiver," as it should. The heavy oak doors bellied like sails in the wind. The costumes were typically of the operatic kind, such as Caran d'Ache and other caricaturists like so much to portray. The truth is that I had made an ideal for myself as to what the music and the performance should be like and yesterday's representation never agreed with it.

Now there is still Don Giovanni to hear and then I come home . . .

. . . For 2 days I have been pursued by an idea, stronger than any previous ones ; that, as the natural result of quite fifteen years' development, I *must* write an Italian opera !

It seems to me now to be the right thing to do, and were it possible, I would gladly give up all the Meyrinks, Shaws and Gobineaus [1] for it. I feel that my style will unfold and come into full bloom there, for the first time, and I shall reach the place where I ought to be.

The question of a libretto is a difficult one. I thought of Boito, and of Italian short stories, witty ones, but it is safer to take a ready-made stage figure (such as Falstaff). Goldini is no good. Gozzi, hardly, but perhaps—there is very much to think about here too. Perhaps you will write about it . . .

The 5 hours' travelling and playing were a bad cure for the nervous condition I was in yesterday.

When I got out at the so-called *Berlin* station at Leipzig, I went straight to the Phonola . . . Then, by the time I had played

---

[1] Refers to opera plans.

the programme for the settled fee, played an encore, written out a testimonial, signed two photographs, listened to Godowsky and myself in the machine, and also sat for a photograph " at the Phonola " it was 4.30, round about six hours since I had left the Anhalter Bahnhof.

This, combined with the " oppressive " weather, produced headache. The testimonial that I was asked to sign was already typed and read as follows : " I regard the ' DEA ' as the crown of creation." I said nobody would believe it, and, of course, wrote one of my own. . . .

I almost wished I was stopping in Leipzig, and I even saw a poster which promised a brilliant " May festival in the Palm Garden." At eight o'clock I was so tired that I looked upon a seat in a first-class carriage in the train as Paradise ; whereas the idea of waking in Leipzig on a Sunday morning struck me as something very unpleasant. So I made a quick decision and took the train to Vienna—and I have not regretted it . . .

VIENNA, 16 *June* 1908.
. . . I sweat over my little love duet—to-day it begins to " dawn." Night reigned on Sunday and Monday. I comfort myself with Flaubert—*he* tormented himself. How does the theory of genius and ease hold good in his case ? This older edition of " St. Antony " is *quite different* from the last ; and *it*, too, is the *revision of a youthful work*. It took him 25 years to do the three versions, from 1849–74 ! When he read the first edition to his friends he said to them beforehand, " If you don't shout with enthusiasm, nothing can move you." The reading aloud lasted four days, after which the friends, tired out, said to him : " We think you ought to throw that into the fire ! " The book then lay fallow for seven years, and was then rewritten to his satisfaction. Only the scandal and the law-suit against " Madame Bovary " gave him the courage to publish the *second* St. Antony. This second is the one I am reading now. The third and " last edition " comes 18 years later, completely different.

That Mozart should have written Don Giovanni in 6 months makes one ashamed of one's slowness ; and Flaubert's 25 years of labour give one pricks of conscience about one's rapidity.

Never, never, can one set up a rule when it is a question of art.

Every stroke of the pen demands its own conditions. . . . In new works one avoids the old mistakes but makes new ones again, because the problem is always changing . . . ' With the beginning of every new thing one is timid and awkward again . . .

VIENNA, 18 June 1908.

The trouble was in the text. The " sitting for the portrait " had to go, it would have torn the threads. Now the duet is finished ! Everything runs on wheels now. The form very rounded off again. Thusmann has just entered unexpectedly and uttered his horrified " But ! " in falsetto. Now there are still three pages of text to complete the act . . .

" St. Antony " is interesting. What a good ballet could be made from Brueghel's pictures of " The Temptation of St. Antony." From some such painting Flaubert must surely have got his first impulse. I believe it is a colossal theme for a ballet ! If one had time ! If I were only 10 years younger !

Perhaps you can write a few lines every 2nd day so that question and answer alternate . . .

To-day is Corpus Christi, the 18th June 1908.

VIENNA, 23 June 1908.

DEAR GERDA,

This letter was written for myself only and not sent.

Your FERROMANN.

DEAR FRAU P.

Your remark, that I was too serious a man to write a comic opera, made me think over it. To me it sounds like censure, but as I know you meant no such thing at the moment, I must attribute it to a disparity in our ideas of what seriousness is. I feel much more seriousness in humour than in tragic " Spanpanaderln." To me, the Meistersinger is more serious than Cavalleria ; Figaro more serious than the Prophet ; Leporello is the creation of a more serious mind than Fides ; Don Quixote more profound than the " Kampf um Rom." Lack of humour in a poet is just as bad a sign as an exaggeration of the pathetic, as in Victor Hugo.

Only psychological tragedy suits Beethoven ; his handling of a tragic situation is quite dull. A tragic situation requires a

133

conflict between *at least* two people, whilst a psychological one takes place in a single person. Beethoven would have been the man for a higher kind of comic opera. Aphoristically : Humour is the blossom from the tree of seriousness. One sees it in Shakespeare and in Ibsen. Therefore it would be pretentious of me to write a comic opera.

VIENNA, 27 *June* 1908.

. . . I believe that most people are natural : also that an inclination towards " dissembling " is natural. By " natural " people you mean those who are most like you, in your own being. Who are clever without being designing, and not literary in speech, and who have a certain big current of feeling. But Frau B is very natural ; yet if you were to think and write in her way, you would dissemble. Ysaye's pose is his true nature (which you cannot bear). A storyteller must go through an endlessly long and complicated row of exercises in dissembling before he reaches artistic naturalness. How could Balzac describe 4,000 people correctly—of whom, perhaps, only ten bear any resemblance to himself—without dissembling ? A born criminal, who lives virtuously, is unnatural, a Jesuit. Naturalness is a great strength and for that reason is to be admired. Weaker people (that is to say, most people) on account of conditions, education, and interests, are obliged to practise dissembling. Unnaturalness is often the wish to imitate a certain ideal, for want of a character of one's own.

And finally I believe that only someone quite alone and quite free can be *quite* natural ; and *who* is placed in such a favourable situation ? . . .

The day before yesterday, Thursday, at the end of a strenuous class, Kapff came and detained me for another two hours, with the most pessimistic bankrupt kind of conversation. I can't help it, but I can't have anything to do with people who have finished with life. Digging into the past is repulsive to me ; either one has done something which one could never do better, or which one could do better now. Either thought is irritating. I felt neither friendship nor sympathy for Kapff. I should have liked to make him a present of a revolver. It is the first time I have felt so hard. Is that bad ? . . .

Yesterday I finished off the first *three* acts of the Brautwahl.

134

It is exactly two years since the day on which I finished the text. In Vienna I wrote *80 pages* of the piano sketch. Now only the final scene is wanting . . .

VERONA, 9 *September* 1908.

One could weep over the condition of this country. The sun shines down perpendicularly, and dazzles and oppresses, without cheering. The people, idle and careless, curious and unfriendly gather together and criticize passing strangers. On the steps of beautiful palaces the poor people sleep like animals. The shops are closed most of the day, barricaded with shutters and locks. The women, uneducated, and without taste, look neither to the right nor to the left, and only betray a lack of *naïveté* . . .

" O Italia, Italia mia,
O fosti tu men bella
O almen più forte ! "

VERONA, 9 *September* 1908.
(Second letter)

. . . In the evening I went to Parona, a pretty, extremely old patch of houses by the river, wonderfully situated. There I enjoyed the sunset, the rising of the moon in a crystal-clear sky, and eating and drinking out of doors . . . The heat still flourishes. I feel well, pleasantly lonely. Think of you with love always.

VERONA, 9 *September* 1908.
(Third letter)

The towns are corpses, but the country is *alive*. The best example : *Siena*. I wonder, too, whether the towns have *gone backwards*, or if they have stood still since the Renaissance ? I almost think the latter. In the life of the public anyhow . . . Looked at closely, these old buildings are *not* better than ours of to-day. With few exceptions, the majority of them are quite ordinary. A heresy ! But in Italy the modern buildings are bad. I believe—and the idea is really good—that, as in music, not the theme but the co-operation of all the means in the com-

135

poser's mind constitutes its value ; so, too, the " charm " of Italy exists in an infinity of coinciding conditions. And the charm is there. When you come out of the theatre in the evening, as I did to-day, and see the " motionless " beauty of the sky outside, in contrast to the sham lighting on the stage ; the houses tinted red by the glow from the lamps below, silhouettes vanishing round corners and disappearing into inconceivable nooks, the moon triumphing above the fantastic shapes of roofs, and the singing one has heard inside making the consciousness of the quietness more acute—all this is nothing and yet more than it is elsewhere.

Dear Gerda : a great idea dawned on me this morning. I should like to give this Italy a national opera, as Wagner gave one to Germany, and which the Italians have not got yet. I feel that I can do it, and that it will be my life's work . . . Mozart could have been the Italian classic, but they scarcely know of him here. I shall think it over well . . .

MILAN, 13 *September* 1908.

. . . I have been considering Italian women a little, and have come to the conclusion that their behaviour is the result of their lack of male relationships. They only know their brothers and uncles ; the harmless uncle, the terrifying uncle, the comical uncle. If, occasionally, they meet their brothers' friends, then certain themes and certain expressions are eliminated from the conversation. By brothers and uncles they are treated like children, and by friends with a formality which always produces the same tone. But with the exception of these contacts men just remain in categories for them. For them, there are men who are " sympathetic," " handsome," " worthy of respect," and " dangerous "—all from hearsay, and the existence of men remains a legend in their girlish dreams which takes on some kind of untrue shape. The women only talk amongst themselves, and the circle of talk turns like the hand of a clock round the figures. In connection with the enjoyment of travel in Italy, I find these conditions where " femininity " is left out most oppressive. And how much of it should I get out of a visit to Frl. F or Frau G here ? Worse than nothing.

But these are only reflections " in between," so to speak, for I have thought of other things ; for example, I have *written down* my ideas about Chopin. Further, I have read a biography of Leonardo which—dry as it was—stimulated me very much. I must finish reading the Mereschkowsky book one day. I thought that he (Leonardo) might give me the wished-for figure for my Italian opera. The historical background of the *Sforzas* is big and one could make Leonardo the central figure of the action, like Hans Sachs in the " Meistersinger." The episodes, when he arranged the festivities at the court of the Sforza and invented many clever mechanical devices for them, are quite reminiscent of the rôle of Faust in the puppet play by Herzog von Mantova, which Goethe also used in the second part of Faust. The milieu, principally Milan, seems to me to be suitable and rich. I shall think more about it . . .

But first of all, the Brautwahl. To-night I go to Basle, where I expect to find a letter at last ! . . .

LONDON, 5 *November* 1908.

. . . The sea was as smooth as a mirror, and it was a mild night. In the end, we arrived " before time." The first immediate impression of London this time was not very pleasant ; I only saw a collection of quite small things—(like certain long symphonies which are composed in four-bar phrases)—I found Vasari's essay on Leonardo quite touching, beautiful in language and feeling, although quite poor biographically. Mereschkowsky's book, too, has good things in it (as, for example, the diary by Giovanni Boltraffio) ; as a work of art it is not bold or connected enough, but full of good intentions. Leonardo's figure and epoch become more and more important in my eyes ; they seem to me to give the most worthy *national subject*. I shall stick to this idea and try to build up a new and more perfect kind of theatre music. I should like, then, to work at it very conscientiously for, perhaps, five years. For I feel that a riper, more independent person has been formed in me, in the way that new teeth grow behind the still firm and healthy front ones. There is an abundance of material in the subject. How worthy of love such a subject is ! I must know still more about it before I begin. How beautifully Leonardo himself says, " Love is *knowledge* of a thing ; the deeper the knowledge, the more powerful the love." . . .

I have taken the book by the cultivated barbarian, Mereschkowsky, too much to heart.  It became less and less possible for
me to read it as literature—especially towards the end (in spite of
the author's praiseworthy efforts, it often reminds one of Baedeker)
—nor to regard it as a possible source for my own plan which
is just beginning to dawn ; but it increased the strong feeling
I already have for Leonardo.  Perhaps I was mistaken when I
thought that, in this figure, I saw some similarities with my own
much smaller one.  It plunged me into a feeling of almost
despairing sadness.  I am still under this impression to-day,
and it seems to be grotesque to be obliged to dress up in order to
play two old pieces in that miserable, large, round, Albert Hall.
Altogether this English tour promises much moral misery, and
it makes an ugly picture.  One sees oneself constantly beginning
afresh, with old tricks, and getting older all the time.

I am still young enough to begin something quite new, but I can
see no end to it all, and I rack my tired brain to find a way out.

Perhaps it is wrong to pass on this mood to you, but to whom
shall I talk if not to you ?  To suppress it is difficult.  I should
like to catch hold of a bit of the coming art of music, and where
possible, sew a seam in it myself.  I feel more and more clearly
that in the future all our present chirping will be defined as a
" prehistoric " epoch.  It can only be hoped that mankind,
before it is too late, may turn away from this stupid urge towards
quickness, excessive bigness and possessions, so that great artists
may still arise.  It is a bad omen for the future that types should
exist like R.S. who (even in his art) is a cross between an artist
and an industrialist.  And yet I almost think that in the new big
music machines will be necessary too, and will be assigned a share
in it.  Perhaps industry, too, will bring forth her share in the
artistic ascent.

" There will be wings."

With this prophecy of Leonardo's, which is just beginning to
be true in our day, I close more hopefully . . .

NEWCASTLE, 10 *November* 1908.
. . . Life here is horrible, grey and joyless . . . Everything sleeps in me, but at the same time I dream unquietly of
unattainable things, big works, beautiful countries—and Rest ! . . .

LONDON, 17 *November* 1908.

(In the train from London to Leeds)

. . . Lately, in albums, I have often come across my signature in the year 1901 and I have *rejoiced* over the progress I have made since then . . . The most active musical life is to be found in London—and Berlin—but there is only reproduction. . . .

MANCHESTER, 20 *November* 1908.

Your little letter arrived in the artists' room here, and produced its good effect. The concert passed off satisfactorily. Richter has given the Directors to understand that he is not so young as he was 5 years ago and can no longer do the whole work. But he promised to provide a deputy himself. This is no other than Cosima's son-in-law who conducted yesterday. In the meantime the " tired " Richter took a theatre rehearsal in London ! The wife of the new conductor is Cosima's daughter Isolde . . . This woman, who already has white hair, looks beautiful, good and refined. She was very friendly towards me : told me that Frau Cosima had heard with much joy and gratitude of how much I had done for Liszt's compositions, and that she sent me her greetings. That was a beautiful reward for me . . .

The previous evening Kubelik played here, with Landon Ronald . . . Kubelik, at a distance, looks like Beethoven, and near to, like Director Reinhardt of the Deutsches Theater. He is small and slender, like Galston. I heard him for the first time and was astonished to find how *little* there is of anything sensational in this violinist's playing : it is on the contrary rather conscientious and monotonous and not very attractive. Who can understand the public ? . . .

It is difficult, in the midst of a hundred silly little cares, to find the right mood for completing the Brautwahl, but I never let the work go quite out of my thoughts . . .

LONDON, 23 *November* 1908.

. . . You must have sent the newspaper cutting chiefly on account of the grotesque Chinese Emperor story. But Sardou's disclosures about Dante on the same sheet were remarkable. Machiavelli is not quite to be trusted—he was (in spite of his powerful intellect) a little the same type as my father.  I am just reading A. France's new book " L'Ile des Pingouins," in which he makes a very ironical attack on history.  As it is impossible to make an exact picture of a person long dead (even about contemporaries one learns nothing true), it is best for the public to form an ideal for itself which is uplifting, and in this way it will believe in *something* beautiful.

Legends seem to me to show the hidden urge towards perfection . . .

# 1909

Yesterday, sea and sky were radiant, blue and yellow ; everything moved, fluttered and blew in the fresh wind. To-day it is quiet and grey. Beautiful as Triest is there is something in the atmosphere that is not noble ; big new thoughts could never originate here, and it oppresses even those who are gifted. I was afraid to come here—meanwhile Mama is out of danger and Papa gets better slowly. . . . This time it is bad for me in Austria altogether. I can seldom be happy here. It has too much against it in all sorts of ways and, in addition, these stale memories . . . I have had another vexation too. Two unknown Italian gentlemen have published a drama, " Leonardo da Vinci " ! ! It is true it is a miserable concoction ; but my idea is deflowered and profaned. Am very sorry . . .

VIENNA, 13 *January* 1909.

. . . I have come back feeling really sad. I become more and more solitary and am glad if nobody knocks at my door in the hotel. Occupation I can *always* find. To-day I have done all kinds of things, amongst others I have sent a clean copy of the piano piece [1] to Paris . . .

VIENNA, 14 *January* 1909.

. . . I received your dear letter in Triest, it did me so much good . . . The sight of both my parents in bed with a folding screen between them, becomes a more and more vivid picture in my memory. Papa is like a child of three and if for two minutes nobody stands beside his bed, he begins to scream

[1] Nuit de Noël.

. . . He is terribly pale, keeps his head very bent, and can hardly see anything any more—— The doctor, compassionate nurse, and an indescribably ugly maidservant, take it in turns to be with them. The cousins have given themselves endless trouble, especially Carolina (she is living in Triest again), whose dexterity and patience are beyond price. The weather is miserable. In spite of that, there is a kind of springlike feeling in me which will not be kept down. . . .


LYON, 16 *February* 1909.
. . . Lyon is more beautiful than Milan and nobody knows me here. Unfortunately it is a severe winter, frost and snow. Bordeaux is not an uninteresting town. But the level of culture (if one comes from Paris) is very primitive and provincial. The art of " beau parleur " is highly esteemed. Of course the interest in vine growing is the chief thing. Such sentences as the following prove this : " J'avais fait suivre le Lafitte au Mouton Rotschild par le respect dû à son ancienneté et ne voulais pas déranger l'ordre naturel, d'autant plus que le maître (that was I) donnait une préférence légitime au Lafitte : mais—entre nous—je trouve le Rotschild supérieur."
That is what the president of the concert society said to me at a lunch at his house . . .
The great number of beautiful and well-dressed women at the concert was striking. Of course, everyone from Bordeaux was there. An old musician, whom I had already met at Erard's, a man of head, heart, and great goodness, begged me, after this lunch, to go to his house for half-an-hour . . . He lives in a small round *place*, which must certainly have stood there for 100 years ; round it are one-storied houses ; and it is very quiet, for neither man nor carriage goes by that way. He has made the house inside very pretty and comfortable. Besides his wife, a young woman, dressed in deep mourning, was there, very beautiful and with an air of distinction . . . A singing pupil. And the old man begged me imploringly, but proudly, to allow her to sing. She sang 4–5 songs by Fauré in a warm deep voice, with great feeling and taste and very expressive play of the features. There was something noble about her ; it reminded me of Donna Anna in Don Giovanni. This little interlude left behind the memory of something tender and almost

fantastic ; fantastic, because it does not belong at all to the character of our time, but goes back rather to the epoch in which the little *place* was built.

MILAN, 19 *February* 1909.

It is in his writings and notes that one first really begins to read about Leonardo. From them, one gathers that he already had an idea of the aeroplane, the screw propeller and the diving apparatus. He wanted the Venetians to regulate the " Isonzo " in such a way that artificial flooding could be organized to hold back or to destroy enemies.

They did not allow him to do anything.

And it went through my mind as to whether the dramatic idea could not be grounded in this. As one plan after another fails, one after another, the people turn away from him, but " he," always solitary and isolated, obtains an increasingly higher and freer point of view until, at the time of his death, he attains his highest wisdom which proves to be prophetic. For one does not want just a dramatic biography. What do you think of that ?

The concert yesterday was beautiful, but rather beyond the understanding of the audience.

GENOA, 27 *February* 1909.

. . . There has been cold and snow the whole journey—ever since Bordeaux. Even in Nice it snowed. The trains here are slow, uncomfortable, always *over-full*, always late, the luggage is often left behind. . . . The journey gave me the opportunity of seeing for the first time the coast which one calls the Riviera. In spite of the frightful weather, it seemed to me to be one of the most beautiful countries I have ever seen. And one day I propose enjoying it in peace with you . . . In front, the sea ; behind, the picturesque high mountains ; between them, terraces with palms, lemons and vines ; there are old towns and grey sunny villas alternately, everywhere.

Nice—which I could only see for a couple of hours in the evening—seems rather amusing and lively. One notices a tendency towards extreme " superficiality." Its situation is, of course, magical. Monte Carlo comes *first*, when one travels from here, so that I was able to throw a glance at this spot where the civilisation is so monstrous, and which has been so generously ornamented by nature.

On the journey to Nice I had a dream. In it, I came back from a very early walk in the country, between 6 and 7 o'clock in the morning, to a small place which looked like a street (a sort of suburban Boulevard). At an open window, on the ground floor, I saw Dr. Leopold Schmidt standing, with half a cello in his hands. This cello was cut through the middle, from front to back and from top to bottom, like a pear which one shares with a neighbour at table. When I asked what he was doing, Dr. Leopold Schmidt said : " I am studying the source of musical sounds." I find wit in this dream.

Pity that it is so cold and grey here. I think in Italy one can only give serious concerts in Rome, Bologna and Milan ; piano recitals, at any rate. These latter will now be the next and last towns. Treviso, Nice, Genoa were artistically unsatisfactory. . . . There is a feeling of spiritual misunderstanding between what is expected from me, what I give, and what the puzzled public absorbs.

I have such a longing for your letters. With the exception of Anzoletti, there is no one in Italy who *knows* me ; they look at me as if I were a strange animal. It is sad that there should be such a distance between me and the Italians. I have been too far away from them, for too long a time, and my culture seems foreign to them. I shall write a special preface to the Italian edition of the Æsthetik . . .

Papa is up again !


ROME, 3 *March* 1909.
Yesterday I heard the third act of " Aida." It was touching, comical, sad, but also beautiful. What an audience ! The ladies dressed up like dummies in shop windows, and the men in the audience joined in, in the singing ! For them the singer is the chief thing. A beautiful sound, a good cadence, bums ! enthusiasm, interruption, bis ! . . .


ROME, 6 *March* 1909.
. . . I am very nervous, just now, when travelling, and have the continual feeling that time is slipping by me (even if I make every possible use of it under these difficult circumstances).

This makes me bitter sometimes (though not against *you*) and consequently unjust. I will try not to be so any more, but be pleased when you are pleased. I take a great deal of trouble to act in the right way, but my life is many-sided and in this respect rather complicated. . . .

Already the conflict between what I should like to do, what I could do, and what I must do is very worrying and keeps me in a continual state of tension. But perhaps everything is for the best like this, and who knows if it may not be the means of preserving my energy and even increasing it.

As regards Benni. . . . Lenau is no reading for him, it is poison, like Schopenhauer and other pleasant despairers. He should only read what spurs him on, not what disheartens him. He should go on reading Shakespeare, for that is good for sense of form and imagination and is fine literature. On the whole, he should read things that are not pessimistic or erotic, but above all, what is artistically *good*. Don Quixote, Goethe's poems, Kleist, Gottfried Keller, the 1001 Nights (erotic, certainly, but this is hardly noticeable amongst the other wonders), Benvenuto's Life, Dickens and Edgar Poe, early Ibsen, and the German romantics ; but not these black, pessimistic, suicidal authors ; no Lenau, Schopenhauer, Werther, Leopardi—the " Suicide Club " of literature. I have written a little autobiographical sketch in the Italian language and sent it to Anzoletti, it is written on 4–5 sheets of notepaper, up to my 6th year. It is quite amusing and written humorously . . . I am longing for home ! !

BOLOGNA, 7 *March* 1909.
. . . I am going through difficult days, even though they are made easier by a very warm reception everywhere . . . Sgambati was very charming to me, and invited me to lunch. After I had played the Sonata he kissed my hand and said I quite reminded him of the Master ; more so than his real pupils. . . .

Tagliapietra and Anzoletti are here again in Bologna. It is the time of the *elections* (le elezione) and the whole of Italy is in a state of excitement. It is only party agitation ; whatever the result, the country will not change . . .

Dear Gerda, I am not going to write much, because I am very tired. I think of nothing but trains, programmes, and the end of the journey. I am out of touch with everything, only the piano-playing goes well, I hardly seem to play with my hands any more. Whatever I perform, this playing makes the same strong impression everywhere . . .

MILAN, 9 *March* 1909.
. . . I have just come straight from a visit to *Boito*. They have suggested giving the *Brautwahl* in Italian and I went to him for advice. Boito is no longer young and his principal thought is for what remains for him to do himself. At last, after nearly 40 years, he seems to have finished his *Nerone*, in earnest. In spite of all that, he showed a friendly interest in what I had to tell him. He thought the project would be fairly easy to carry out.

My ideas agreed with his : about dramatic art, about Wagner. He predicted good things for my work. The first, and perhaps the greatest difficulty is the *translation*. And much time can be lost over it. On the other hand, he seems to think that publishers and theatres are certain to be interested. It was a pleasant hour I spent with an able, gifted, and kindly-disposed man.

Yesterday I had a very strenuous day, four hours' travelling and 2 hours' preparation for a relatively new programme. The concert lasted another two hours . . . There is no question of "taking it lightly," the people expect too much and there are men of authority everywhere. On the contrary, I have taken the greatest trouble.

The concerts in Rome, Bologna and Milan were also very successful.

To-day I go to Triest—still four stages before Berlin !

VIENNA, 14 *March* 1909.
. . . I have been moving about every day since the 4th March. I admire my own elasticity.

On the 4th  Concert in Rome
        5th   To Bologna
        6th   Arrived early and concert
        7th   Second concert
        8th   To Milan *and* concert

| 9th | To Triest |
|-----|-----------|
| 10th | Arrived mid-day *and* concert |
| 11th | Journey to Fiume (5 hours), concert; after the concert left for Budapest. |
| 12th | Arrived mid-day. Evening concert |
| 13th | Went to Vienna |

The success in Budapest was the same as it has been everywhere this year . . .

I am so far away from every normal condition, that I cannot tell exactly how I feel. I think I am exhausted. I notice that because I have had so few *creative thoughts* lately. . . . But I believe that after 4 days at home I shall be myself again. I did not want to leave you without news, felt the necessity of writing to you . . .

I am writing to you again—still to-day! I have just come from Bösendorfer, on whom I called. I remembered that he had built a piano (thinking of me) and that I had neglected to go and see it.

I have accustomed myself gradually to making use of the pauses during the journeys and, in spite of the extraordinary amount of work I have done, I wished to give pleasure to the good old man. I even had much pleasure myself, for the instrument is unusually good, big and beautiful.

Bösendorfer I found *very* fresh, and happy as a child, without being in the least childish. May he still be able to continue so for a long time to come! Although I do not like old people very much, I must say it was a great comfort to me to find my Mother up. Though weak and visibly more fragile, she was clear and active-minded, and so good! She blessed me, saying: I bless you for bringing so much joy and help to your Mother. God will reward you and everything you do will succeed.

The time I spent with Sgambati and Boito was a wonderful experience. One might say: Truth lies in old age; for, as the kernel of the whole person, it alone survives, and there is not enough physical strength to hide it. . . .

Oh! . . . I am so tired and so out of the rut of my straight line! . . .

147

*(Addressed to Varese)*

BERLIN, 20 *July* 1909.

. . . To-day I wrote the first sketch for a treatise on Melody-formation.

No time for everything! Looked through the Diabelli Variations again. It would be a fine task. . . .


*(Addressed to Varese)*

BERLIN, 21 *July* 1909.

This morning I attacked the old rascal Manasse . . . The days roll by like a Phonola-roll : if you attend very closely, interest and expression can be put into it. But if anything is overlooked it is too late to put it right, and unless you are careful the roll is finished—almost unheard. . . .

I am reading Plato now. . . .


*(Addressed to Gargnano on Lake Garda)*

BERLIN, 28 *July* 1909.

To-day the " Lokalanzeiger " contains the news of Blériot having flown across the English Channel. I know now the names of a good half dozen such " big birds," and it is to be hoped that the youth of the future will be turned aside from piano-playing by the new racecourse. But the Jews will stick to playing the piano, for it is not dangerous ; and they will confine themselves to playing :

> Si oiseau j'étais
> A toi je volerais.

. . . To come back to the aforesaid bird, it seems to me that the act of having flown the Channel is beautiful and important —but it does not surpass that of Wright's flight : it is only more sensational . . .


FLORENCE, 7 *August* 1909.

. . . This town is not so beautiful as it is reputed to be. Perhaps it was only at the time when the principal buildings were put up that they seemed original and very magnificent ; especially to the Florentines themselves, who have never suffered from patriotic shyness . . . The dome of the cathedral is the

only thing that still gives an impression of grandeur and originality, especially if one looks at it from a point where one cannot
see the façade. The sculpture is often bad, and what is good
is hidden ! . . . Some of the houses which are seldom mentioned have wonderful proportions, and if someone made a proper
study of them the result might lead to a beautiful type of architecture for towns. Messel has done something like this. But
he sticks in his period as far as the Empire and Biedermeier styles
are concerned. It was phenomenal how art flowered in Tuscany,
and that alone explains the present-day exhaustion. Poets,
from Dante and Boccaccio up to Carducci. Amongst sculptors,
Giotto, Michelangelo, Leonardo, Benvenuto [Cellini], Verrocchio,
Donatello, and a whole Milky-Way of smaller stars. Amongst
scientists, Leonardo, Galileo and prominent doctors and lawyers.
Musicians, Guido Monaco, Monteverdi, Cherubini up to—
Puccini (!). Rulers, Cardinals, Popes, a Machiavelli, and great
generals—one can even count Napoleon Buonaparte amongst
the Tuscans.

But now they are a small people composed of astonishingly
uneducated, provincial tradesmen, with a blockade of prejudices,
antiquated customs and opinions, and a ridiculous number of
conventional phrases, which make a kind of island of the culture.
But the *country* is heavenly . . .

Here is a little episode which is worth relating.

Yesterday evening there was only one guest in the Restaurant
Bonciani. He was a priest, wore gold pince-nez, and was scrupu-
lously, almost elegantly, dressed. Not far off fifty, rather an
intellectual face, the middle of his head shaved and the remaining
hair in fantastic little bunches on each side ; he was reading a
French newspaper. He addressed me in Italian which did not
sound quite natural. A street band was playing outside, and the
waiters had hurried to the door. " The excellence of the service
has to suffer on account of enthusiasm for art," he said, turning
to me. I found the beginning of the conversation rather pro-
mising, and we talked from one table to the other. He had come
to Italy 32 years ago and preserved, so he said, " a pleasant
recollection " of the time. He remarked that he had not been
a priest then, and so I concluded, without asking further questions, that it must have been the story of a woman. " 32 years
ago ! You were not born then ! " said the priest. At this
moment the old waiter who served me threw in the remark,

quite short and dry, " You are forty-two." This remark surprised me. Then the priest proceeded to praise the wine, and developed a beautiful rhetorical eloquence :

" This wine," he remarked, " is not so good as Lachrymae Christi, nor Falerno, nor the wine of San Marino, but it is an agreeable wine." I thought of the Abbé Coignard. Finally he talked about music and said he had done a little composing himself. The figs were eaten and I stood up. " Perhaps we shall meet again one day," I said. " No," he said, quite decidedly, and tapped on the table with his finger, " this evening." (Hm.) " I don't know," I said " Adieu," got up, and bowed . . .

BÂLE, 12 *August* 1909.

I am sitting in the Drei-König Hotel in Basle and feel very well to-day, thank God. It is sunny and fresh, outside and inside, and I am like a convalescent smiling afresh. The theory that it is necessary to be very great in order to bear greatness (even in the form of enjoyment) is a universal truth, and one must be strong in order to feel that strength is pleasant.

The temperature and the abundance of everything in Italy were too strong for me in the condition I was in when I came away. It is no use going to Italy in the summer in order to make a recovery ; it is only good as a place to rest in after recovery !—then, by all means ; but I needed to collect strength and not to strain what I had of it, and it nearly prostrated me. Yet to-day, I feel—as a kind of reaction—a good effect from being in Italy. On the way here I found an excellent and charming edition of Cazotte's " Le Diable Amoureux." The way in which some books are got up invites one to read them, more than others. This one—published in the forties—almost " woos " readers. So I have allowed myself to be led to Cazotte easily and shall have finished the book before my return home. The first chapter is " captivant " (which means more than " fesselnd " in German) and I have thought of making it into an original kind of opera or pantomime. Who knows ! ?—" Le Diable Amoureux " is a beautiful title anyhow.

Dear Gerda, I become good when I think of you, of you all, of my room in the tower, and of " safe " Italy. I shall drag myself on another two stages or so, and then we shall have a happy time.

Manchester looks the same as ever. Below, slippery ground, black and shining, animated by ugly people (God knows why they exist) and loaded carts, walking, rolling, rattling ; the genius of cheerfulness banished to an inaccessible remoteness ; the roofs and towers of the town vanishing ghostlike into the grey fog. What is the point of putting clocks on the towers ? One can never read the figures on their faces. I feel so strong and creative and suffer because I am unable to work. There is still a small amount of less important work to do, the Liszt Polonaise and the new notation to edit and similar things.

The walk across the desert in the " Zauberer " I should like to represent *scenically*, if possible : at first an empty stage perhaps, with effective decoration ; then the wandering, exhausted Kassen enters and the voices of the unseen spirits of the magician and the young woman are heard respectively, enticing and warning. The cauldron in the first act must be there *from the beginning* ; instead of the Magician pulling gold out of it (which is not impressive enough for the audience) the whole cauldron must change, under thick smoke, into a showy statue of Buddha. Such things, and others too, must be thought over, fined down and enlarged, even in the words too.

What do you think about it ? Please send me a copy of the libretto on the journey to Germany. . . . I am only waiting for the moment when I put my foot on land at Flushing . . .

COLOGNE, 8 *November* 1909.
It was strenuous, from Bradford to Cologne . . . The crossing was as smooth as oil, only delayed at the beginning by fog. The sky was clear when we started, and then I enjoyed the most remarkable picture I have seen in the whole of my life, perhaps. The splendour of the stars was magnificent and I was absorbed in looking at it. And—Listen !—Instead of the sky looking as it usually does, like a concave hemisphere, with little holes for light in the ceiling—all at once I saw endless space above, and the planets floating in it, some higher or lower, nearer or further away, in groups, cascades of varying intensity in light, colour and size. It quite moved me, and then, as if man were not allowed to glance into such a mystery, suddenly a wall of fog

got up on every side and—my shadow fell on it ! That was an experience.

And I had a number of smaller pleasures too . . . In London I saw a fascinating picture of the great Pitt. Anything like the clarity and intelligence in his look I have never yet encountered. The riches of nature and of earth are distributed in the same way. Thousands go short in order that one can be so endowed. I mean (in case I have not said it clearly)—there is a certain quantity of intelligence allotted to men and it is unequally distributed.

To-day I received, at last, the translation of the first act of the Brautwahl from Anzoletti. It is extraordinary. The language is splendid and the understanding astonishing. He has a clear head ! With a few alterations it will fit the music and perhaps this will sound still better with Italian words. The Brautwahl seems to be lucky. Egon has also offered, of his own free will, to do the piano score, which is very important for me. What a pity that I cannot carry on all these things now, quietly and persistently to the end ! That is the only thing that pains me. Do you know that the Petrarca-sonnet had great success in the Gewandhaus ? Senius sang it. Oh, Columbus ! . . .

BUDAPEST, 3 *December* 1909.

On the night journey from Berlin to Vienna, from Nov. 30 to Dec. 1, I met Herr Hertzka. Had already seen him some time before, the unmistakable Austrian would-be artist, hurrying to and fro, everything in fluttering movement on his extremely mobile person, hair, beard, cravat and cloak. At last he could stand it no longer and introduced himself : " Hertzka, Director of the Universal Edition A.G., Vienna." And the conversation span itself out till far into the night, and we hit upon much that we had in common. We spoke of the 2nd part of the Wohlt. Clavier, of the Brautwahl, and finally of Schönberg too. He wanted to do everything for me.

In Vienna, early, I had a visit from Bösendorfer. He was fresh and clever, warm and open ; his visit did me good. Then in the evening, at the concert, Kapff, old and ill, made such a sad impression that I made him a present of 100 gulden. I could not see such misery, and it seemed as if I were paying a debt . . .

The success was enormous. I was recalled six times. Early

the next day to Budapest. Have played extraordinarily well here . . .

And now on to Lemberg and soon to Berlin again ; these two days have been a little too much for me. I am thoroughly jogged and jolted and in playing, too, I have given out much (especially here). How everything accumulates in life, the further one goes ! How much there has been in these two days ! They feel like two weeks. An abundance of things, but difficult to deal with. People take very much from one, thinking all the while that they give. Soon—I think—I shall be ready to be alone . . .

I kiss you in my inmost thoughts, for in this medley you alone stand firm . . .

# 1910

(*Addressed to New York*)

CHICAGO, 15 *January* 1910.

My window faces the sea, and I overlook an endless flatness of shining ice and snow. A white desert! Boundless and hopeless. And behind me lies the town, just as black as this is white.

I sit the whole day in the hotel ; my most serious occupation is regulating the central heating. The result to my art is that I oscillate between headaches and freezing. The moment when the headache stops and the freezing begins is indeed " ganz scheen," as Caufall would say. I try other work too, but only second class. Middelschulte is going to bring me an essay by Bernard Ziehn to-day, on Bach's uncompleted fugue. Comes very à propos. They are both distinguished men and—in order to fill up the time—I have written a nice essay about them for the Signale, and called it : " Die Gothiker von Chicago, Ill."

To-morrow, I go to St. Paul. . . .

From Minneapolis to New York it is as far as from Berlin to Petersburg ! Patience . . .


(*Addressed to New York*)

MINNEAPOLIS, 20 *January* 1910.

. . . There was beautiful winter atmosphere in St. Paul ; it is a pleasant town. Minneapolis has only been established 50 years and has 320 thousand inhabitants. These are the wonders of the new world.

I am studying counterpoint again, for which Chicago has stimulated me very much. It is a beautiful weapon which one must be able to handle. But it is difficult to concentrate when one is constantly having new rooms and surroundings . . .

(*Addressed to New York*)

CINCINNATI, 19 *February* 1910.

. . . I have altered the plan for the Fantasia contrappuntistica (on Bach's last and greatest work). I shall not begin with a Fantasy, but bring into the fugue itself everything in the nature of fantasy. It will sound like something between a composition by C. Franck and the Hammerclavier sonata, with an individual nuance.

I miss you and don't know whether it is better or not, without being able to reach you, to know that you will still be another week in America. You have been so good and made everything easier and more beautiful for me . . . May everything good be with you. Be happy. I believe everything will go well now . . .

(*Addressed to New York*)

LOUISVILLE, 22 *February* 1910.

. . . Starting this evening, the journey to Kansas-City takes 24 hours ! If the South begins with Louisville, then the promise is a bad one. Dirty, bad hotel, no respectable entrance hall, and niggers of the lowest type. It is unnecessary (yet I must say it) to wish you everything, everything good and pleasant on the journey. You leave a gap here and a most golden memory. . . . Don't worry about me, my work keeps up my courage. The fugue is becoming monumental. After that I shall start working at my opera . . .

NEW ORLEANS, 27 *February* 1910.

When I received the telegram from Hanson : " Your wife started in glorious sunshine, parting from the excellent lady difficult," I was sitting in Kansas-City and had (moral) cramp in my heart, which has remained with me all these days. . . . Meanwhile I received both your very dear and interesting letters ; the practical hints I have observed minutely, and I am now writing a little analysis of Turandot for Mahler. I think I shall be able to hear the rehearsal and the idea refreshes me ; when you read this, it will already be over . . . Yesterday evening, after a journey of 27 hours, we arrived here. The South ! It has always a new, surprising and indescribable magic. My sense of pleasure in change of scenery has been blunted, but here it is stirred afresh and the mere idea of being by the Gulf of Mexico fires my blood—as if I were a novice in travelling. Immediately, as in Italy, a feeling for doing nothing with the highest justification sets in. We walked about, without overcoats, until midnight ; it was difficult to decide to go to bed, and everything was so lively during the night that sleep was impossible. Everything takes place in the street, everything is open, the negro population is very numerous, but besides that, one hears all languages, sees types from all countries, and the figure of the American business man looks just as out of place here as the only sky-scraper does, which is my hotel. . . .

NEW ORLEANS, 1 *March* 1910.

Your letter from the ship has made me quite tender. To-day is the first of March. I intended finishing this monster fugue in February, and I *have succeeded*, but I shall never undertake such a thing again !

I write to announce this good news. . . .

ATLANTA, 3 *March* 1910.

New Orleans did not quite come up to expectations for, first of all, the water is 100 kilometres away and, secondly, it is a cruel climate. It is like an exotic sister of Triest . . . Why do people torment themselves by living here ? No wine, no theatre, no connection with the world (even New York is like a foreign country here) and yet ! it is not only the money that holds them fast, but, as everything goes to prove, the South !

The softness, the warmth, the misty evenings, and the eternal summer ; the strange little houses, consisting almost entirely of open verandahs, the service of numberless black domestics, which everyone can keep, and in which some of the characteristics of slavery still survive. The women are beautiful and are, I believe, the chief interest, apart from business . . . This has been one of the worst towns and I shall be glad when I am out of it . . .

The fugue is the most important of my piano works (with the exception of the concerto)—I have still two days in which to make a clean copy.

It consists of :

        First    Fugue⎫
        Second    ,,   ⎬and the working out of the three
        Third     ,,   ⎭
        Intermezzo
        First variation
        Second variation
        Third variation
        Cadenza
        Fourth Fugue
        Coda

You see the plan is unusual.  Every note " sits."

I read your dear letters over again until I receive new ones . . .

To-day you will see land !  Your visit here was exceptionally beautiful ;  perhaps you will be able to enjoy being at home too.

I received the final letter from Basle yesterday.  The thing is in order.  The Concerto will be played too.  We have many a good thing to look forward to . . .


DAYTON, 3 *March* 1910.

## THE REALM OF MUSIC

### *An Epilogue to the New Æsthetic*

Come, follow me into the realm of music.  Here is the iron fence which separates the earthly from the eternal.

Have you undone the fetters and thrown them away ?

Now come.  It is not as it was before, when we stepped into a strange country ;  we soon learnt to know everything there and nothing surprised us any longer.  Here there is no end to the astonishment, and yet from the beginning we feel it is homelike.

You still hear nothing, because *everything sounds*.  Now, already you begin to differentiate.  Listen, every star has its rhythm, and every world its measure.  And on each of the stars and each of the worlds, the heart of every separate living being is beating in its own individual way.  And all the beats agree and are separate and yet are a whole.

Your inner ear becomes sharper.  Do you hear the depths

and the heights ? They are as immeasurable as space and endless as numbers.

Unthought-of scales extend like bands from one world to another, *stationary*, and yet *eternally in motion*. Every tone is the centre of immeasurable circles. And now *sound* is revealed to you !

Innumerable are its voices ; compared with them, the murmuring of the harp is a din ; the blare of a thousand trombones a chirrup.

All, all melodies, heard before or never heard, resound completely and simultaneously, carry you, hang over you, or skim lightly past you—of love and passion, of spring and of winter, of melancholy and of hilarity ; they are themselves the souls of millions of beings in millions of epochs. If you focus your attention on one of them, you perceive how it is connected with all the others, how it is combined with all the rhythms, coloured by all kinds of sounds, accompanied by all harmonies, down to unfathomable depths and up to the vaulted roof of heaven.

Now you realise how planets and hearts are one, that nowhere can there be an end or an obstacle ; that infinity lives completely and indivisibly in the spirit of all beings ; that each being is both illimitably great and illimitably small : the greatest expansion is like to a point : and, that light, sound, movement and power are identical, and each separate and all united, they are life.


TOLEDO, 5 *March* 1910.

When you consider that I was still in New Orleans on the 1st, have played in two other towns in between, and to-day have a concert again here in the north, you will gather what an amount of travelling there has been !

There is nothing, anywhere, so inappropriate as the name of *this* town. Toledo ! ! But the spring makes even the impossible beautiful and the weather is glorious.

I am still intoxicated by the " great fugue " I have finished— I shall be sober again soon ; and something else will come to take its place.

Now from the 9th to the 13th I shall move like a pendulum between New York and Boston or rather—when you read this —I shall have moved ; for one writes about the future and reads about the past ! Which of the two is real then ? It makes one's brain reel. (Moreover, a telegram for the West arrives earlier than it is despatched.) Because of this I was able to find out early in the morning, in Dayton, to my great joy and ease of mind, that your boat had arrived in Cherbourg at 4 o'clock in the morning. Judging by the punctuality, the voyage must have been fairly good. Now you are over the English Channel, my friend for many years and many *hours* . . .

6 March.

. . . I have had two weeks of hard work (almost three) since I left you in New York. And the great *change* in the *climate* has been very trying . . . It is fine, here in the South. It is a world in itself. About Berlin, for example, one hears *nothing* ; there is not the least connection with it any more, nor any kind of dependence—without exaggeration, it is as we feel with regard to Peking. They talk of New York as of something quite, quite distant, a big, big town which has many pleasures and where the people lead a mad life. But of that, too, the South remains *completely independent.* After providing for the necessities of life (which is easy) the rest consists of much sun, a little laziness and love-making and a naïve desire for external elegance. And the South is so powerful, that one understands it at once and admits that it is right, is moved by it oneself. I said all this to X, who remained cool ; he did not understand it, and it was as if (unconsciously) he were envious that people could live comfortably without the noise and hurry and the 1000 sufferings of the average man in New York. Envious that one should be allowed to remain quiet without someone else being immediately in front of you ; envious to see so much room for everything and even a little piece of space left free for the late-comers, and with some air between too !

I tried to explain to X that in the old culture industrial inventions were the *result* of growing necessities. Whilst in America the invention is made and a use for it is thought out afterwards, so that the public can be made to feel that it is a necessity. How in Europe the railway arose from the wish amongst towns and nations to have communication with one another, whereas here the railways are made first and then the towns are built.

I tried to explain to X that industry altogether—important as it is economically—is yet only a means to attain practical ends, but here it is an aim in itself and the real reason for the activity is not the making of a million unnecessary articles, but the employment of a thousand workers to do it. I tried further to explain to the good X, who listened so attentively whilst shaking his head from time to time, how the American thinks out nothing for himself and does not work out his own *ideas* and *understanding* of a thing if it is not his business.

For that reason he takes the laws of religion, of art and of morals, for granted, like traditions, or as they are presented to him by clever, cunning people and he becomes as obstinate and limited as a peasant. Politics interest him only so far as they are an active power on the stock exchange and his only personal interests (personal ! that means the same as the millions of other people have got with whom he mixes) are the family, " honour " and patriotism. This explains why the American likes to " join up " with those who are unknown to him and who will converse with him ; in hotels, in trains, in the street ; because he is certain of understanding him, of finding that the other has the same standard, the same opinions as himself.

I believe that this expresses the whole psychology of the American fairly well. What strikes me this time, and which I did not notice before, is the necessity for cordiality and warmth in the Americans, and that is a beautiful impulse which reconciles one to them.

I babble like this because I am so tired ; it is to be hoped I have not bored you . . .


BOSTON, 12 *March* 1910.

It is still impossible for me to hear anything from you and this—although I know it cannot be otherwise—is almost more than my nerves can bear, strained to the uttermost as they are.

" Dear old Boston " stands on the same old spot as always, and my mood is very like it was in 1892–93—my two flowering years ! ! " Away, away," barks the dog in Anderson's " Snowman."

Christian Science has a big ostentatious church here in the middle of the most elegant quarter ! It cost $1\frac{1}{2}$ million ! . . . They have stolen the architecture of the church from Italy again, although the taste is not altogether good. The cathedral in Berlin would rank very high here as architecture. One is obliged to remind oneself of something like this in order to find the way back to a standard . . .

And the bare streets ; either quite empty or filled with a mass of Plebs, compared with whom the Berlin working man is an aristocrat ! The world is joyless here, and it is, so it seems, hopeless to think that it will ever be any better. Not the land of " unlimited possibilities " but of " impossible limitations."

What a pity that you did not hear Turandot under Mahler. In the end I remained there for the evening ; it seemed to me to be unjust towards Mahler to go away. With what love and unerring instinct this man rehearsed ! Artistically, and humanly, it was both gratifying and warming.

The performance was perfect, better than all the previous ones, and the success was great. It is true the papers did not wish to take it quite seriously, but the world is full of errors and misunderstandings.

Most of the music of the Magic Flute, too, is only a kind of lightly coloured illustration. And arias like

> " Der Vogelfänger bin ich ja "

cannot be valued much higher than that.

The important position given to the Brahms Violin Concerto, too, in this programme was exaggerated. In the first place the piece is stolen from Beethoven (what *I* call stolen), and secondly, although it has the appearance of being big, it is patched together in small bits. I thought of two comparisons in connection with Brahms. The first is that of a little mountain lake into which a stream flows on one side and goes out again on the opposite side, without disturbing the calmness of the lake. The other comparison occurred to me by remembering how similar Ludwig Spohr's position was in the musical world of his time ; and the similarity of the gifts of both composers . . .

NEW YORK, 14 *March* 1910.

Two letters from the boat at last ! They are so dear and good and you say that the voyage was beautiful.

To-morrow I am going to Boston for a recital. After that the dates are still uncertain. . . .

15 *March.*
. . . The whole of my " local " biography is printed in detail
in the Symphony programme. These programme books are
very well done—Turandot was a great success. Frau Mahler
herself fetched me from the box in which I sat half hidden. " Do
go, give Gustav the pleasure." And I went on the platform as
shy and " unused to it " as if I had never stood in front of an
audience before. . . .

NEW YORK, 17 *March* 1910.
The Boston Recital yesterday was a little winding up, a kind of
" full stop and comma " in the tour . . .
*Everything* in Boston was just as it was before, the same people
using the same words, and even in the sleeping car the same old
fat nigger, who wears spectacles now. . . .
I played as well as I possibly can play. The success was great.
To-day I really feel as if everything were " completely over "
and it would have been right if the tour had ended now. The
dates, as I said, are quite uncertain, but Hanson will not let me
off the Brooklyn Recital, 28 April. There are six whole weeks
till then, which would be enough time for a big tour really.
I shall close my letter for to-day, for I am over-tired and quite
exhausted. . . .
I have opened the closed envelope again because your *extraordinarily* dear letter from Berlin has just come and been received
with equal love by me . . . Your dear words and feelings have
given me the strength to go on further, when it was threatening
to fail me.

COLUMBUS, OHIO, 21 *March* 1910.
Every day makes the time I have to spend here shorter.
One advantage in America is the quick business methods. " I
should like to have that printed ; I should like to have that in
the paper " and it is already done . . .
I am glad it is beautiful in Berlin ; nowhere is it so beautiful
as at home.
When I come again in two years' time and have acquaintances
in every town, from New York to " Frisco," everything will feel
easier.

162

COLUMBUS, 22 *March* 1910.

*About Red Indians.*

I spoke to a Red Indian woman. She told me how her brother (a talented violinist) came to New York to try and make his way. " But he could not associate his ideas with the question of daily bread." How much good it does one to hear of such a sentiment in the United States !

Then she said that her tribe ought to have an instrument something like this : A hole should be dug in the earth and strings stretched all round the edges of it. I said (in the spirit of the Red Indians) : An instrument like that ought to be called "the voice of the Earth." She was quite enthusiastic about this.

Miss Curtis was formerly my pupil in harmony. Do you remember her in New York ? She has devoted the whole of this year to the study of Red Indian songs and has brought out a beautiful book. She gave it to me " In remembrance of the first performance of Turandot in New York." She is a fine, cultivated, rich girl. . . .

The Red Indians are the only cultured people who will have *nothing to do with money*, and who dress the most everyday things in beautiful words.

How different is a business man from Chicago compared with this ! Roosevelt is called " Teddy " by him ; and by the Red Indians " Our great white father."

NEW YORK, 24 *March* 1910.

Your letters are not just a little distraction for me, but, as you know very well, they are a very great necessity. Every new one brings relief ; every interval between them makes a tension. I have written to you a good deal—but it isn't always possible, for an engagement list like the following quite finishes one off ; and yesterday I could do absolutely nothing :

| 20 March, | 6 o'clock | Departure from New York |
|---|---|---|
| 21 | 9 ,, | Arrival in Columbus |
| 21 | 8 ,, | Evening concert |
| 22 | 12 ,, | Mid-day departure from Columbus |
| 22 | 7 ,, | Evening arrival Pittsburg |
| 22 | 8.30 ,, | Evening concert |
| 22 | 11 ,, | Evening departure for New York |
| 23 | 9.30 ,, | Morning arrival in New York |

163

Please look closely at the 22nd March. Is it worth while? One starts going through America with a full sack which gets torn, and one strews half the contents on the way.

If Pittsburg were not so incomparably smoky, it might be a remarkable town. In the centre of the lower part of the town there is a serpentine road, four miles long, going up the steep hill which leads to the upper aristocratic quarter; the road is open on one side, so that as one goes up and the town lies further below, one sees more and more of it. We drove in an excellent motor-car in the twilight—it was quite fantastic. It is *Carnegie's* town and he built a concert hall for it (the most beautiful in America) which cost 2 millions. Everything breathes of great wealth. There are ten or twelve enormous columns which bear the roof of the entrance hall, each is made out of one single piece of black marble and is worth 4–5000 dollars. The hall was quite full . . .

Now I must tell you about Mr. C. F.'s " System." It is the most cunning one I have ever heard of, a patent of patents—in comparison, Uncle Benjamin's " machine " is primitive. F. keeps a *school for the development of piano teachers.* (Just think of the endless wheel which turns continuously without achieving anything!) F. himself gives instruction to the 12 most gifted students *gratuitously* ; in return for this they have to give instruction to the remaining 3–400. But F. receives the money from the 3–400. Wonderful! Admirable! Unique! . . .

NEW YORK, 25 *March* 1910.

A hot summer's day with a warm dusty wind and summer scents.

All the orchestras have given their last concert, and I have to hold out for another month and practise, too, in order to convince people that I can play the piano! I am furious to-day, and feel as if I were being exploited by everyone.

The people in Hamburg are in a hurry [1] and have written five letters in one week, after having kept silence for three months.

But haste has nothing to do with my work. Either it must be quite good or I don't do it at all. I try to keep to that standard. Everybody works for the next moment and lives as if it were a

---

[1] About the production of " Die Brautwahl."

164

question of Eternity.   The contrary of this seems more right to me.

Forgive this explosion, dear good Gerda.   I would rather write more to-morrow when I am calmer.   I should like to say at once that I mean nothing bad.

Coat of Arms :

26 March.

Continuation of the letter, but not of the bad humour, although I go to Chicago this afternoon, and then for about a 40 hours' drive on further to Colorado Springs.   It is *a pity*, a great, great pity that I can get no letter all this time and already I have been many days without one.   To-morrow is Easter Sunday and nothing will be forwarded to Colorado Springs on account of the distance.

The beauty of the Coloured Springs (almost like an illuminated fountain—I wonder if I shall be reminded of the Viktoria-Luise-Platz [1]) is so renowned that I am expecting much pleasure from seeing them . . .   I shall be there on the 1st April ; it is probably the most fantastic place in which I have ever spent my birthday—up to now.   It is a pity, for someone is certain to remember the day and I shall hear nothing.   I must not spin counterpoint round this subject or it might become an Elegy, almost a Berceuse Élégiaque.   Let us say rather : a new year, a new aim.   And you will help me further as you have helped me so beautifully up to now.

DES MOINES, 28 March 1910.

Yesterday was a hard day, indeed the last two nights and days were both very strenuous.   The heat in Chicago was very great, which made it more difficult to play, and concert-giving and concert-going did not at all suit the time of the year (and the day !).   It was Easter Sunday.   I was sad in the morning and

<hr />

[1] Busoni's flat in Berlin.

165

thought of other Easter Sundays. I was completely alone, nervous from 19 hours' travelling and at first everything went badly; but when I heard that there would be many musicians at the concert, and that Mr. and Mrs. Rothwell (Conductor in St. Paul) had remained expressly to hear me, then I pulled myself together and it was all over with " take it lightly."

This was the programme:

> Waldstein Sonata
> Brahms Paganini
>     (encore: Liszt-Paganini Variationen)
> Chopin Sonata B minor
>     (encore: " Butterfly "—Etude)
>     (2nd encore: Terzen-Etude)
> Erlkönig
> Au bord d'une Source
> 6 Rhapsodie
>     (encore: Campanella).

The audience stopped and clapped until the piano was closed and the lights were put out. You see, that was real work and showed (apart from fugue playing) about everything that one can do on the piano.

The Erlkönig and Sixth Rhapsodie have been " newly renovated " and I shall now play them again. I believe I have made something out of the 6th, especially. Then I enjoyed a meal, and for it had the company of Middelschulte, Stock and both the Rothwells, who are all pleasant and intelligent.

Middelschulte was charmed with the finished fugue and its plan. He said the idea of variations in between is quite new and the plan out of the common.

In the evening, at half-past nine, I came on here to Des Moines, which is a horrible town in a paradisical country. The spring is in full bloom. To-morrow I am off to Colorado Springs which they say is beautiful, and where I shall be on the 1st April. The whole affair should have ended there really.

*Denver* lies *eleven* miles from Col. Springs, but I must travel the whole way back (as far as Boston) and then back to Denver, which makes about 5,000 kilometres extra!

Unfortunately I can compose but little, hardly at all: the journeys eat up too much time.

I think of you and of you all even more than usual. . . .

From the standpoint of a touring artist, the concert yesterday was very satisfactory—full house, a feeling of excitement and enthusiastic criticisms. The heat had reached the highest point for the year. I was dead tired. But a beautiful piano, good acoustics, and the feeling of great expectation in the hall hypnotized me for the two hours I was on the platform.

From the standpoint of a thinking artist, no longer young, it was an unforgivable waste of strength, time and thought, which can never be recovered, in order to make a momentary impression on a small number of insignificant people.

Taking it all in all, again Chicago seems to me the best town in America. Boston is too much like Leipzig, and New York is disintegrated by excess of pleasure. An event there passes as quickly as one of those dried flowers which children blow away. " A beautiful flower," the children say—puff—and only the stalk remains in their hands, and they throw it away. Transitoriness ! but without it new blooms would not be possible.

Only there must be no *hurrying* transitoriness which shames us. For example, like Debussy's " L'Après-midi d'un Faune " which I heard conducted by Mahler the other day. I said to someone, " This music is the picture of a beautiful sunset— *it fades whilst one looks at it . . .*"

I have to wait here for the 6 o'clock train to Colorado Springs and will try to fill up the time. But whether it is the spring, fatigue, or the atmosphere of the West—for the last few weeks I have been able to accomplish nothing ! It is understandable, but none the less to be deplored. . . .

I still have 9 concerts and exactly one month before the tour is " completed." But I need not practise any more, just keep the playing going. The latter has changed a little. One involuntarily responds to the demands for a brilliant technique which are made by the Americans. Well, with me that cannot be the cause of serious harm. I have also learnt, at last, how to attack the 1st movement of the Waldstein Sonata which never went quite as I wished. And I have played it for almost thirty years ! !

These two last sentences ought to be written out and hung up in Conservatoriums. . . .

We arrived yesterday evening—instead of mid-day—five hours late. I had hoped to get some pleasure from this place, but it is nothing more than a health resort, so far as I can see up to the present.

A large, expensive hotel, gardens laid out in an artificial style, pretty scenery in the background—that is all one finds here, and the hours seem so long that people don't know what to do with them. Hot days and shiveringly cool evenings ; and the sunsets being shut out by high mountains gives a touch of melancholy.

Instead of edelweiss, chamois brushes and stag horns—as medallions, letter weights and watch cases—they sell Red Indian handiwork here (perhaps from a German factory). It is like Baden-Baden, or some place like that—only one wonders why it is necessary to travel *two sun-hours* further west just to see this !

For here we are so much nearer to the Pacific Ocean than to the Atlantic that there is more than 8 hours difference from the Berlin time.

I have never yet been so far from you and just before the 1st April, too. But what a journey ! ! It has opened my eyes and brought an extraordinary light to bear on my conceptions of America which were still unclear ; and has given me the key to many unsolved problems. Now I know much more and I see quite different things.

We travelled for *twelve hours* yesterday, through table-land ; as if we were going through a sea : the view from all sides was boundless, an endless distance, and—for the whole 12 hours— there was neither *house, nor tree, nor water* ! ! ! I saw then the big fundamental reason : America is not built over yet because almost everything has yet to be begun : the few showy towns running along the coasts are only a shell, and the kernel of it is missing : Chicago is the *inside crust* of this shell and then comes : Void. Some such idea was already beginning to dawn on me, on the way from Memphis to New Orleans, but I put down the condition of the country there to the climate. But now I am bound to admit that America is young ; that it is not yet born. It was a revelation. Now I am pacified about America : it still has work to do for centuries to come. Shall I really travel again to Denver from New York on the 19th ?

I am so sad without letters, and so tired ! ! Have you had the letters which I have sent almost daily ?

I have a longing for you, for home, for peace, for my work—
but am too enfeebled to enjoy looking forward to it. It will all
change, and my next letter will sound quite joyful, dear Gerda
. . .

COLORADO SPRINGS, 1 April 1910.

I began the new year of my life well for I got up at 7 o'clock.
At this hour the landscape was quite " Segantinish " to look at——
I have been obliged to give up my intention of resting here
for 3–4 days. It is not so easy to bear this altitude of 6,000 ft.
without any transition stage. It takes away one's breath (literally)
and the nights are horrible.

It is about 8 o'clock here, so in Berlin it is not quite 4 o'clock
in the afternoon. Perhaps some intimate friends are having tea
with you and you are speaking of me. I can see the picture in
front of me . . . Now it has passed, and I see the sharply
defined white and brown mountains again in front of Segantini's
grey-blue sky and I am conscious of *where* I am—but, after
looking at it a long time, I forget and feel myself, bodily, in the
Engadine and think :

Behind the mountains, there is Italy——

And I knock on the mountains as on a wall and from the other
side (as if behind a door) I hear Anzoletti's voice saying : " What
is the matter ? Oh, Ferruccio ! " . . .

I am completely alone here, and that is better than being with
people half of whom are friends and half strangers. I have
traversed—town by town—exactly a third of the earth and now
there is 8 hours' difference in the time !

No year in my life has been so full up as this one which is just
over : the richest in work, experiences and achievements—and
I feel that I am still going upwards. Everything good, my
Gerda, is with us.

From memory I cannot count up exactly what I have done
during this year.

Amongst my own compositions are :

> Die Stücke an die Jugend
> Berceuse
> Bach-Fantasie
> Berceuse élégiaque für Orchester
> Die Grosze Fuge

The New Notation
1st volume Liszt Edition
180 pages of the Brautwahl score
Frau Potiphar
Many Essays for papers
Numberless letters
Adjudicating for the " Signale " prize.

*Concerts* :
Tour in England
   ,,   ,, Switzerland
   ,,   ,, Austria
   ,,   ,, America (played 35 times)

Then, there was the performance of the Concerto in Newcastle, of Turandot in New York, of the quartet by Petri, and smaller things.

Plenty of experiences. . . .

Please add to it the thousands of kilometres of travelling.

(I worked well at the opera to-day.)

All hope of post is over. Now they will send nothing after me from New York. I travel back to-morrow as far as possible uninterruptedly for 3 days and 2 nights. Then I shall find the letters.

(This day seems to have no end.)

I send you all I can think of, of beauty, goodness and love : I know you are thinking of me now . . .

NEW YORK, 6 *April* 1910.

At last, yesterday—the 5th—after a lapse of ten days ! your letters could reach me again, and I am enriched by them . . . The expectation of the post has been my only thought during this week of complete enervation :—nothing remained in my brain but this . . .

Your dear words—intended for the 1st April—have done me an extraordinary amount of good. Returning to New York and reading about your feelings was half like " being at home" . . .

In the West when I saw a farmer behind a plough I thought : There ! that is the most primitive form of well-being ; just add to it sleep, appetite, love—and some beauty—these things never change and not an ounce is added to them by anything mechanical.

Why does a " skyscraper " look wrong ?

Because its proportions are wrong in relation to the size of people ; and because the conception of the building as a whole is not in right proportion to its height . . .

The book by H. H. Ewers is, of course, the same that I bought once at the Anhalter Bahnhof . . . The German critic has come to grief altogether over this book, and at once talks about E. A. Poe—this man who was a martyr to misunderstandings. " A new Poe," she cries ; but there cannot be a new Poe ! It must either be someone whose work is *different* or *worse*. In the whole history of art there is no such thing as a second example. What a number of " new Chopins " there have already been ! . . .

The volumes of Strindberg were very welcome. He is a poet, has thought, development in his work, and also personality. But it seems to me that a something (important) is missing, only I have not yet found out what and where it is. A thousand thanks for the books . . .

The new notation has found an opponent to whom I was obliged to reply. I am proud that I can write English so well. I have written this letter quite alone (that is to say, the printed one enclosed).

Enclosed are cuttings about Boston and Pittsburg, the " daughter " of Busoni, and Chaliapine's wonderful make-up as Don Quixote in Massenet's Opera (he is the last man to touch this subject).

And for to-day I must take a warm farewell. . . .

WASHINGTON, 8 *April* 1910.

A beautiful town, and a fresh, " sparkling " spring morning . . . If only there were no recital ! The climatic torture of Colorado Springs has fairly " beaten " me—the three days' travelling from there has not exactly cured me, and I had had enough without both these superfluities. . . .

That Klimt's work shows a similarity with Donatello's bas-relief does not surprise me. Art is like a game of chess ; the same moves, with the same men, and on the given field of the chessboard—and yet no games are alike. The " Klimt-Dona-tello " similarity probably has its source in Byzantine art, in the East anyhow, like all art, with the exception of music, and that is because it does not copy forms but is the expression of mood.

Verrocchio—as I have said many times—had all the later styles in him (up to the Rococo). Rodin has certainly been influenced

by him. How nice it is that you are so satisfied with the arrangement of the museum ! " Handicraft " is to art as tilling the soil
is to harvest.

I am very proud of, and am very strengthened by, my new
counterpoint studies (I have worked hard at harmony too) and
that makes one skilful.

In music one cannot *teach* Composition, but one can *practise*
it ! " Practice makes perfect "—there is always something true
in proverbs. One is born an artist, but has to educate oneself
in order to be a master. That has often been said already, but
if you don't pay attention to it, may good luck be with you on the
journey to brilliant mediocrity ! . . .

BOSTON, 12 *April* 1910.

. . . I have just come back from a motor drive from Cambridge where I and Mr. Byrn visited *Dolmetsch.* He looks like
a little faun, with a handsome head, and lives in the past.
He builds pianos, Clavecins and Clavichords. The Clavecin
(the English harpsichord) is magnificent. I made capital out
of it at once and, first of all, brought the instrument into the
Brautwahl (when Albertine accompanies herself on it) and,
secondly, begged for one to be sent to Berlin. They are
beautiful outside too . . .

To-day I wrote a kind of letter of appreciation about America
to Hanson for publication.

The recital was yesterday and it was very good . . . Then I
had guests to lunch, then Dolmetsch. The time gets filled
up . . .

TERRE HAUTE, 14 *April* 1910.

. . . Your letter comforted me very much, for everything is
on such a low level here, that this Terre Haute ought to be called
Terre Basse.

One is hardly on the way to feeling reconciled when another
blow throws one into a state of opposition . . .

I have also seen the number of the " Signale," with the piece
in it which won the prize : it is, looked at as a whole, what I call
a heap of misery. No good ever comes out of a thing like that.
There are four or five fugues in it (certainly four) and with such

a miserable theme, what sense is there in turning it round 12 times ? And then giving it a prize for composition ? . . .

Washington is a really beautiful town, with an artistic plan, laid out by a Frenchman a hundred years ago . . . The country is radiant in its spring beauty. Now I shall soon know it all. Not just the few towns on the " Pacific " coast.

Hanson in his reply to-day says that my little letter about America is " magnificent " . . . God, but I have a feeling for the country ! I have sacrificed three years of my life here, and shall be obliged to sacrifice as many again, and Benni was born here, and they have received me very heartily, and if everything goes according to plan I shall have to thank them for my little bit of wealth ! I cannot " overlook " all this any more !

I shall close my letter on this D major chord, that it may gladden you more than the others I have written of late which were very depressed . . .

Literary P.S.

This Strindberg is a fearful man ! I have read the book of plays called " Kammerspiele " (which he calls " Dramas by a man of sixty, in 1910 ") and I must say they make me hold my breath. But if the wisdom which comes with age only makes one bitterly angry and allows *only* bacteria to be seen in every drop of water, so that every joy in the flowing well of life is destroyed ! then let us remain foolish or die young.

What Strindberg sees is terribly true, but he arrives at his truths by way of unimportant details. That will always be the weakness in his great talent. His amateurishness in music is laughable. The technical certainty is imposing. His taste plays him stupid tricks. He writes about unpleasant things and has not got the humour necessary to make them enjoyable.

I wonder if it is possible to perform these plays ? . . .

ST. LOUIS, 16 *April* 1910.

Yet another 26 hours towards the West and then—eastwards, and gradually homewards . . .

The " Musical Courier " emphasizes the fact that I have brought a new tone into concert life. After the second tour I believe I shall possess enough authority to make experiments here too. Here is something which occurred to me during a conversation with X yesterday. It *must be* possible to realize everything that people think of (however daring it may be) : for the power of imagination is made up of things which *exist* and the idea itself proves that somewhere or other a reason for it *already exists*.

Telling X that one day someone would discover an apparatus which would make a piano *tune itself*, made me think this out. " That is impossible," said X quickly. I said, " Everything is possible until the opposite is proved." And the realization of my idea must be possible, *because it came into my head*. And it is the combination of many things which I have already seen and of which I have heard. They can build an instrument now which registers automatically exactly how much the *strings slacken*. That is the first step towards my idea.

It is impossible to talk to X in symbols ; he takes it all literally. If I say, " Do that for me to-day, you won't lose anything by it " (it is a free day), X looks in his pockets at once to see if he has lost anything.

Or if I say, " You don't know the charm of the wine countries—wine makes the poor rich : " X says, " The wine industry ? "

" To build up," for him means to put up houses : " To feel rich "—to possess money : " To stand alone," to have no companions for meals and no financial help : " A good concert "—a full house and many encores. It is astounding. The Americans and Red Indians can learn nothing from one another.

And this occurred to me too ; one discovery *destroys* an earlier one. Since elevators came into use here they have ceased to use steps. In towns, squares and gardens have disappeared because people live in the suburbs. Or : the necessity for applause ceases when listening to a gramophone ; or : the art of fortifications is lost because of the invention of cannon : there is a dearth of literature because there are so many newspapers and monthly magazines ; and so on—one could make a dictionary of it all.

And this is the way one babbles when one is tired . . .

DENVER, 18 *April* 1910.

Denver is really quite nice and is a little centre, but to get here one has to travel across the Steppes, past tents and young men on horseback, who are beginning a completely new life. With

174

horses, pistols, tents and a couple of ploughs, they make a new way through difficult country. And these courageous, primitive instruments of civilization are badly nourished and have only the meanest pleasures of life to cheer them. There is something grand in it! It makes a great impression on one! Splendid fellows, in spite of the lack of cultivation which can be seen in the expression in their faces. Tall, strong and agile, and not bad or dishonest . . .

I had a beautiful idea in the train yesterday. I thought I would arrange the great fugue for orchestra. Transcribe the choral prelude (Meine Seele bangt und hofft zu dir) as an Introduction to it and let this recur as a reminiscence just before the Stretta in the fugue.

" It would be a great work ! " But who will give me a second life ? . . .

The opera has to be worked out most carefully and occasional improvements, completions, and enlargements have to be made. I *will not do it in a hurry.* . . .

Here we are again, 5,000 ft. up. I had a bad night, the air takes away my breath.

From here I begin to move slowly homewards now : I have still 100 things to wind up during the last week. People meet my wishes in every espect. I need only express the wish. There is much that is good in the country. The artistic side of it is *small* and that makes many things easier. With my concerts and Wüllner's, the whole concert season was provided for. On the whole, that would be unthinkable in Europe, wouldn't it ? . . .

I wonder if Mexican lace interests you ? I understand nothing about it. I really don't know what to bring away from here— one can't stick sky-scrapers and suspension bridges in one's trunk——

I am certain that our reunion will be a very, very beautiful one . . . What about the summer holiday ? England ! Switzerland ! Hm. . . .


DENVER, 18 *April* 1910.

If Chicago is the heart of America, then Denver is the appendix. Such a blind alley ! One knows nothing of geography if one does not travel ! . . .

175

I will try to translate something I read in an Indian story because it sounds so far away from everything of *this* country :

" And I could tell thee stories, that would make thee laugh at all thy trouble, and take thee to a land, of which thou hast never even dreamed. Where the trees have ever blossoms, and are noisy with the humming of intoxicated bees. Where by day, the suns are never burning, and by night, the moonstones ooze with nectar in the rays of the camphor-laden moon. Where the blue lakes are filled with rows of silver swans, and where, on steps of lapis-lazuli, the peacocks dance in agitation at the murmur of the thunder in the hills. Where the lightning flashes without harming, to light the way to women, stealing in the darkness to meetings with their lovers, and the rainbow hangs for ever like an opal on the dark blue curtain of the clouds. Where, on the moonlit roofs of crystal palaces, pairs of lovers laugh at the reflection of each other's lovesick faces in goblets of wine : breathing as they drink air heavy with the fragrance of the sandal, wafted on the breezes from the mountain of the South : where they play and pelt each other with emeralds and rubies, fetched at the churning of the ocean from the bottom of the sea. Where rivers, whose sands are always golden, flow slowly past long lines of silent cranes that hunt for silver fishes in the rushes on their banks : where men are true and maidens love for ever, and the lotus never fades."

What do you say to that ? It brings tears to my eyes.
" But there is no such thing," X. would say.
O disillusionment ! O Poetry !
They are as opposed as poor and rich.
A cowboy has just galloped past my window on horseback. I love having the writing table in the window, one is alone and yet in contact with the world outside. Unfortunately " the dear yellow car " has just passed by too, which wakes me out of dreams *everywhere* in America.

Here the spring is late, the trees are not in bud yet. But we had the company of the Mississippi for a couple of hours, on the journey from St. Louis. What a view ! Big and beautiful at the same time. The season, the sunset, the virginal purity of this immense beauty makes an unforgettable picture ! One shudders at the thought of people interfering with it . . .

I have spent some very pleasant hours here with *Stock* . . .
He is a very intelligent and able musician : he also has a certain
serious idealism and is very conscientious. At the same time a
dear fellow and obviously honest.

Good God, the method they have here of turning people into
celebrities makes one's heart sink into one's boots. Is it possible
such a small, ordinary person like X can really be a great artist ?
Even from an " opera singer's standpoint " ? I cannot believe
it, and I have never heard of her being extraordinarily good in any
of her rôles. But every nigger knows her name. And if you
give them Debussy with his three muted violins, one half-muted
horn and a melody consisting of two whole tones—they are
transported with delight !

It is true that such errors have existed in all ages, and to be
popular means, " to be on everybody's tongue." We have
experienced it with Mascagni and Grieg and—outlived it.

The day before yesterday at the last symphony concert I heard
the following programme :

> Overture, Fliegender Holländer
> Symphony (III), Brahms
> Till Eulenspiegel, Strauss
> Aufforderung zum Tanz, Weber-Weingartner
> Overture 1812, Tschaikowsky

Of all these, Wagner's youthful work is the one which stands the
test of time best, and is the strongest too. The symphony by
Brahms made an unhappy impression on me : it is a ghost of
the Leipzig school. (And it is not long ago that I heard the
*very first* performance of this symphony in Vienna. At that time
people felt as if they were standing before a sphinx.)

Strauss's Eulenspiegel sounded like a modern Papa Haydn in
his most naïve mood, making the old Vienna aristocrats laugh
with him.

I let Weingartner and Tschaikowsky alone, and went for a
walk in the snowstorm, when I had leisure to reflect.

As you read this letter I shall be, I think, already on the boat
and you will know—from the telegram which I shall send and
which you have already received (that always confuses me !) that
I start on the 3rd, and that I shall have started—enfin. Kant is
right ; time is only an idea. I have still got a lot to do till then
and to my poor head it seems to be even more than it really is.

Life has taken another turning, this time an outward one and I am not yet clear about its significance—and whether it will harmonize with the inner turning.  I thought I had finished with the glitter of external things and I hoped, in my own home, to seek for what I could not find outside—and now it seems as if everything wished to begin all over again.  In any case one cannot complain of boredom . . .

NEW YORK, 29 *April* 1910.

Now it is over, the farewell concert took place yesterday evening in Brooklyn ; a good finish, the hall sold out, the atmosphere festive.  But it finished off my nerves—look at the programme ! [1]

And look, please, for a moment at this time-table, and try to go with me in thought :

| | | | |
|---|---|---|---|
| 25 April | 10 o'clock | Evening leave Chicago |
| 26 ,, | 9 ,, | Morning arrive Cleveland |
| 26 ,, | 4–6 ,, | To Oberlin |
| | 7–9 ,, | Concert there |
| | 9.30–11.30 | Back from Oberlin |
| 27 ,, | 2 a.m. | Leave Cleveland |
| | 6 p.m. | Arrive in New York |

After yesterday's concert I could not get to sleep till 3 and at eight to-day I was out of bed again—because I could not rest. And now comes the so-called recreation !  God help me !

After having actually been a " Preacher in the Desert," in the " deserted West," the cultured public of Brooklyn was in a way refreshing . . .

Now America has been discovered for the third time (and by an Italian again !).  I only missed investigating that little piece of coast on the " Pacific " Ocean . . .

I have an enormous amount to do during these days, and the boat goes 2 days sooner than I expected . . .

All good wishes for a joyful, happy reunion, beloved wife, and may all goodness and love be with you until then and for ever !  . . .

[1] It contains Beethoven's Waldstein Sonata : Brahms' Paganini Variations : The B Minor Scherzo : 2 Nocturnes in F Major and E Minor : The A Flat Polonaise by Chopin : The Abegg-Variations by Schumann : The Erlkönig : Campanella : and the 6th Hungarian Rhapsody by Liszt.

# 1 9 1 1

It was spring when we left New York, and here to-day the cold is pitiless and there are immense masses of snow . . .

The day before yesterday, in the evening, at the Italian Restaurant I sat next to Prince Troubetzkoy, a man of great personality ; with a cardinal's face !

Last Sunday, the " Boston Herald " had a cutting from the year 1863. Amongst the musical news, one read :—" Adelina Patti is still singing " (!) : further on an announcement that Messrs. Steinway had bought a piece of ground in 14th Street in order to build a house of their own. No word of the Boston Symphony yet. Teresa Carreño plays " The Mocking Bird " at the " White House " (as a child). The pupils and friends of *Mercadante* had arranged a festival for him in Naples. That was 48 years ago. Adelina Patti is *still* singing, Carreño *still* playing, Steinways have reached a high position, but where is Mercadante ? Do not look back, is what I say . . .

NORTHAMPTON, 15 *February* 1911.

. . . It was quite beautiful in Montreal, winter weather such as you like (but too cold). Very good concert, and the people whom you know all sent you hearty greetings.

That we are in New England to-day is unmistakable. The servants in the hotels are old girls in spectacles ; it reminds one of a hospital. God punish grumblers, they are his most wicked servants !

I am rather at the end of my patience, but I must not be childish, so I pull myself together.

I miss you everywhere, but am glad for your sake that you are

179

at home, and that you need no longer run round with me like a tight-rope dancer . . .

I hope to earn some reward and to be able to enjoy it, when I see you again . . .

I sat in the orchestra yesterday, and heard " Don Quixote " by Richard Strauss. It is a work which has great qualities ; commonplace in the lyrical places, unusually exciting in the grotesque parts, naïve in a boorish way and yet on the other hand too cultivated : badly put together as regards form, but the daring texture of sound is excellent. On the whole, one of the most interesting works of our time and the richest in invention ; perhaps the composer's best work. I listened with attention and in places with the greatest pleasure. But I should like to hear it conducted by Strauss himself. I could see in Turandot how much is spoilt by X's conducting. No *illustration* of Don Quixote has quite satisfied me, Strauss does not either ; but I believe it belongs to the better, more intellectual, and less literal ones.

I admit willingly that beside this work, Turandot, mutilated as it was, is less brilliant, and happily I have developed enough to be able to recognize this myself. Strauss reminds me of Tiepolo and I feel the reaction of the Cornelius school coming, but perhaps without the stiffness and awkwardness of the " Nazarenes." Possibly the appearance of Palestrina after the early Netherlanders would supply a better parallel for the change we may expect to see.

I am looking forward so much to my work in the summer and autumn. My concentration has been absorbed here, by always having to overcome a feeling of impatience, and the dislike of compulsion. I am like one who is obliged to lie with a broken leg : but who has nothing else wrong with him, and waits until he can walk and move about again. I say once more, I must not throw away my good years.

The position in my development as a composer would already be quite different if it had not been for the long interruptions and having to connect up again so laboriously. I have only four months in the year in which to produce some better work and then I have to take a little step backwards. I don't complain, I only want to be clear about it . . .

To-day I hope you are in England and that you are light-hearted and well . . . There are still ten more days in February, which will be busy ones for me and which will pass quickly. After that, every day makes a day less in March. La peau de chagrin ! or the ass's skin . . .

NEW YORK, 19 *February* 1911.

. . . To-day I walked for three hours down over Bovary as far as Brooklyn Bridge ; quite interesting but not exciting and not nearly so picturesque as Amsterdam, for example.

Witek said something very apt about his impressions here. " I am surprised," he said, " that there is so much that is old-fashioned, almost mediæval here." Mr. Pickett was rather sentimental in Boston, and sighed, " Old Boylston Street " in the tone of voice in which a Viennese would exclaim " die Schtêfans-kirch'n."

The Americans like to pretend (adopting a warm tone) to see something old in their country, which inspires affection. " The dear old place, you know." . . .

In Boston yesterday, I became acquainted with young Bock of Bote and Bock, who expressed a wish that we might work together.

Yes, but what shall I give him ? American Concert programmes ! With fingering !

S. " gossips " in a humorously benevolent way about Reger in the " Sonstags Staats " newspaper : but the way in which he abuses Strauss' Rosenkavalier is almost indecent. Whatever critics write, one always asks oneself, " Why ? "

Turandot " pleased " in Boston and was praised in the papers. I wish very much that it could be put on the *stage*, for *that* is the only place to which it belongs.

This thought has already improved my mood.

I am expecting your news quite impatiently, but I shall still have to wait . . .

NEW YORK, 22 *February* 1911.

The day before yesterday, in the evening at Schirmer's it so happened that not only Dr. von Hase was there, but also a son of Zimmermann's. It is comical, for they are my three publishers.

At dinner Mahler said something very good. " I have found," he said, " that people in general are better (more kindly) than one supposes." " You are an optimist," here interposed a fat American woman. " And more stupid," Mahler concluded, quickly, addressing the lady.

The first performance of the Berceuse took place yesterday evening. Toscanini came.

After two recalls for Mahler, I was obliged to bow twice to the audience (from my box). " The audience doesn't like the piece, but it likes me," I remarked. The Berceuse belongs to a type of music which does *not* suit Mahler so well as the rhythm and drums of Turandot. But the piece is effective, and I still almost believe that it can achieve a kind of popularity.

" Like a fine coloured Japanese woodcut," said Schindler.

There was no Celesta, instead of it an upright piano—didn't sound so bad as I feared.

It is almost uncanny, the way in which the dates are getting filled up.

```
February 23rd, Boston Symphony, New York
         24th,     ,,          ,,     Brooklyn
         25th,     ,,          ,,     New York
         27th,     ,,          ,,     Hartford
         28th, Recital in Boston
March 2nd, Afternoon Soirée at Frau Untermyer
             (Count Apponyi as guest)
             Evening Recital at Brooklyn
       5th, Recital at Chicago
       6th, Des Moines
       7th, Omaha
       9th, Kansas City
      10th, Sedalia
      14th, First Concert in California.
```

Now I must practise. I have four *different* Recitals and three different Concertos to play.

Others things I want to do—from now on—have to be crossed out.

Think a little of my worries, and love me . . .

NEW YORK, 24 *February* 1911.

. . . In the Italian Restaurant I met Consolo, the pianist, who knows Prince Troubetzkoy, and I got to know him too.

GERDA BUSONI, 1911

Close to, his face looks " clean-shaven " ; one thinks (although one sees him for the first time) that one must have known him before with a big beard and that he must have taken it off suddenly.

He is simple, interesting, original, but has the same kind of naïve, philosophical, quiet obstinacy, that all Russians have, who think, or wish to think.

He was born in Italy (and speaks more Italian than Russian) and has a Swedish wife. Lives in Italy—Paris—Stockholm and (least of all) in Russia. Reads no books at all, for some Russian-philosophical reason which is not clear : is in favour of everything natural and open-air (theoretically), but smokes and gives exhibitions in New York.

Consolo is very sympathetic, tactful, and cultivated. It was one of the nicest " evenings " I have had in America.

Mahler can *not* conduct the repetition of the Italian Concert himself to-day . . . When you read this, I shall probably be between Omaha and Kansas City. One sees the world. . . .

NEW YORK, 25 *February* 1911.

I seem to have a clear head again to-day (it has not been clear for a long time and I was *very* unhappy) and so I write to you with a newly awakened joy of life. How good it is that the earth goes round. Yesterday I had much to do, and yet too little. You will soon understand why.

At two o'clock I was asked to conduct my Berceuse myself, Mahler ill and absent.

The concert began at 2.30, but it was almost four o'clock before it was my turn to stand on the platform for those ten minutes.

A rehearsal was arranged at 6.30 in Brooklyn for the Todtentanz to-day. . . . Back again at ten o'clock and at 10.30 I was in Astor.

In this way, I was obliged to waste eight hours in order to be employed for three-quarters of an hour. The work itself was rather pointless and did not further anything. It is like sharpening a pencil which is already sharp.

This evening I shall probably be with Toscanini, who, it seems, was charmed with the Berceuse. That may help the Opera—when once it is finished.

And *when* once it is finished, my own work will begin. . . .

183

Collectedness belongs to Art, freedom to travelling. If one unites Art and travelling, both are losers.


NEW YORK, 28 *February* 1911.
Last Sunday (the 26th) I was at Toscanini's. He lives in a private suite in a big hotel and keeps his own Italian cook.

It was the most pleasant evening I have spent, since you left. The food was excellent and the conversation animated and interesting, right up to midnight.

Consolo was there. I played them the Sonatina, the Mephisto Waltz, the St. Francis legends. I was brought still more into the right atmosphere by a Steinway which thunders and *sustains the tone* (it is so long since I had this pleasure !). Toscanini is the most intelligent musician I have met up till now (with perhaps the exception of Strauss). Tremendously lively, quick, far-sighted, and artistic.

He repeated whole pages out of my æsthetic. I mean, he spoke my thoughts and did not say one word which I could not corroborate with my whole heart. He seemed to have a particular sympathy for me, for (according to Consolo) it is seldom he is so communicative.

He looks scarcely thirty years of age, but he is forty-four. His blindness is a fable. He does not even use glasses. His memory is a phenomenon in the annals of physiology ; but this does not impede his other faculties as is often the case with such abnormalities. He had just studied the very difficult score of Dukas' " Ariadne et Barbe-Bleue " and the next morning he was going to take the first rehearsal—from memory ! But such achievements must wear him out ; he is a bundle of nerves . . . I hope with all my heart that life will bring me still more closely in touch with him . . .


NEW YORK, 1 *March* 1911.
So *this* day has arrived, and this month, too, will come to an end one day ! But to me now it seems so far off as to be unattainable . . . I must prepare a new programme for Brooklyn, so there is no pause at all—I am freezing from fatigue. On the third I must do all the packing up for the West, for I do not

come back again to New York *for a month*.  There will be no
prospect of any thought or similar luxuries.  The evening walk
is suspended.  Perhaps in California—but there too, so much
is crowded in, and it is, strictly speaking, the question of a
" Début " again.

" How long will this go on ? "

CHICAGO, 4 March 1911.

I have read with great pleasure about the beautiful impressions,
of the pleasant hours in England and of your cheerful and re-
ceptive feeling.  It is, perhaps, the first time too that you have
been able to be happy *alone* ; and again it occurs to me that
everything that pleases lies in oneself and nowhere else . . .

I am all the more pleased that you have felt so well over there,
as you have missed nothing here.  It is only a hurried repetition
of everything.  Now, it is true, comes the promised California,
like a Fata Morgana ; the Land that is praised so highly (perhaps
praised too much) but there is neither the time, desire, nor freedom to enjoy it and I am prepared for a disappointment.  Here
are the dates :

| March | 5th | Chicago | |
|---|---|---|---|
| | 6th | Des Moines | |
| | 7th | Omaha | |
| | 9th | Kansas City | |
| | 10th | Sedalia | |
| | 14th | Los Angeles | |
| | 15th | Pasadena (suburb) | |
| | 17th | Los Angeles | |
| | 19th 21st | S. Francisco | The Pacific Coast. |
| | 22nd | Oakland (suburb) | |
| | 25th | Seattle | |
| | 26th | Portland | |
| April | 31st 1st | Cincinnati | |

I am reading a long novel by Wells, this time a serious one.
The changes in this man are wonderful and this book must put
him in the first rank of novelists.  He brings deepened feeling
to it and a stream of ideas ; he keeps his humour (freed from
common-place humour) and gives the feeling that he has digested
the experiences of life.  What pleasure to watch such a development ;  what happiness to experience it oneself ! . . .

185

Dear Gerda, I write every day, but you must reckon that the letters are always one day further away from you. But then, nearer again and nearer until the last one arrives at the same time as your deeply loving and grateful

FERROMANN.

DES MOINES, 6 March 1911.

In Brooklyn, Boston, Chicago, the recitals were sold out. In both the last towns I played very well. Yesterday, in Chicago, particularly so. Six recalls after the Liszt Sonata! I am not *practising* any more now. I can do no more and there is nothing more new to be done. The last two weeks were very hard and I feel exhausted.

My head feels burnt out . . .

Travelling and concerts go on now, until the 1st of April. Hanson now is agitating about the next tour . . .

KANSAS CITY, 9 March 1911.

. . . I am convalescent to-day, after a severe attack of influenza (or something similar). Hanson's people have been pitiless and I have been obliged to play with fever and pain and last night was the first time since the fourth of March that I have had a long enough night's rest.

Now it is all rather better; the weather is so lovely that one can sit with the window wide open and enjoy it . . .

My ideas slumber, I am morally blunted, physically feeble and generally depressed and everything looks grey.

All the same, Fräulein Curtis received a half-awake letter from me, about making use of the Red Indian motives. I believe my idea of beginning quite gradually with them is right; with small experiments at first (like attempts to fly).

It is absurd to make a Symphony with Indian melodies, after the Leipzig model (like Dvořák), or a Meyerbeer-ish opera (like Herbert's recent one). It needs a great deal of study to get inside the Indian life.

I thought at first of putting one or two scenes into one act, with Red Indian ceremonies and actions (very simple) and to join them together with one of the usual " eternal " stories; mother, son, bride, war, peace, without any subtleties. It

186

requires the highest kind of subtlety to listen to music of that kind and to reproduce it correctly.

I owed Miss Curtis some such small " sketch," for she had taken much trouble to write out and explain the melodies.

Possibly, it may not remain a sketch. I have been looking so long for something *unusual* and short for my next work.

Up to now, the book by Wells *gives* what it promised. " I feel we might do so many things, and everything that calls one, calls one away from something else." This is in it amongst other things. There are five hundred very closely printed pages, and so far I have hardly finished 150 ; for they are closely thought, too, as just that little sentence shows. As far as I have read, the book gives the impression of an autobiography, just as good as Rousseau's Confessions or Alfieri's Vita (scritta da esso stesso). Looked at like that, it is the truest form of novel. It is also written in the first person. The title, " The New Machiavelli," refers to a statesman of genius, who, in retirement, makes a record of his ideas . . .


SEDALIA, 10 *March* 1911.

When, to-day, I received your first letter from home (after a whole month !) I cried. The children's welcome must have made you happy. I am better, things look more cheerful again. Yesterday, I had a dream about a place with the high and light name of Montesole, in Tuscany. It was no dream, but a conversation with my " friend," Walter. I will tell you more about it. To-day, I must quickly put into words my joy over your letter and show you my happy face again, again, after the bad, grey weeks. I kiss you all and say Auf Wiedersehen.

Your FERROMANN, PAPPAFERRO, MANNPAPPA

(which sounds Indian too).


LOS ANGELES, 13 *March* 1911.

We left Sedalia on the 10th, midnight, and have been travelling until 2.30 to-day—the 13th. The route took us from the State of Missouri, past Kansas, Colorado, New Mexico, Arizona, to California. Most of the way (for almost two whole days) we travelled through *desert*, enlivened somewhat by a background of mountain chains (now and then with fantastic shapes) and red rock.

I was passive (still convalescent) and the three days passed—completely thrown away, it is true—but peacefully !

To-day, about mid-day, there was some vegetation to be seen at last ; at first wild stumps of palms and cactus in the sand, and then suddenly, the richest culture of orange groves. The town is an American provincial town (at least at first sight) with sky-scrapers, and the usual street sights. It is a fresh wonder to me every day how *such* a town, so tasteless and bare, could be built in *such* a country. Why must this marvellous gift of Nature be besmeared in such a way ? The most unsympathetic people, Japanese or Jesuits, would have built something more beautiful. What is this pride they have of being " practical " ? . . .

I am writing to you to-day about my arrival, and when you read it I shall be in the East again ; so these complaints will only have a sense of the past, or an abstract sense, and you must think no more about them. But the moment is uncomfortable, and will it be a comfort later to know that it went by miserably ? Besides, you feel with me *now* (even if we cannot be in direct contact with one another). Sometimes I think you are right and that the North is more cheerful . . .

LOS ANGELES, 15 *March* 1911.

## MELODY BELONGS TO THE FUTURE

It can be said—contradict it who may—that Wagner was the first to recognize melody as the supreme law, not only theoretically. On the whole, the older art of composition suffers from a neglect of melody. Unconsciously we feel another standard in the classical works and we do not measure them so strictly.

The broad strokes of the brush found in the later symphonic compositions are missing in the pre-Wagner music. There the " eight-bar sentence " reigns supreme, which, for our feeling, seems a short breath. The quality of the music, too, within these eight bars is more primitive than that of the symphonic music.

With Beethoven, this strikes one most forcibly in his *Second period*, which is the weakest, and is exemplified in its principal compositions, the 5th Symphony, the Waldstein Sonata, the Appassionata, and the three Quartets, Op. 59.

I should like to repeat—and let them contradict me again—

that in Beethoven's first period feeling conquers helplessness ; in the third feeling stands above the mastery which he has gained. But in the second period feeling is overshadowed by symphonic breadth and symphonic brilliance. Beethoven, in his second period, exploits the forceful ideas contained in the first.

The heroically passionate defiance of the " Pathétique " continues to be the basis for all pieces similar in feeling (only more extended) in the following period, headed by the Fifth Symphony. But the melodic element does not keep step with this extension and gets lost in—what shall I call it ?—a kind of table-land of modulatory and figurative eloquence. I am thinking, for example, of the working out in the first movement of the " Appassionata " where the persistent rush and intensity of temperament fills the place where the content should be.

In this case it is more as if the thrilling eloquence and infectious conviction of an orator were making the effect, rather than his theme or the wealth of his ideas. It makes an effect, accordingly, on larger masses of people and with a more direct impact. Temperament disguises not only the content, but the feeling too ; although it may not appear to be like this.

The deepest feeling needs the fewest words and gestures. It is an historical commonplace, repeated like a continuous cinematograph performance, that as each new composition appears it is accused of a lack of melody. I have read this kind of accusation in criticisms after the first performance of Mozart's Don Giovanni, Beethoven's Violin Concerto, and Wagner's operas. And it is always taken for granted that the increase in technical complications is the reason for the decrease in melodic invention.

It almost seems as if technical mastery makes its effect by being unusual, whereas melody is only perceived as such when it appears in commonplace and familiar ways.

*But as a matter of fact Mozart, as a maker of melodies, was richer than his predecessors ; Beethoven broader, more ingenious than Mozart, and Wagner more voluptuous than Beethoven* (if perhaps less noble and original).

Beethoven himself in his *third* period—at times in the string quartets—dissolves the rigid symphonic mechanism into melody and—psychology. Wagner was more material ; and it is against this materialism that some living composers are trying to re-act.

Immaterialism is the true being of music; we are on the track of it; we wander through narrow underground corridors at the end of which a strange, distant, phosphorescent light gives us a glimpse of the passage leading out into a marvellous grotto.

When once we have reached the vaulted room in nature's mysterious palace, then our souls can learn to soar with speech; and it will sound for ever, like a blossoming and exalted *melody* . . .

LOS ANGELES, 15 *March* 1911.

This is one of those days when one waits passively for sunset, in order to put one's head, which is heavy and indolent, out of doors. Clothes stick; one doesn't like sitting, one doesn't like standing, and least of all does one like lying down.

It is a great error to suppose that because I am a good (and also effective) artist, I should—or could—be brought into contact with the Public (in general)!

Artists have as much to do with the public as religion with the church. I mean, religion belongs to something inside, something personal (like talent); the church is an " Institution," ostensibly for the average masses, in reality for the benefit of the priests. Wells tells his countrymen similar truths (at last) in his excellent book.

This has given me the greatest pleasure ever since the 27th February, when I bought it. Listen how finely Wells has developed.

" That something greater than ourselves which does not so much exist as seek existence, palpitating between being and not being, how marvellous it is! It has worn the form and visage of ten thousand different Gods, sought a shape for itself in stone, ivory, and music and wonderful words, spoken more and more clearly of a mystery of love, a mystery of unity, dabbling meanwhile in blood and cruelty beyond the common impulses of man. It is something that comes and goes, like a light that shines and is withdrawn; withdrawn so completely that one doubts if it has ever been."

In the middle of writing sentences like these, I received a telegram from Hanson : " Congratulations on the great success in Los Angeles, means very much for the future." My God !!

190

. . . Am I then someone who seeks a future in California ? But perhaps he means California's future. (I wish it every possible prosperity.)

And just à propos, I read in Wells :

" Most of the good men we know are not doing the very best work of their gifts ; nearly all are a little adapted, most are shockingly adapted to some second-best use."

To-day, I had the idea (very uncertain and visionary) of an Indian Rhapsody for piano and orchestra.

Monte-Sole is a small estate in Settignano, where my friend Walter, from Kansas City, used to live, and it is to be sold. They made my mouth water by talking about it, and I will investigate the matter. I find pleasure in the name alone. Besides this, Settignano is in one of the best wine districts (it lies behind Fiesole, I believe).

Enfin, you see my mind begins to wake up a little. To-day has been the first free day, without travelling or concert, for three weeks. (I have discontinued practising since Chicago) . . . If only it were not so hot ! It is like an illness and I have hardly recovered from the hellish week between Chicago and the journey here . . .

I kiss you and the boys, you are very near to me . . .

Los Angeles, 17 *March* 1911.

One breathes again. It has become cool. I only received " Die Ratten " by Hauptmann, yesterday. I have read it, but am still too close to the impression to be able to look at it. It may seem strange, but as I read it, I kept on seeing Zille's drawings. There is much in it, and something—something important —is missing. Don't know yet what. It is very alive. In the list of Hauptmann's works, the " Versunkene Glocke " has the greatest number of editions. O,o ! . . .

The palms in the middle of this American town make an improbable effect. English-American industry, and tropical vegetation ! Like a volume of Byron amongst account books.

I shall soon turn my back on it all. To-day my nerves are quieter ; they were strained to breaking point. . . .

The only time I was in Nice, there was snow. Here it is cool and cloudy. They have given me no time or opportunity to recover from influenza and so I have dragged round the remains of it with me. I am too tired to long for new impressions, or to enjoy them ; but from what I have seen up to now, it seems there is nothing here which might not be found in Italy ; and much that Italy has is to be sought for here in vain.

I played yesterday, four hours after my arrival from a twenty hours' journey. I played well and had a success. I have to travel another thirty-two hours from here to Seattle ! It takes three days, or more, to get to Cincinnati from Portland !

. . . Chickering, without any scruples, wished to send me to Honolulu. That is *no* exaggeration, for yesterday, their representative really made the suggestion ! ! " It is a very interesting trip," he said.

It is sad that I receive no letter, and it is oppressive. I hope every day, every day. It is really like a bad dream. I feel as if I were being posted like a parcel . . .


S. Francisco, 21 *March* 1911.

It is indeed—or rather, it should be !—moving to see this town half in ruins and half new and unfinished, defying the elements, if such an expression as " moving " can be applied to any American undertaking . . .

It was not the earthquake but the fire, which broke out in fifty places at the same time, that made the disaster. In order to isolate the fires, they blew up the houses which lay between, with dynamite. It lasted five days . . .

It is spring the whole year here, and mediocre people without any deeper interests or ambition have nothing left to wish for. Imagination, of course, belongs to " wishing." If I were rich, said the idler, I should look out of the window all day long, and spit . . .

A group of musicians has settled here . . . (German and Italian) . . . The Germans attacked my playing. They are busy " keeping up the traditions " on the Pacific Ocean ; conscientious people ! What harm a rat-hole like Leipzig can do ! The Italians behaved very patriotically. . .

S. Francisco, 22 *March* 1911.

Yesterday came the fat letter from you . . . A smaller one would have given me equal joy !

The battle of S. Francisco ended yesterday. " Busoni won the battle," says one newspaper . . . And to-day another said, " When I am somewhat older, I may become a serious artist yet " . . .

Now, as things are better, I can tell you that the day before yesterday, and yesterday, I was quite miserable.

There are still a couple of big journeys, then—Glory to God in the highest and peace on earth,

Deinem gewisz gut-gewillten

Dich liebenden Ferro-Mann.

Seattle, 25 *March* 1911.

We have got quite a long way north again. Yesterday we travelled through " regular " Tyrolean or Styrian scenery, with wet fir-woods and a rainbow against banks of clouds. To-day, too, the sky looks as it does in the mountainous parts in Austria ; stormy, with the sun breaking through . . .

Your letter of the 8th has just come . . .

On that day I was in bed in Kansas City, with raging influenza . . . In Los Angeles the heat finished me off. The journey here from there lasts two whole days and two nights.

From California onwards, the niggers have almost disappeared, and in their places there are masses of Chinese. They serve in the hotels, sometimes Japanese, too.

The little voyage from S. Francisco to Oakland over the bay was quite beautiful, but for me not exciting, for I was no longer susceptible to impressions. For this reason, I have almost no impression of California ! . . .

It is true that I have suffered very much this time and every-thing becomes more and more difficult for me. To confine my years of intellectual strength and to cripple them in this way, is torture to me. Added to this, I see nothing of life, and have no pleasures. (Just a good hotel is like a present from destiny.) . . .

My coat of arms, the ass's head with a garland, I shall soon hack in pieces.

I have corresponded with Miss Curtis about the possibility of developing the Red Indian melodies, and I have pointed out the radical faults in all the attempts to use them up to now. To-day she writes to me : " Your letter is like your book.   A few words which disclose a view from the mountain top."

Unfortunately, one cannot do everything oneself.   I constantly think of those words in Wells's book : " *The most excellent being adapted to some second-best use* " . . .


CHICAGO, 30 March 1911.

. . . This evening we go to Cincinnati (in order to celebrate my birthday).   How I shall play the E flat concerto by Beethoven there, without fingers, without mind and without rehearsal, God knows.   But so much has been all right up to now that this will be all right too.   Mahler has not conducted since the 21st February.   Spiering took his place on the 24th and remained and will remain until the end of the season.   It was very creditable that an averagely good violinist should show so much *présence d'esprit*, and was able to carry through the performance fairly well.   But——!   The behaviour of the New York audience and the critics over the matter will remain in my memory as one of my most painful experiences.

The sensation made by a leader of an orchestra being able to conduct unprepared, has made a greater impression on them than Mahler's whole personality was ever able to do !   Spiering has been exalted to the position of one of the greatest conductors, and they have spoken quite seriously about his continuing to fill the post.   *Not one word of regret has fallen about Mahler's absence ! !*   One reads of such things happening in history, but when it is a personal experience, one is filled with despair . . .

In the train I had much time to think and I thought of many things.   I believe that I thought to good purpose.

I have almost accounted for the omnipresence of time ; but I have not found out why we humans think of time *as a line* going from backwards, forwards, whilst it must be in *all directions* like everything else in the system of the world . . .

I have thought of many other things.   And I always come to the conclusion that our music is only a lot of chirrup ; this idea is no longer merely idealistic, for it can be proved logically.   No, I do not write magazine articles on purpose ; but all these questions crowd into my mind more and more and time is getting short.   I must not throw a whole month's work to the winds again, as I have done this time.

I think with *serious* joy of the journey home and I have the feeling that my most important period is beginning and that it is, I suppose, the *definitive* one. The joy is not less because it is serious ; on the contrary, it is deeper. It is deep and beautiful, but it has lost all its youthfulness, like Rembrandt's later self-portraits. Possibly, I shall be different again at home, and more like I was before. But however it will be, I rejoice inwardly with you all and myself, more fervently even than usual . .

CINCINNATI, 31 *March* 1911.
*Night.*

. . . It is half-past twelve midnight in Berlin half-past seven : perhaps the household is already stirring and it is the 1st of April. I had quite a nice evening with Miss Burston, the first human evening for an eternity . . .

Petri gave an enormous Busoni Recital in Manchester ; I only received the programme . . .

1 *April, Morning.*

. . . Now I am going to have a little lunch with the Italians here . . . I shall write more in the afternoon. I think so much of home, it is seven o'clock in the evening there.

1 *April, Afternoon.*

I was cunning enough to ask for letters in the *other* hotel, and happily, there lay a bundle ! The news about the Brautwahl has given me great pleasure—more pleasure than anything. Of all the letters, the one from Lori was the most full of sentiment, and the simplest, and for that reason, the deepest in feeling.

. . . It is still the 1st of April, but it will soon be passed—" Be off, be off," said the watch-dog.

Many have written affectionately, and here, too, the people were very friendly. . . .

NEW YORK, 7 *April* 1911.

. . . To-morrow I shall go on board. There, in tranquillity, I shall think out different things. I should like so much to have repose ; but—I give it up . . .

195

*(Addressed to Göhren auf Rügen)*

BERLIN, 10 *July* 1911.

. . . To-day the morning was beautiful and productive ; I have always postponed doing the worst part of the score ; but now I must put up with doing it—and—go on to the end. It is so quiet up here, and the sun added to it gives an impression of Sunday. Sometimes, life seems so beautiful ; as if it were one long holiday.

Yesterday evening, at eleven o'clock, I stood in the light of the full moon, in front of the mystical doors of the County Court building ; the street was quite empty. It was like the atmosphere in The Magic Flute . . .


*(Addressed to Göhren)*

BERLIN, 15 *July* 1911.

Now to-day one of the most difficult sections is finished and there are 70 pages of MS. ready for printing . . .

Yesterday old Councillor Hase paid me a visit. We got on excellently with one another. Life has made him softer too. Now his sons begin to criticize him, and he implored me to go on with the Liszt Edition, so that they may not think he has undertaken something impossible. The Hungarians are quarrelling amongst themselves about this. Bartok is taking part in the Liszt Edition now . . .


*(Addressed to Göhren)*

BERLIN, 17 *July* 1911.

. . . I have read Balzac's letters and Die Hoffnung auf Buddhismus. I have reached the point now of looking upon teaching, philosophies, and religions, as works of art, and I side with the art that has the best preacher. I hardly think that the individual will be happier or wiser for any of them, amongst the masses. I find that the shoemaker in the Bible, in the Thousand and One Nights, or in old Rome, is always the same shoemaker. And the artists, the priests, and the courtesans are the same.

When the soldier with a Bible in his left hand strikes out furiously with his right ; or a Saracen cuts off heads whilst he talks about Mahomet ; it is just the same thing.

Again you have a letter with a magazine article in it ; but

there is nothing new to tell you, and I don't need to talk of myself to you ; and it would be superfluous to assure you of my love, because you know that I always am and always remain your . . .

FERROMANN.

(*Addressed to Göhren*)

BERLIN, 18 *July* 1911.

Please be patient with this little essay.

On the whole, I have always thought very well of our epoch and considered it artistically interesting. But the impressions and the mood in which these impressions are formed fall together on to the floor of one's soul and it is only later, when the mood has changed, that they can be separated.

Now, in this epoch, I see a real supremacy of its " three powers " :—

Money,

Industry,

Sport ;

After that, Jewish activity threatens to be supreme ; the wish to pull individuals out of the masses and to stamp the individual into the masses. Money and Socialism try to eat each other up, like Siegfried and Fafner ; Fafner and Siegfried.

Industry, with its noble aims of cheapness, quickness and mass production, is quixotic. . . .

I wanted to tell you about these little reflections, as I tell you everything. Do not consider it dry . . .

(*Addressed to Göhren*)

BERLIN, 20 *July* 1911.

. . . The score has been my only thought. I have been sweating over this part of it, for it was five years old and badly put together. Now it is quite tidy. After this comes the *last part*, but that is very important and complicated ; but better composed. And then, a long, big, deep sigh—(of relief).

VARESE, 4 *September* 1911.

I have now decided to remain in Varese until I make the return journey . . . The landscape here is most beautiful ; the air very fresh. Everything pretty and pleasant . . .

Thanks for the newspapers. In the " Allgem. M.Z.," a Dr. Friedhof [1] has tried to *bury* my Fantasie (Kleist calls a joke like that " Shakespearean in character "). He remarked that there was a modern current running through the work, which was not like Bach. " But how intelligent you are," says Mark Twain, in a similar case. Or like Brahms, " Every donkey notices that . . ."

VARESE, 5 *September* 1911.

This is the fourth night running that I have slept badly. It exhausts me . . .

Books don't stimulate me ; the Goncourt Journal does, it is true ; but it always makes me melancholy. Staying in this hotel here is really nice and the weather continues to be brilliant. It is a memorable summer . . . I miss the piano, even if I do not play . . .

There is a new entertainment building, with the lovely Italian name : " Kursaal." That characterizes present-day Italy. Amongst the attractions are—Roller Skating (in Italian, Skating Ring). They irritated me so much there, with their stupid, vain faces and the lifeless carriage of their bodies, that with my whole soul I wished that one of them might tumble and do himself some damage. Five minutes after, the " Master " fell and tore his left trouser completely in two at the knee. Was it my fault ? " They will say you have the evil eye," said Anzoletti. (They hold out their first and fifth fingers to keep off " the evil eye.")

*Afternoon.*

. . . It is the old story, I can sleep after I have done good work ; if I do *no* work, I become nervous.

The evenings here are not refreshing. It is like slow murder. Only the landscape is magical (in these moonlight nights) . . . But it would be psychologically interesting to know why during peaceful periods I have fewest ideas, and become unpeaceful myself.—Query—.

But of all summer resorts or similar speculative places that I know, I find the *nicest* here. I find my impression confirmed again ; that it is the country that is most alive in Italy, not the towns . . .

[1] The name means " churchyard."

198

(*Addressed to Stockholm*)
VARESE, 9 *September* 1911.

. . . I have moved to Anzoletti's.   I couldn't bear it any longer in the hotel, after six nights without sleep and in anxiety.   Last night I went to bed quietly again and slept.   Ratschi-Potschi !

Varese pleases me more and more ; and it is very varied.   I am in a continual state of amazement over the landscape.   The people are friendly, the women very pretty . . .

Have taken up my work again . . .


(*Addressed to Stockholm*)
BASLE, 13 *September*, 1911.

. . . But I am very uneasy.   There is so much to be done and the opera has stuck (I knew it would !) . . .   Hope on ; hope ever . . .

# 1912

LONDON, 15 *March* 1912.

It went very well yesterday, lasted two and a quarter hours. Adagio and Fugue Op. 106 and the Liszt Sonata were especially successful. For the first time I was able to practise five hours undisturbed the day before. The Paganini Variations [by Brahms] have become " faded," old maidish ; although they were quite charming in their youth. Too little in them for virtuosity, or for serious music. Chopin's Ballades keep fresher, but the 2nd and 3rd are remarkably badly composed . . .

I have allowed myself a small reward ; the first edition of *Gulliver*, which I have found at last. It cost 70 marks, but it is worth it and may increase in value.

I do not find that London is so *beautiful* this time, although what one sees in the streets is quite different from anything one sees in Berlin. As the people speak *softly*, the quality of the sounds one hears is different from Paris and Italy. To make up for that, they love to hold concerts and services in open places here ; it certainly doesn't sound like an Italian Serenade !

The barrel-organs, too, are characteristic and so is the whistling to call a cab. But one never hears a human voice raised. Has that ever struck you ?

LONDON, 17 *March* 1912.

Now Sunday has come ; reflection of the English nation ; amputation of life. . . .

Everything repeats itself ; London and Sunday ; exhaustion and books. Just as it was 10 years ago . . .

LONDON, 18 *March* 1912.

I was at the " Futurist " Exhibition and had a thrilling impression from some of the pictures. It is true that not being quite well, and rather nervous, makes me very sensitive. Boccioni seems to me to be the strongest of them ; he has a picture called " the Rising City " which is really great. " Leaving the Theatre " by Carrà is excellent too. And " The Dance at Monico's " by Severini, whose work seems to be very unequal . . .

I had to tell you something about this whilst the impression is still vivid. (Unfortunately I can see that these people are already becoming old-fashioned.)

Anyhow it has refreshed and delighted me.


HAMBURG, 25 *March* 1912.

After the first incomplete impressions I have good hopes.[1]  I heard half of the 2nd act in the orchestra and saw some of the scenery. The sets are *very pretty*. The instrumentation sounded well, although the orchestra is still uncertain and makes mistakes.

Frl. " Albertine " would like to accompany herself on the piano ; but I hope to prevent this !  At 5.30 we have a rehearsal with piano . . .


HAMBURG, 26 *March* 1912.

The rehearsal at the piano yesterday was very delightful. Thusman and Manasse are excellent. The Finale of the 2nd Act they sang particularly well. The scene by the pond, too, I listened to with pleasure. The mise-en-scène made one realize that Reinhardt has spoilt us.

All the same, it will look quite well. I should like to have the moon at the close of the Pond Scene, and that seems to make difficulties.

" But we bought a beautiful new moon ! " the stage manager called out to the machinist.

The problem of how to produce the magic play of sparks has been very well solved ; the Church vision will also make an impression.

For the first day, anyhow, I had a number of beautiful impressions. I am going to the theatre again now. Auf wiedersehen, dear Gerda, I believe it will be good !

[1] This refers to the rehearsals for the first performance of the Brautwahl which took place 12 April 1912.

Yesterday evening was very full of impressions ; and I had expected hardly any.   For, first, I read a good deal of Villiers' book ;  then, in Hamburg, by accident, I tumbled on Act III of the Walküre (I am allowed to go on the stage unhindered) ;  and finally I met William Steinway in the hotel, with whom I discussed many things.   The book " L'Eve future " is very unusual ;  with its mixture of subtle thought and leaning towards " baroque," it is startlingly original, and has many reminiscences of other works ; and for me, it is especially remarkable, because it contains a lot of problems *which I have already considered myself.*   Its descent from Poe (Ligeia), Hoffmann (der Sandmann) and Wagner (exorcism of Kundry through Klingsor) is obvious.

What I heard of Wagner's yesterday *sounded horrible to me* . . . I *could* not wait for the beautiful ending which reconciles one to the whole.   These Valkyries and these spears which are always being stamped on the ground ;  the senseless movements and the nonsensical immovableness ;  the orchestration which at times says too much and then too little—drove me out before Wotan began to take his leave : and—the libretto—— !

I am just going to the rehearsal, will write later.

Now the rehearsal is over.   It was taken at the piano.   The Church scene sounds *very* good ;  all my youthful recollections of the Catholic atmosphere are in it.   Leonhard is developing. He stands better on the stage.   I mean the singer.

Yesterday I took an unopened letter with me.   It was from Lessmann, for my birthday, addressed to the " Herr Composer " . . .

I still hope that all will go well.

I am extremely glad that you are coming to-morrow ! . . .

The more work that is put into everything for the opera, the more *wavering* it becomes.   The singing was good when they were alone ;  with the orchestra—less good ;  on the stage—still worse.   *Each* one adds his own little inaccuracies and in the end there is a whole sum of them.

The last two days I have been quite crushed.   The time is (as always !) too short . . .

*(Addressed to Ringgenberg bei Interlaken)*

BERLIN, 20 *July* 1912.

I am in a pleasant mood, although the weather has become grey, for (this is the principal reason) to-day I have finished another small work which is good : " Der Fantasia contrappuntistica Kleine Ausgabe " to which, as introduction, I wrote three Variations over the same choral (Allein Gott in der Höh' sei Ehr'), which are quite new.

Then to-day I received a letter and book called " Franziska " by Wedekind, from Munich. The Director of the theatre wants music for it, to be played between the acts ; perhaps written for organ or a quartet. What do these theatre people, painters, and the like, really think that music is ? Something parallel to obscuring the light, which can be used as padding between the acts. The organ is not at all suitable for the Wedekind play, as far as I have read it ; for it seems to me that the attitude towards life in it is satirical and daring. That would be a misfit ; like Grieg, when in all sincerity he wrote funeral music for Peer Gynt.

I will send you the book as soon as I have read it myself and please tell me your impression of it.

The " Rising City " hangs in your room. The picture grows on me more and more. It is very thrilling and the painting very skilful . . .

*(Addressed to Ringgenberg)*

BERLIN, 24 *July* 1912.

You have written so beautifully, that it made me feel quite pleasant and warm. I send you back all my love with equal warmth. . . . During the last few days I have been busy with the Wedekind. It is a Faust parody. Have thought over a plan, including orchestration, and how long it must last ; and even sketched out the operetta and music. For before I decline to do it I must know : Why——

What do you think ?

Reasons for doing it :

1. Small and quite delightful work.
2. A big première.
3. Perhaps helps things in the future.

Against it :

1. Perhaps the whole trouble will be in vain.

2. It may be thought I am joining the Wedekind circle and cause misunderstanding.

3. It will spoil my own Faust idea for myself.

Will you tell me your opinion ?

There are 12 small numbers to write, as I calculate, for an orchestra of only 20 (that attracts me very much). . . .

(*Addressed to Ringgenberg*)

BERLIN, 28 *July* 1912.

I have had an idea just lately ; it was an idea for a sonata with the following plan : Chaos—Restless work—Cheerfulness—Rest and beauty.

Prelude—Fugue—Scherzo—Adagio.

I am going to refuse, I think, the Wedekind Faustina (or a " discourse against love ").

Only wait for your opinion.

BERLIN, 29 *July* 1912.

Your letter has strengthened me in my decision to let the " Franziska " go. I knew I should ! ; and to-day I wrote to Munich to refuse. . . .

(*Addressed to Ringgenberg*)

BERLIN, 3 *August* 1912.

. . . I have been occupied with smaller things in between. For if I began a big work now I should have to put " the Secret " [1] on one side ; and I am just in the right mood for it, intellectually and spiritually.

My plan for a sonata would not be so suitable for a string quartet. *Power* and *contrast* in sound would be lacking. Besides this, I have a feeling of duty towards the " piano " ; I must give it a turn. For a quartet I should have to have a different train of thought . . .

[1] A proposed opera, " Das Geheimnis," to a libretto by Karl Vollmoeller.

*(Addressed to Ringgenberg)*

Even the imperial post has caprices ! Two letters and a post-card from you have just reached me, *at the same time* (to my great joy). Because of Sunday ! . . . Where is this Sunday in nature's calendar ? Although the origin of this human arrangement was founded in religion, it is not " belief " in religion which is harmful . . . (the bad thing is to hide one's nature and be intolerant towards others). But what harm is there in " believing " and what help is to be got from " not believing ? " When I—with many struggles—had got materialistic teaching well into me, I thought I had achieved wonders ; but I was no happier, rather less so ! And how is it with Schopenhauer's philosophy ?—Still worse. Religion, so it seems to me, is like clothing ; everyone must cut it to suit their own bodies, and wear it without giving too much offence to the passers by ; in fact these should find it pleasing. . . .

Everything is rather clearer now. Yesterday I finished the Brautwahl suite (a good piece ! !). The changes I have made in the opera will not take more than 2 weeks. In September I shall be free to prepare for the season. The (business) correspondence is tedious and endless. . . .

PARIS, 11 *August* 1912.

The mornings in Paris enliven one's pulse and stimulate thoughts and the " Déjeuner " rounds them off delightfully. But in the evening where are the Berlin lights and flowers to be found, and the Berlin youthful high spirits ? The little Parisian dresses in black even in the summer, and she disappears from the streets directly the shops are closed. Then the everlasting cocotte appears who, fundamentally, is just as soberly thrifty and positive as, collectively, all these Mademoiselles M . . . of whom the female part of France is composed. Compared with Berlin, a summer night in Paris is almost gloomy. The " average " man's expression is really more stupid than elsewhere. On the whole the woman is stronger, more energetic and cunning ; only sees her aim for quite a short distance ahead, and is constantly on the " qui vive."

On the first day of my arrival (Friday) I lunched at Foyot, because the feeling on the other side of the Seine appeals to me quite differently. " Here one reads books ; on the other side one reads newspapers," Widor said to me—whom I met at lunch. When I told him what brought me here he made a remark which is typical of the French outlook. " When you are a landowner, you will be one of us." A landowner is something so solid, respectable and unchangeable. . . .

I decided yesterday (Sunday) to drive to the Gare de l'Est, but as the driver at this command replied, " Not further than that ? I should prefer to go into the country," it occurred to me that I could make the trip in the motor-car, which I agreed to do at once. We went through the Rue du Faubourg St. Antoine and out through the Parc de Vincennes. The road passes through two or three villages and went through blooming, cultivated, not strikingly picturesque country.

The house, which was the attraction that brought me from Berlin, is pretty and cheap ; but it requires *as much again* as the original price to be spent on it in order to make it inhabitable.

Towards evening I came back, dined well (the fresh air had stimulated my stomach but been injurious for my head) and spent quite a stimulating evening, by myself, until midnight, on Montmartre.

The evening before that I spent quite differently and I will tell you about it in its turn. We must do everything in order.

On a previous evening (that is, Friday) I had met Vollmoeller on the Boulevard. He addressed me in Italian and said, in Paris he was always reminded of the superiority of the Italian over the Frenchman . . . He had had a long conversation that day with d'Annunzio. We made appointments for the following day (1) to lunch together ; (2) to discuss the libretto in detail ; [1] (3) to meet d'Annunzio. Through a misunderstanding we did not meet for lunch. The discussion took place at tea time and made me feel hopeful about my work. (With so much on hand I am a new man again. The endless number of details to be considered ; the continual planning and replanning makes me quite young again !)

Late in the evening we went to the Hôtel Meurice, rue de Rivoli, a sumptuous hotel. D'Annunzio's welcome was warm and his manner that of a man of the world. He was in dress clothes and pumps, and in the company of society people, two ladies and two gentlemen. A very beautiful Italian woman, who

[1] The " Geheimnis."

was naturally kind, was there and her name intoxicated Gabriele almost foolishly. She is called Donna Beatrice di Toledo, Marchesa di Casafuerte ; and certainly it sounds like a whole play by Calderon. The four went away immediately after the usual compliments ; " Je vous ai applaudi " and " quand vous reviendrez à Paris " . . . And we remained behind, three of us, including the Olympic one. D'Annunzio is sympathetic, quick and lively of thought ; a charming narrator. A little " scented " and affected and at the same time sometimes shy and abashed. He informed us about his newest piece, which he wrote especially for Mlle Rubinstein ; and because of this there is so much mime and so many dances, that it requires as much music as a pantomime.

Whilst he talked he unfolded such an array of rich pictures and colours that one became quite enchanted ; although in the end one had to confess that he had only put together a series of designs, costumes and ceremonies. He intimated that he would have liked me to write the music . . . But Vollmoeller said to me afterwards that it would have been an unsuccessful labour. He does not believe in d'Annunzio as a playwright. (He, d'Annunzio, is very dependent on ideas of success, hence his immeasurable respect for Wagner and—even for Puccini !) D'Annunzio and I separated very warmly, with many germinating plans, and this meeting has pleased me very much.

So I have fulfilled my little mission and shall turn, without haste, towards home. I am so glad I shall find you all together ! . . .

PARIS, 12 *August* 1912.

. . . Yesterday I bought something very rare, almost unknown and of great beauty, for 25 francs ; that is, 12 pictures on the Legend of the *Wandering Jew* by Doré, in the original edition. They are very strong and as woodcuts are also unusual. (I thought at first they were lithography.) Published 1862, just 50 years ago, at the same time as the first edition of the " Misérables." This style-less epoch has now become " historical " and we can see a definite expression in it. In France, anyhow, the epoch was important. (I believe in Austria, too.) Early this morning, in bed, this aphorism occurred to me :

" Because they ran in front of them, those who were left behind only saw their backs and, therefore, thought they had no faces."

Had a long and serious conversation with Vollmoeller yesterday evening, chiefly about literature. He considers Stefan George *the greatest* poet of our time : " He guards the linguistic conscience of literature." He does not think so much of Goethe as I do. I said : " How wonderful a verse like this is : Stürzen wir uns in das Brausen der Zeit ; how it must have *sounded* when first it was written, coming after such writers as Klopstock and Gellert ! The idea of joining time together with noise, move-ment and sensuality was unheard of up to then." He agreed. He always finished up with the refrain, " You are a better man of letters than I." In the same way d'Annunzio welcomed me by saying, " I know that you are a philologist." . . .

I am still wandering about without any aim to-day and to-morrow. . . .

You are all most warmly greeted at home ; we four will soon be sitting at the round table (which is too small) . . .

PARIS, 14 *August* 1912.
I went round the opera house for half an hour yesterday, and studied the plan of it. As far as I can say about architecture, I think the form genial and the execution of it masterly. The ground plan, above all, is grand ; and it was a splendid idea to put this ground plan under Garnier's bust in the place of an inscription. Every line which the walls follow was put in its place with the greatest certainty and clarity. The decoration is heavy and conventional certainly ; perhaps Garnier was less of an artist than a pure architect, and much can be put down to the account of his period. Who knows, however, whether they will not say he was right about everything, later on. It is certain that what he had to do was to preserve the representative *French* style and to accentuate the national side of it, and for that he was obliged to put on state uniform.

I have never seen the inside of the house, but it seems that the big staircase is unique in construction.

The curve of the façade is perfect ; the *mind's eye* carries it on at either side.

" What a work of art keeps through the ages is its *form*," said Vollmoeller to me.

To-morrow, I think, I shall start for home . . .

Even without piano-playing, it would have been a horrible journey. I was in pieces when I arrived . . .

Ysaye plays next Sunday in the Albert Hall (with Backhaus and Melba) the—Gounod's Ave Maria.

The newspapers gathered the following news about me : (1) I had finished a new opera ; (2) arranged the Berceuse for cello ; (3) am hopelessly ill.

Thank God, to-day, in spite of 2 bad nights, I am quite well. To-day is my " half " birthday, the 1st October.

The playing goes well. I almost think it interests me again ; consequently it can still be improved or changed . . .

PETERSBURG, 6 *November* 1912.

I remained behind, very sad.[1] I went on foot from the station to the hotel ; it took me an hour. Later, I walked for another two hours in Moscow, this town with its (for me) foreign language, amongst a crowd composed of students, suburban people and cheap cocottes. In appearance, I thought the town could be compared in a certain way with Edinburgh or Venice. Melancholy as I was, the ugliness of it disturbed me and I decided that towns—like works of art, like everything really—are incomplete and deficient, never right in character and always unfinished. Man's optimistic wish to admire allows him to overlook a thousand atrocities in favour of one idea, which has been inspired by a few beautiful and characteristic things in a place. If one feels in a state of opposition, one can see most things in Moscow and Venice as ugly. In short, some stimulation being taken for granted, the impression lies in oneself . . .

The concert was a memorable one and was perhaps even more imbued with a spirit of festivity than in Moscow. Here, too, it rained flowers ; there were laurel wreaths and they called out " Campanella." I played as well as I can play . . .

The 78-year-old Cui (who I thought was dead) was at the concert. The wife of the critic Ivanoff, who is a sister of Frau Sgambati, greeted me. The hall was quite full. It would have been inhuman had I not felt a good deal of emotion. I gave myself up completely, too, to my playing ; so that to-day I am not up to very much . . .

[1] After Gerda Busoni's departure.

I start this evening for the first Riga concert. It makes it a little easier for me that they speak German there.

The long-promised Schirmer edition of the Chopin preludes is giving me a great deal of thought again. I should like to put many of my ideas into it. . . .

RIGA, 7 *November* 1912.

It was a glorious thing to get your letter this morning (at 7) and other letters too . . .

Robert Freund writes very beautifully ; amongst other things he says . " The Sonatina took me captive at once. The very unusual harmony just suits the fantastic, mystic character of the piece, and gives the impression of a natural, spontaneous intuitiveness.

" I ask myself why I cannot get in touch with Schönberg whilst even the most daring things you do seem quite natural to me. Is it because of the incompleteness of his form, the short sentences and lack of interest in his themes ? You are the true Futurist in the sense that your influence is for the future—etc."

RIGA, 8 *November* 1912.

It is quite comfortable and quiet here . . . There is some Empire architecture here too ; it is remarkable how this style suits all climates and nations—probably because it is impersonal.

In general, a town such as this is more prepossessing than any of the towns in Russia, which are disconnected in form and where all the splendours of the State seem to be displayed on pedestals in the midst of poverty.

An excellent bookshop, an equally excellent wine shop, are flourishing oases. Riga reminds one most of Königsberg ; the long riverside is very lively and picturesque. Market stalls, steamers, sailors, poor people—a wide perspective.

It seems there was a moment after the revolution when the Letts tried to push themselves to the fore. . . .

They have asked me by telegram to give a 3rd concert in Petersburg. Don't think it tiresome of me that I refused. I should have been obliged to go to the station immediately after the 3rd concert in Moscow and go as quickly as possible to Warsaw from Petersburg. This is my third letter since you left. Really, looked at closely, I am a little martyr. Not only must I always do what I am opposed to doing ; but do it too with all my concentration and strength.


RIGA, 9 November 1912.

If I look out of my window (it is the morning after the concert ; it is snowing and everything horizontal is white) the impression I get is like an incorrect but similar copy of my time in *Helsingfors*. It reminds me of how, from " Wrede's Hus " [1] I looked out on to the little garden laid-out in front of the theatre. And, for a moment, it seems as if there had been no lapse of 23 years. Memory is one of the greatest mysteries to me. In this case it concentrates on one small far-away point and springs over thousands of impressions.

The power of forgetting and remembering clearly again in many cases ; the helplessness of the will, even when it might be of the greatest importance to remember ; and the sudden return of memory, often through an unimportant trifling cause —all this is too little studied and has hardly been explained at all.

We spoke with Wetzler about Toscanini. The latter believes that in his case memory is visual. That is to say, he remembers the picture of the score, as it is printed, and with him it is almost automatic. A photograph in the brain.

I know, in my childhood, that I saw the *turning over* places when playing from memory and that a piece, quite well known to me, seemed strange in a new edition. Then there is a kind of " finger memory " ; the fingers run along the usual road like a dog, and I might make a mistake as soon as I thought consciously. I believe that the memory is almost the only cause for being in a state of excitement before a public performance. If one is excited, one is afraid more than anything of " forgetting " ! . . .

From outside it seems so still and quiet here, and yet on all sides the people almost eat each other up with jealousy. These continual little battles and annoyances must consume them more than the big agitations in the wider world. (One learns to understand Strindberg well.) And here desire is added to it all. The people burn with lust for life ; the men with unsatisfied ambition

---

[1] Busoni's first flat in Helsingfors, 1889.

and the women—— I noticed this with both men and women yesterday evening !

Dear Gerda, for few is it so beautiful as it is for us. Let us be thankful and happy. . . .

ST. PETERSBURG, 10 *November* 1912.

There is nothing to be done about it. I have been almost forced to give the third concert in Petersburg. Read this letter, which is really very flattering.

Your

" ST. PETERSBURG, 26 *October* (= 8 *Nov.*) 1912.

" DEAR MR. BUSONI,

" Excuse us for approaching you once more, in spite of your decision. We believe the reason for your refusal is founded in the fact that you do not wish to over-tire yourself. We should like to propose, therefore, that you give up playing to the students in the Conservatorium and instead of this give a third concert here. In your own interests we consider a third concert to be quite indispensable, and we were really very happy when an accident gave us the chance of getting the hall for the 6 November. It is a fact, that during the last 10 years no artist has had such success here ! and it would be unforgivable not to use it to the fullest extent by failing to seize the possibility presented of your giving a third recital.

" If you had the tenth part of the conviction we have of the necessity of a third concert here you certainly would not hesitate to give it. We shall deeply regret it if we cannot realize our aim, and you cannot be converted to our opinion. Taking all this into consideration, may we be allowed to beg you once more to telegraph to us at once respecting your decision ?

" In the pleasant hope that it will turn out to be in favour of our proposal, we greet you with the best wishes,

for Andreas Diederichs,

F. KOEHLER."


ST. PETERSBURG, 10 *November* 1912.

On the whole, Riga was a pleasant intermezzo ; sometimes I love such towns, with their quiet church squares, crooked alleys and old buildings ; but I have noticed that *everything pleases me better as a memory.* Memory is sometimes a master in the art of overlooking petty details. Remembrance gives us the artistic picture of what has been experienced. One should learn to compose from it. It is like a marvellous sketch. I remember how surprised Benni was the first day in Basle when I said to him, " This will make a beautiful memory." Now I see clearly what, at that time, I only divined unconsciously. It is for this reason that one is generally disappointed if the beautiful remembrance of a place takes one to it a second time. The first impression is seldom exact or complete. That was the case with Boston, it seems to me.

Here in Riga, too, they are using sleighs already. The drive to the station in Riga on a winter night—the town looking like a drawing by Wilhelm Schulz, deserted, with old-fashioned street lamps (like the scene in the Brautwahl)—makes such a pretty, picturesque picture in my memory. . . .


MOSCOW, 13 *November* 1912.

For 6 days I had no letter and to-day I found it here ! . . . So you found the Chorus in the prison in Fidelio beautiful ? You " gourmande " ! There is little music that is more beautiful. When Beethoven feels with humanity, his feeling is so strong that he needs very few technical means to express it. The feeling suffices completely. I am glad you have come round to my ideas of the theatre and the style of the inside of the house. The public must be prepared by it for the pomp and unreality. A play should offer something which is contrary to daily life ; it fulfils its purpose when it gives what life has not got. This conception of its purpose is certain to come back . . .

I thought of playing the Delius Concerto myself.

213

After the second concert in Petersburg the people (over 100) stood in a queue from 4.30 in the morning in order to buy cheap seats for the third concert . . . That touched me.

I shall try to cancel Lodz, and in that way I shall be at home one day sooner. I want the day badly, for many things . . .

ST. PETERSBURG, 19 *November* 1912.

I took leave of Moscow yesterday evening (the Liszt programme is much more strenuous than it looks on paper) ; from the concert I went straight to the station. Frau Kussewitzky had provided the " provender." She is an excellent woman. Herr and Frau Diederichs were with her. Here I am conducted about like Serenissimus, looked after like a tame monkey on a string.

Before leaving, I spent the evening with the Kussewitzkys. It was rather a formal evening. Nikisch and Bloch were there . . .

The Beklemischeffs have become my intimate friends. I love them both.

I looked closely at the Kremlin and I remembered your remarking once, quite rightly, that the walls and outside doors are in the old style of *North Italy. They were, as a matter of fact, built by Italians, as all the most important and best Empire buildings were ! !* I came to the conclusion that the Russian peasants have a style of their own, which comes into art, but art has no style of its own. For example, the Venetian song (that is used in Venezia e Napoli) has become a Russian folk song ; workmen from Italy brought it over. It was very interesting to learn all that. A very old and famous church in the Kremlin (whose name, unfortunately, I don't remember) is quite in the style of St. Mark's inside. (My father would have felt triumphant.) The architects of the theatres and the two halls of honour in Moscow and Petersburg were also Italian.

The following story provides excellent material for a novel. You know that the cellist Wersbilowitsch and our old friend Hildebrand (can't you remember his nose ?) clung together for half a life-time as musicians as well as boon companions. Hildebrand finally went back to Denmark, in order to die in his native country. Twenty hours before his death he wrote to Wersbilowitsch and entreated him to give up drink ; pointing to himself as an example from whom to take warning, as his intemperance had ruined him. Werbilowitsch received the news of Hildebrand's death by telegram and the letter arrived *three days later*, so that he had the feeling of its having come from another world. This shook him so much that he immediately gave up drink, the next summer went back to Finland, and after many wanton years worked and studied again seriously.

His friends and acquaintances heard of this transformation and waited with great joy and excitement for Wersbilowitsch's first concert in the new season. The evening came, and W. played the first piece so nervously, messily and incorrectly (formerly he had been so free in his playing and always certain of success), that during the interval, in despair, he emptied half a bottle of brandy almost at a gulp. From this moment he went downhill rapidly again and died in misery quite forsaken by all.

On my last day in Moscow, the two musical favourites of that country, Josef Hofmann and Rachmaninoff, came to see me. I can get on well with Hofmann. He is fresh, wide awake, and moderate in his views, and takes an interest in many things. . . .

Scriabin was very nice in the evening at the concert—(Chopin had heroic aspirations too, but on the whole he remained in his own more limited waters. It is not in Scriabin's nature, either, to compose big scores, but he tries to do it. I don't consider that they will live, but I respect Scriabin for striving for such a high ideal.)

ST. PETERSBURG, 20 *November* 1912.

I am such a remnant of past glory to-day ; was seldom so tired, and still have to play at the Conservatorium—and to be fêted ! The people here have treated me very, very well. I am grateful for it. Yesterday evening it rained laurel wreaths. Perhaps a hundred small wreaths came down from the gallery—it was very pretty . . .

WARSAW, 21 *November* 1912.

You shall have one more letter, all the more because I have been obliged to postpone my departure for half a day. I have put a great strain on myself by springing from the concert platform into the sleeping-car and I dare not do it again, for the last four days have made me absurdly tired. It was *only yesterday after-*

*noon* that I played in the Petersburg Conservatorium and since then I have been travelling for 18 hours. It was lovely, faced by 1000 young and absolutely enthusiastic people, to fulfil a little mission. In spite of the enthusiasm the taste for ceremony which the Russians have did not fail ; it was ceremonious and impulsive at the same time.

I saw Rubinstein's death mask. The greatness in the physiognomy is undeniable and I felt very affected by it.

A Princess von Altenburg (aunt of the German Crown princess) presided. Glasunow was charming and simple. A dozen or so of the people from the Conservatorium were at the station and made a demonstration. My send-off was quite theatrical . . .

I was guarded and conducted about like a prince and could feel palpably how " imprisoned " such a ruler must feel. I enjoyed the solitariness and the silence in the train throughly . . .

The only civilizations in existence (I have thought this before) are those which are beginning or ending. Only one small space in Europe, anyhow, can boast of a *complete* civilization. On the map it is rather like a pinpoint. I thought more about it and discovered the following about America. (Skip it, if it wearies you.) The civilization there came from Europe, and produced on the coast people like Franklin, Lincoln and Poe. Fortune hunters crowded the West and ran wild. When they got rich they required beauty from life, to suit their crudeness and according to their taste. Primitive in intellect, with too much wealth and using it too much for pleasure, these people were the originators of Americanism. And this lack of culture turned back, like a wave, to the coast and inundated the East. I am afraid it will remain like this for a long time . . .

# 1913

How beautiful Turandot could be ! (Would it not be better to make an opera out of what is already in existence ?) But not performed as it was in London yesterday, when I was obliged to come out after the Second Act ! How it ended and whether it was a success, I don't know, even to-day. We shall read about it to-morrow. *It will never be any good for play producers.*

The same afternoon, I heard Mahler's Seventh Symphony, which was a great disappointment to me (and a little satisfaction) —and to-day, a wet Sunday, I heard orchestral music too. Fragments from Wagner, and Le Rouet d'Omphale by St. Saëns. I always enjoy Wagner, the " Dramatist," best in a concert, and the Frenchman's " light touch " always gives me fresh pleasure.

I have composed the aphorism : " Compositions for the theatre should be written but not performed." (My expectations in this respect are good.) I am not so happy as I expected, but hope the Nocturne will be good . . .

The music to Turandot had more success than the play. One can never give people anything that is *too bad* ! Just imagine, an orchestra of some twenty players, who play incorrectly ; some of the music repeated 4–5 times consecutively ; some cut ; the whole performed in the style of variété. And because, for once, there *was too little* music for the stage manager, pieces by St. Saëns and Rimsky-Korsakov were shoved in between my music ! Imagine ! Shall I refuse to let them have the music ? The producer says he has paid, and he is in the right. Go to law ? With whom ? . . . Before the lawsuit is finished, the season will be over . . .

What do you think of Turandot as an opera, and in Italian, after Gozzi ?

Auf Wiedersehen, dear Gerda,

Your FERRUCCIO, who has reached a very uncertain moment in his life.

LONDON, 25 *January* 1913.

This letter will be a little document about an idea which may become very important for me. For the present, I shall be obliged to consider that with the Nocturne Symphonique my list of preparatory works is complete ; which does not mean that with my " daily progress " I do not continually enlarge my musical vocabulary. For considering my age and the stage of my development, I do not think I ought to hesitate any longer before beginning a principal and monumental work, towards which all my previous works have been aiming.

At the same time, I should like to deflect the course of my stream back to its source, and try to make my principal work an important one for Italy, too. But one's grasp has to be very comprehensive, if one wants to reach the heads and hearts of all with one blow !

That is what Wagner intended doing with the Nibelungs, who however were comparatively alien to the German people, and did not hit the mark so directly.

Italy possesses Dante, who is equally valuable to all and who is popular in spite of his greatness ; and even *outside* Italy.

The cinema gave me this idea, when I saw " Dante's Hell " advertised as a film in the " Strand." I should not stop with Hell, and not presume as far as Heaven ; but end with the meeting with Beatrice.

Piazza della Signoria, with Dante sitting on the stone on which he was wont to dream ; a characteristic street scene depicting the time, perhaps, too, with Beatrice passing by. And afterwards some six pictures of the most distinctive episodes : Ugolino, Paolo and Francesca, a couple of pictures with crowds ; finally, the ascent with Beatrice. And, of course, in Italian.

That, anyhow, is something to keep me going for a long time . . .

. . . If I could work, nothing would irritate me, but everything has been at a standstill for more than three months. That leads to self-distrust, as in the years of adolescence . . .

The weather is incomparably beautiful. They have built several beautiful buildings during the last four years, so that the town looks charming this time . . .

The following idea occurred to me : if one admits that there are such things as " presentiments " and " second sight," and if one can look into the future (if only for the tiniest moment and shortest distance), it is logical that one should have the same capacity for looking *backwards into time*. That at least would be an explanation of the so-called seeing of ghosts. Seeing ghosts might be nothing but a momentary and uncertain glance into the past. Everything is made in circles, and it must be the same with clairvoyance too. It is like a Marconi telegraph station, which reaches out to the same distance in all directions . . .

I like to occupy my mind and try to explain these questions to myself. If it does not further anything, it does no harm.

I shall make up my mind to write to d'Annunzio, and almost think that the Leonardo idea would be better for me than the Dante. Your feeling was right again. *Moi, je raisonne trop.*

I believe that this time of interruption is maturing me, after all, and producing a clarity in me about myself. Anyhow, we will interpret it thus . . .

LONDON, 2 *March* 1913.

. . . I am glad you found my little theory about the seeing of ghosts well thought out. It is characteristic of reports about the seeing of ghosts, that one person sees, whilst the others who are with him are aware of nothing. This characteristic, too, is in favour of my theory, because only individual people have the gift of clairvoyance. Enquiries should be made as to whether the same people who saw the ghosts were gifted in clairvoyance in other ways. That would give a strong foundation for my theory.

I am reading Wassermann's new book, " The Man of Forty." It ought to bear the sub-title, " A Book for Men over Forty " . . . It is well written, and in places excellent, but I miss the highest summits of achievement.

Wassermann must feel it himself, and suffer consequently. He said something like this to me once : " I would give the whole of my collected works to have written Balzac's ' Le chef d'œuvre inconnu.' " . . .

LONDON, 6 *March* 1913.

Yesterday evening, I experienced the first pleasure I have had for a long time ; d'Annunzio answered me by telegram : " Very delighted. Say if you are coming Paris for meeting." That has made me feel quite young again and now we will see.

. . . Partly from good nature, and partly from the pleasure I took in doing it, I wrote a Scenario for Maudi.[1] The story of a girl is told in pictures, with the very good title of " The Dance of Life and Death." A music-hall is seen on the stage with a scene in the style of a Beardsley picture ; a dancing hall in Paris ; a dance with barrel-organs in the streets of London ; and the end (in my manner) is mystical ; in a church, in front of a remarkable altar ; on it is a group of figures with the cross in the middle ; right and left, the figures of Death and the Angel of the Resurrection. There is a dance of Death, and much else. It could be very good, lovely, and true ; at the same time, it is made of the stuff which lasts. But—— (All kinds of dances take place ; beginning with a sort of game of tennis, which is danced ; a gypsy dance, pantomime, Grande Valse, and cancan, street dance (on the parapet of a bridge), religious dance, and the dance of death).

I have written nothing for the church part of it yet, for that means oratorios. (It's English, you know) . . .

We went by car to Cambridge, in order to be able to *get back*, for there is no train so late. On the drive there it rained quite biblically, and we lost the way. It was quite amusing really (doing it *once*) and I arrived a quarter of an hour later than the concert was advertised to begin. (Geo. Albert) Backhaus was waiting in the rain in front of the concert hall, to the glorification of his top-hat. He wanted to play the Chromatic Fantasia himself, so that the audience should not be kept waiting ! !

I have the feeling that everything will go well now ; new spring, new buds.

I have finished " The Man of Forty," and it goes off towards

[1] Maud Allan.

the end. The man goes to the Franco-German war at the finish. As the book is not a novel, but a psychological study, the reader asks himself, " In what way can a man of forty save himself, who was *not* born in 1831, and who therefore cannot go to the Franco-German War ? "

(The description of the War is not a big one) . . .


LONDON, 10 *March* 1913.

Yesterday evening, I saw the devil playing the violin, and he was quite different from Liszt's idea of him. He had quite a dark face, almost black, overgrown with a short, thick, and still blacker beard ; two coal-black eyes and a blood-red, thick under-lip. On his head he wore something which looked like a black, round hat *without* a brim, placed a little on one side. He was broad and strong. Under his black overcoat, he had on a woman's skirt which touched the ground. He held his violin in the right hand and bowed with the left. He looked wicked, and did not stir from the spot. He looked dangerously powerful, with an exaggeratedly projecting lower jaw, on which sat the thick red lip. With the exception of this lip, everything was black. But he was no nigger ; perhaps an Indian. That was in the night, in the streets of London.

Meanwhile, three dear, good letters have arrived from you, written with such wonderful feeling. Thank you !

I have just practised the 12 Studies Op. 10, by Chopin, for two hours. I play them quite differently now. (I have mostly played the other twelve.) I am glad to have done it.


MANNHEIM, 26 *May* 1913.

Yesterday evening, Bodanzky and Director Wichert (Kunsthalle) came to the hotel. There was a very good discussion about librettos, Wagner, painting, and some anecdotes, too. Wichert is quick and humorous ; that is to say, clever . . .

He wanted to found a club, " The Gap " (" Die Lücke ") which would start everything pleasant which is missing in the town. He's a splendid museum director ! . . .

I am in a holiday mood now, rejoice at being alone, at coming home, at making order among my books, and among my thoughts too.

The Brautwahl was mentioned with admiration, Bodanzky was very warm, and praised it with understanding. Altogether, we agreed excellently yesterday evening about all the themes under discussion.

Pfitzner scored a very good point, for the rescue of the libretto of the " Magic Flute." He said : " Everyone is agreed about the alleged nonsense in the Magic Flute ; but only one has written a continuation of it and that was—Goethe."

Bodanzky is going to have a new setting made for the Magic Flute, based on the mystical atmosphere of Goethe's second part.

You see, it was a stimulating evening, rich in thought. Like something out of the " Serapionsbrüder " : indeed, very much like that.

I look back on these two months with thankfulness and pleasure, and sing, to my own words and music :

" Alles hat sich wohlgefügt."
(" Everything has fitted together well.")

I am morally strengthened, and hope to do still more work, and hope it will be good. I will make an attempt with d'Annunzio, otherwise I must help myself in some other way.

I am thankful, too, that you could experience everything with me. I never forget that you have been just as good in the bad moments as in the happy ones . . .

PARIS, 23 *June* 1913.

I went to d'Annunzio's house, rue Bassano 11 ; he was in a Japanese woman's kimono, very pale, very absorbed in expression, and aged. He looked like a picture of Mephistopheles, receiving the pupil.

" I am just writing a book, ' The Man who stole The Gioconda,' for the Gioconda is in my possession, and I shall put her back in the Louvre as soon as the book is published." What he then told us is either a conscious lie, or he believes it himself, or—which would be unaccountable—might be true, after all. In any case, it is strange enough to tell you about it here.

" The man who stole the Gioconda comes from a family of mystical painters, dating back six hundred years. He brought it to me to Arcachon " (It is confirmed by the police that he took the Paris-Bordeaux train.)

" This figure had accumulated adoration and love for so many hundreds of years that the passion of many thousands of men had finally imparted life to the picture. It seemed necessary, certainly, to kill a man, in order to give her something direct from the heart's blood, but the mystical action succeeded, and I lived for four days with the Gioconda. My power did not suffice to hold her longer and she vanished. Only the landscape remains on the picture, and in the landscape only *her smile* remains. The gesture of her smile has remained imprinted in the landscape, but the figure has disappeared." (He repeated that with much satisfaction.) " In this condition the Louvre will receive the picture back again."

There is a similar story by Poe, with the procedure reversed. There an artist paints a woman's portrait, until the life and truth of her expression is attained in the highest degree ; at this moment, the model dies, her life having passed over into the picture.

At first he would not quite believe in the possibility of a Leonardo on the stage. " In the same way that I should not give my words to Christ or Napoleon, I do not dare to let him speak through me."

Then, to him, the lack of passion and feeling in Leonardo is opposed to drama.

" A brain, borne by a skeleton, like a burning light in a lantern." But when, as a slogan, I expressed the idea of an " Italian Faust," he began to see the possibilities. " Not an *historical* Leonardo, but a symbolical one." " The Mystic must be added to it." " A series of pictures without dramatic connection."

There I had him where I wanted him to be.

He spoke then of working in collaboration in Arcachon, where it seems the landscape has no decided form. " The clouds are the waves, and the waves are the forest, and it is intangible."

He was very stimulating, but sometimes I had to smile. We are going to see each other again to-morrow.

In contrast to this, a conference of *Marinetti's* yesterday was much more realistic and material. I had scarcely sent off my letter to you, when I met him in the hotel (with Boccioni). Boccioni has exhibited " futuristic sculpture."

The idea is this : To show many movements of a body, with

223

architectural effect, in *one* form. So you see a leg that is lifted, which at the same time moves backwards and forwards while the muscles are expressed in a correspondingly manifold way. There is much study in it, but it looks ugly and unintelligible, especially if the man has a little toy house in the place of a head, for reasons which were explained to me very theoretically by Boccioni. The conference ended in strife.

Compared with *this* art and the incarnation of Monna Lisa as Gabriele's mistress, Schönberg's Pierrot Lunaire is insipid lemonade !

Many impressions ! ! This evening I am going to Pisanella . . .

PARIS, 23 *June* 1913.

The world is full of surprises. Pugno, in collaboration with a 22-year-old Parisian lady, is composing " la città morta," by d'Annunzio. And the strange thing is that d'Annunzio believes in it. He himself says wittily, " Pugno has allowed himself to be fructified by a virgin " ; but all the same, between the aphorism and the fact, there is much room for headshaking.

This is certainly the most interesting part of Paris.[1] I am sitting at the open window, and it is the moment when daylight becomes blue and the lamps shine yellow. Girls pass by, coming from work. The charm of southern Europe is here in this historical city of the world.

I do not think that such a perfect example of this combination is to be met with anywhere else nowadays.

Now I am going to the Châtelet, to Pisanelle, or " la mort parfumée." I shall see Mlle Rubinstein, of whom it is said by one that she cannot speak but can dance ; by another that she has a beautiful body, but cannot dance ; by a third, that her body is not womanly, therefore not beautiful. She is just like St. Sebastian, pierced with arrows by all . . .

PARIS, 24 *June* 1913.

Yesterday evening, Théâtre du Chatelet ; full house, mostly women. Big orchestra, dilettantish music, music-making which was suitable for everything and for nothing. Curtains with large patterns à la Reinhardt. Behind the curtains, yet another curtain.

[1] Hotel Restaurant Foyot.

Tam-tam signal ; the first scene is a hall from the Kremlin. How did it get to Cyprus ? It was painted by Gospodin Bakst (of the Russian ballet).

Fräulein Rubinstein is also Russian. Half the audience, I noticed, consisted of Russians. A former beauty who sat next to me addressed me as Mr. Chaliapine. I made my excuses. " But what a resemblance ! I know him personally." It makes one realise *how* people *see* things.

The first act is tedious, and produces no effect. A beggar woman sings off-stage and also speaks off-stage. It is obvious that the singer and speaker are two different people.

The second Act is a harbour. It is entirely red ; red walls, red ground, red ships, and some blue water in between. A slave (Rubinstein) has lost her way ; a young King arrives and gives her his white mantle and his white horse, and Fräulein Rubinstein rides off in triumph. She has neither danced, nor spoken, only stood on the stage, tightly swathed in some sort of stuff with a square pattern.

Third Act : an unintelligible scene. A number of nuns come in, and so it is obvious that one is in a convent. Is it a convent court-yard ?

I was so tired and so irritated that I went out in the rain. There was nobody in the streets, although it was only half-past ten. The rue de Rivoli, with its long row of lamps (one in every arch), looked almost gruesome.

I know that Pisanelle will be smothered in roses in the last Act. Hence the name, " la mort parfumée " . . . A lot depends on colours with d'Annunzio. Brown Arabian women with red roses ; white horse, white mantle. He also brings in a number of handicraft things, too.

The French language on the stage is horrible. This declaiming of words like *blasphème, innocente,* with a long, neighing sound on the accent and the exaggerated *e*-mute, in the long run sounds like bad singing.

The whole play seemed old-fashioned, declamatory, pathetic and motley ; full of excitable gestures, long tirades, inexplicable stabbings, deaths, and screams. Melancholy, and without humour, it is like an æsthetically affected Wildenbruch play.

On the other hand, it may be a masterpiece, and I may be admitting myself to be unappreciative. It *is* possible. (The succession of artistic emotions has been too rapid during the last few days and I am partly confused and partly blunted by them . . .)

PARIS, 26 *June* 1913.

If I, like d'Annunzio, could say with an absolutely contented smile, that I am not happy, on the contrary, that I am very *un*happy, I should say with an equal amount of inward satisfaction, that everything is being more successful for me in Paris than it really is. (D'Annunzio looked quite blissful as he added, " For how could I create if I were not unhappy ! ")

This town affects one in various ways, like certain women, who are unsympathetic and yet can charm ; and others who are very sympathetic and clever, but leave one cold. Paris has characteristics belonging to *both* sorts. (Unfortunately, the weather is grey and cold.)

How old-fashioned and over-ripe this Paris is. Every kind of interest is to be found here, and profound indifference is shown to them all. Perhaps d'Annunzio belongs *here*, like Oscar Wilde and Meyerbeer.

On d'Annunzio's bookshelves there are books, old and new, about Cyprus, for example. In each volume, three or four long strips of paper were placed as markers. Very probably he uses these places when he needs something—for his own book ; he does not *know* things, he gets the knowledge as he wants it, (he is, of course, an artist, not a scholar !) and has a quick intuition for what is suitable or important.

I noticed very clearly the other evening how much the streets in a town are classified by the lighting. The important ones brilliantly lit and the others less so. All the principal streets are defined by the stronger light ; whilst by day everything is light. By avoiding the darker roads, one is surer of finding one's way by night than by day. What a long time it takes to arrive at such a simple solution ! . . .

PARIS, 27 *June* 1913.

Yesterday, d'Annunzio invited me to late dinner. He had a big Russian woman with him, (who was the essence of amateurishness) who behaved well, however . . . He said that he was

226

going to die in two years' time (looking as he did when he told us about his four days with the Gioconda), whereupon the Russian woman made great eyes, startled and imploring, and I simply couldn't help laughing rather openly. When he saw that he was not believed, he smiled too, and said, " Yes, but it is so," and with the smile he gave up the game, but stuck to his point by adding, " Whether you believe it or not, it is so."

The worst thing is, he wants to hear some of my compositions in order to adjust himself to them (so he says) but really in order to examine them (is what I feel)—it is senseless, and depressing, and I don't know how to get myself out of this situation. Possibly, I may go away suddenly, and leave everything just as it is. (To you I need not explain that.)

D'Annunzio describes R. as being an ordinary unintelligent business man ; and yet he insists on making the whole thing depend on *him* to a certain extent. R. himself comes here to-morrow, and I do not believe that I can endure a meeting. I know I am not being wise, and I will still think it all over ; but I have had enough of it ; drinking poison under pretext of being invited to a glass of wine.

At the same time, from d'Annunzio's conversation, I feel convinced that as soon as he began writing his verse might give me the deepest pleasure. But to me his feeling for the mystical and his practical ideas are incongruous. All the same, he is quite right when he says, " Why should we plague ourselves for three or four years, when we can do nothing with the work when it is finished ? "

That is how things stand, and I shall have come to some decision by the evening . . .


(*Addressed to Alt-Aussee*)

BERLIN, 16 *July* 1913.

. . . I played through the Liszt things eagerly ; it is remarkable how few and how simple are the forms which he uses for his technical passages. (All other " piano composers " want to do too much and fill out to excess.)

I work daily, and hope to be able to produce something for you . . .

*(Addressed to Alt Aussee)*

BERLIN, 18 *July* 1913.

Haschke sent a beautiful consignment of books on approval to-day. Amongst them, Delacroix's pictures to Goethe's Faust (which please me more and more) and a rare edition of Lichtenberg, with etchings by Chodowiecki. And the *official* appointment from Bologna [1] came to-day, too. It is a beautifully composed letter . . .

Berlin changes the places of its buildings as one changes furniture in a house . . . Changes here are generally " improvements "; whilst in Paris, almost everything new is uglier than the old . . .

The Red Indian themes are not very pliable or productive. I shall have to put a good deal of my own into the Rhapsodie.

(After a final examination and revision, the Nocturne Symphonique seems to me to have reached a kind of perfection . . .)


*(Addressed to Alt Aussee)*

BERLIN, 20 *July* 1913.

I have nothing to report, the weather is bad, my mood passable, but my mind becomes clearer every day. I sleep very well and the Red Indian Fantasy progresses. Yesterday, I busied myself with translation, because I wanted to make Benni acquainted with two of Poe's poems . . .


*(Addressed to Alt Aussee)*

BERLIN, 22 *July* 1913.

. . . The Red Indians are passing by, and thoughts begin to move.[2] To-day, I began putting down some thoughts about melody again. Perhaps they will interest you.

Absolute Melody : A row of repeated ascending and descending intervals, which are organized and move rhythmically. It contains in itself a latent harmony, reflects a mood of feeling. It can exist without depending on words for expression and without accompanying voices. When performed, the choice of pitch or of instrument makes no alteration to the nature of its being.

Melody, independent at first, joined the accompanying har-

---

[1] As Director of the Liceo Musicale.
[2] Busoni was composing the Indian Fantasy.

mony subsequently, and later melted into inseparable unity with it. Recently, it has been the aim of polyphonic music, which is always progressing, to free itself from this unity.

In contradiction to points of view which are deeply rooted, it must be maintained here that melody has expanded continuously, that it has grown in line and capacity for expression and that in the end it must succeed in becoming the most powerful thing in composition.

At the time when operas and salon compositions were " abounding in melodies," the quality of the melody and what it had to express were at their lowest level, because it had to be possible to cut the melody out of a musical composition and separate it from the remaining constituent parts in the easiest and most intelligible way ; leaving—a spoilt folk-song.

---

Transcription occupies an important place in the literature of the piano ; and looked at from a right point of view, every important piano piece is the reduction of a big thought to a practical instrument. But transcription has become an independent art ; no matter whether the starting point of a composition is original or unoriginal. Bach, Beethoven, Liszt, and Brahms were evidently all of the opinion that there is artistic value concealed in a pure transcription ; for they all cultivated the art themselves, seriously and lovingly. In fact, the art of transcription has made it possible for the piano to take possession of the entire literature of music. Much that is inartistic, however, has got mixed up with this branch of the art. And it was because of the cheap, superficial estimation of it made by certain men, who had to hide their nakedness with a mantle of " being serious," that it sank down to what was considered a low level.

(*Addressed to Alt Aussee*)

BERLIN, 23 *July* 1913.

The weather is cool, but it has been clearer the last two days, and even sunny sometimes ; I hope it is like that where you are too and that you are enjoying it. It is a joyless existence I have been enduring for almost two weeks now . . .

I can't seize the passing moment and although I know that many ideas that occur to me are good and beautiful, I am not completely conscious of them, and allow myself to be con-

229

fused by details. (And I have worked so hard to overcome this.)

There are brief moments when I feel I have strength and freedom and I have a presentiment of happiness. Thank God, I am well, think clearly, and have time in front of me . . .

I work every day, and I have reached the critical moment in my piece where many ideas have to be forced into one form. I hope it will go well . . .

HEIDELBERG, 17 *September* 1913.

I will make a kind of diary out of the letters to you during the coming time ; write in it daily even if I don't post daily.

Cold and wet welcomed me here but, to make up for that, I was greeted at the station by the charming Frau Lilly (formerly Meyer) who chanced to be there. It was such a friendly greeting that I interpreted it as a good beginning. Leaving yesterday was very difficult, for I felt I was going to territory only half-known, and that, I think, made me uneasy.

I told Frau B. too (when I wrote to her about her new life) that one *incessantly* begins life afresh.

This morning I had a similar feeling to the one I had when first I went to Leipzig. What a pity it is so grey !

I thought out a beautiful edition for the " Nocturne Symphonique," with an etching and other things. But it will not be possible. When I look round for " etchers " Klinger is always in my mind as the principal one . . . One notices for the first time, clearly and distinctly, how much one values a painter when a decision has to be made about a purchase or a commission. For example, I value Boccioni very much, but I do not want to order a title page from him. . . .

During the night I could not get free from a certain two-part imitation. I turned round in bed hoping the passage might appear in the inversion, but it remained obstinate . . .

HEIDELBERG, 18 *September* 1913.

Yesterday it rained in a way " that makes all pigs clean and all men dirty " (as Lichtenberg says). To-day it is a sunny, fresh morning and I feel in a mood for travelling to unknown destinations ; I am suspended between the past and the future, sail between two banks, move in space, and Heidelberg is only a name, for I am nowhere.

In an old catalogue I found a " livre mystique " by Balzac, 1835—unfortunately sold already (for the unworthy price of six marks). It is unknown to me and must be rare. Perhaps it contains the first print of " La Dernière Fée " and " Séraphita." I almost regret having announced my visit to Bodansky. He throws me back into reality. I think I shall go there this afternoon and to-morrow, probably, go on further southwards. This last word contains so much ever-recurring magic, that just to use it is to become a poet. Scenery is always beautiful when it is enlivened by the sun and if one knows that one is not bound to the spot. . . . I feel so youthfully indeterminate to-day. Quite happy and almost without weight.

You were so very dear, you are so good ! . . .

HEIDELBERG, 19 *September* 1913.

When I went to see Bodansky yesterday evening he was already in the theatre conducting the " Sommernachtstraum " ; so we only met after the performance. . . . B is going to put Turandot on the stage, this season if possible. We spoke of the Sommernachtstraum music and of how he had commissioned Zemlinsky to write music for Cymbeline.

" If I were a Norwegian "—I began, and at the same moment B said, " *You* should write the music for Peer Gynt. Would you do that ? I don't perform Grieg's music for it."

This attracts me very strongly, but how can I catch the Norwegian atmosphere ? It does not allow of such poetical treatment as oriental theatre music ; the country lies too near us for that. It must be " genuine " and a foreigner cannot catch it.

As his knowledge of various musical compositions increases, Bodansky is continually changing. In his youth everyone was supplanted by Wagner. At present he is enthusiastic about the " Huguenots " which he is just studying.

The new generation begins to show opposition . . . things are better for them than they were for my generation, who from birth were obliged to drag round Wagner on their shoulders !

But, as I feared, all that, interesting as it is, has torn me out of my abstract condition . . . I came back to Heidelberg at one o'clock in the morning, and slept for ten hours. This

231

afternoon I shall travel further. I think I shall make a stop in Basle. The sky is making a bitter-sweet face. This inertia which seems to have got inside me makes it difficult for me to continue the journey.


GENEVA, 21 September 1913.

I did not write yesterday ; the night journey, too short and without a sleeping-car, fatigued me very much. But the feeling when I arrived in Basle the night before—I mean the feeling of the town—was so petty and tedious that I did not want to have anything to do with it. So I took the next train in order to get away from it at all costs.

This town, too, is hard to put up with, and its interests quickly exhausted. One should be economical with life. One does not read an unimportant book a second time, and in the same way, when once the contents of a place are known one should not return to it. (One should not act otherwise with people really, but there, consideration, feeling and destiny all join in and have to be reckoned with.) It was all the more delightful for me to find Benni fresh and clear, and in a surer condition than he had been at any time of late. We found pleasure in saying nice things about you, and you were with us in the otherwise unsympathetic hotel room whilst we had tea. And now, by chance, A is there and B is waiting—and so good-bye to all soaring travelling flights and excursions into the abstract for which I hoped : sentinels stand at the side of the road everywhere, take something from one and say, Halt !

I was intensely moved by reading the Urfaust, that is, the first version of Goethe's Faust, where all kinds of things are still missing and the Gretchen story is the principal theme. It is so original, alive and first-hand (the greater part in prose), that one can hardly contain oneself. How well it is held together, and how carefully the apparently simple verses are fashioned to support it.

In this fragment at the end, for example, (after Mephisto's cry " She is judged ") the following " is saved " is missing. Can you understand what an enormous step in Goethe's conception of life these 2 words imply ? . . .

Dear Gerda, à propos Goethe, I found such a wonderful copy here of the " Ausgabe Letzter Hand " in 55 separate volumes for the price of 10 frcs !, that I took it although I already possess it . . . On the way, in order to practise Italian, I read Carducci, who makes war on the gnats and strikes at them with his lyre . . . and an excellent little book by Schopenhauer " über Schrift-stellerei und Styl " in which he abuses the critics in an edifying manner, and therein is in agreement with Carducci. . . .

GENEVA, 22 September 1913.

At last : radiant, fresh autumnal weather . . . To-morrow I shall go on further ; I don't know where yet (theoretically I like to imagine I have unbounded freedom), probably I shall stop once more before Bergamo. I forgot to report that I got out at the Baden (German) railway station, and that this station is planned in a new way and has an entirely new and monu-mental building. It is built in the new, flat, " Greek " style, without ornaments and capitals, very elongated and with a square tower. It is a very good construction. Using the word " new " makes me think with ironical melancholy of that letter of Liszt's giving an account of the " modern " façade of the old Cathedral in Geneva, which is in the taste of Napoleonic times. It annoyed him at that time, and to us now it is historically remarkable. All the same ; it's good that we possess a " modern " style. Letters written in the seventies and eighties could have had nothing to communicate about that ! . . .

Arno Holz, too, thinks he has created a modern style. I let a bookseller seduce me into buying his " Ignorabimus," and of the 200 pages I couldn't read more than ten . . . His preface ends : " *Written in the year in which impotence was trumps* " . . . The honest fury of Schopenhauer's abuse (" scoundrel," " block-head," " charlatan," " ink-slinger ") never sounds vulgar because it comes from the heart out of love for something greater than himself.

MILAN, 24 September 1913.

This day whose light has never before been seen, I arrived at seven o'clock in the morning. I used the beautiful hour in watching " das Erwachen der Stadt " (the awakening of the town). But here there is nothing in the awakening to charm the mind and senses. It has much more the effect of taking a toy out of a box and standing it upright. After that, the little machinery

233

begins to run round in a circle. There is nothing between Geneva and Milan for which it would be worth while " to break the journey." It is, by-the-bye, almost too short a run for a night journey . . . Good weather. The trees are autumnal already and it is fresh, but still I am able to write by the open window . . . I may go on to-day to Bergamo where I hope to find your letter . . . Berlin must be very beautiful now ! ? . . .

MILAN, 25 September 1913.

I wrote to Serato and whilst I wrote—unintentionally at first —the end of a Beethoven Cadenza (for violin) occurred to me ; then the beginning ; and when I had closed the letter, the join for the two bits occurred to me too. In this way I had got the whole Cadenza complete (only in my memory, it is true, without a piano and even without manuscript paper) . . .

Amongst books I found a very beautiful " Novellino " (Geneva, 1765) on yellow paper in vellum ;  " Les Nuits d'Young " with two copper-prints by Deveria, a Don Quixote with engravings by Horace Vernet, and the first edition of Musset's novels.  I did not buy the Geneva Novellino in Geneva, but here.  The Goethe ought to be in Berlin by now—very worn outside, but wonderful inside, original bindings, which one would prefer to keep as they are.

I shall go to Bergamo this afternoon and, probably, (after another two days) to Bologna. If only I had one person there with whom I could talk freely, and who " knows " me, it would be much easier for me. Serato or Tagliapietra would have done quite well. Perhaps I can get Brugnoli to come over for a little while. Yesterday I saw Boito go by in a carriage—otherwise no one . . .

BERGAMO, 26 September 1913.

Already it seems a little strange to be writing in German. I arrived here directly after sunset. The drive in the town was full of fantastic impressions, quite improbable, and time seemed to have been put back (as it was in Wells' " Time Machine " or in Andersen's " Goloshes of Fortune ").

Up here, this morning, in Augusto's [1] library, it is beautiful

---

[1] Dr. Augusto Anzoletti.

and light.   One looks down to what is nearest, and out to what is farthest ; it is an ideal workroom, in the forenoon . . .

And it was glorious to get your letter.   The other letters were all more or less unimportant . . .

Pfitzner asks if I won't play his Trio, and whether he can have the score of the Nocturne Symphonique.   I have heard that he said to Frau B, with the sigh of a martyr, " What will happen is that I shall perform Busoni's piece and he will not play my Trio." But it will be the other way round, for I am going to play his Trio on the 12th January and I shall take care not to give the Nocturne to a raw orchestra, for the piece is woven with nerve-threads.   Considered as a whole, my years in the forties have been the best.   I feel stronger and more gifted, more successful and independent . . .   This life here, without hope of anything happening, without prospect of change, without sociability, without women—when the day's work is ended and evening falls like a curtain and darkness begins—and the next morning begins again like a thousand other mornings and moves towards the thousandth empty, lonely, dark evening—in spite of all the beauty and individuality of the place, one would be bound to become a furious eccentric here.   It is pleasant, however, to pass a couple of days thus, during this lovely autumnal weather : still, the day seems long, particularly if one gets up at 7 o'clock, as I did to-day.   I am looking forward to your next letter and thank you for the last. . . .

BERGAMO, 27 *September* 1913.

If I look back at some things in my childhood, I perceive that I was an intelligent boy.   When I was twelve, I had a large and beautiful toy-theatre with rather a splendid town scene.   This pleased me very much, but it made me feel sad.   I began to ask myself *why* and found the answer : *Because nobody walked about in it*.   Here, in Bergamo, I cannot help thinking again of that scene.

This town extends unexpectedly.   We walked for quite 35 minutes yesterday all the time between houses and through suburban streets, from Anzoletti's flat to the factory.   We watched the " casting " ; it was a beautiful picture.   The molten iron, the reflections, the men's figures moving in the half-darkness, the fantastic ovens and wheels, and in the background the open doors, and behind that, the sunny landscape.

It is an interesting little kingdom over which our friend [1] reigns. In the evening we walked for another 20–25 minutes behind the house up to an inn Belvedere. By the time we had finished our little supper it was half-past eight, which means there that night has fallen completely and everything is deserted. We plunged into the " tumult " of the new town below, where there is life in the cafés and even a music-hall. The audience consisted entirely of men, which reminds one a little of western America. Although they were all attracted by the two shabby women vocalists, they behaved as if they were quite indifferent and superior, and hardly looked at the stage. This attitude of superiority and boredom in Italy is really a provincial trait, combined with a lack of naïveté. Compared with Bergamo, for instance, Geneva is thoroughly " kitschig " [2] but more cosmopolitan. Of course the separation of the sexes here is to blame for many defects all over the kingdom. Yesterday I was thoroughly tired out, for we were on the go from 4 to 11. At 11 o'clock we took a motor-car at the station and again there was a fairy-like drive over the ramparts, and through alleys so narrow that there was hardly room for the car to pass. Literally, we did not meet one single person on this drive. A " modern " counterpart of Bergamo is Pittsburg in America. I shall never forget the 4-mile motor drive up the mountain to the rich upper town. Down below, as the distance widened, the smoking chimneys and the roofs increased in numbers ; there the " Morlocks " dwell ; up above, we found pure air, marble buildings, parks, and inaction. That beautiful evening, too, at the theatre in Varese, two years ago, came into my mind again, with the candlelight and the beautiful provincial ladies and the festive gala doings in the midst of great comfort.

This letter consists of reminiscences ; if one lived here one would write one's " Memoirs."

It is cloudy to-day ; when the weather is clear one ought to be able to see the Cathedral at Milan . . .

I have looked forward to the post in vain ; here one is more dependent on it than elsewhere . . .

BERGAMO, 28 *September* 1913.
I say farewell to my holiday to-day and look forward with pleasure to work. Yesterday I had violent " stage fright " as

[1] Emilio Anzoletti.           [2] In bad taste.

before an important concert, so that I felt ill. We visited Augusto's establishment and an institute for " graphic arts " which produces all kinds of art and coloured prints. During the last few days I have come to the terrible conviction that the Italians (now) are not a people with a feeling for art. They read, hear, and see badly ; what they build is ugly ; they have no taste in their homes. In all these respects they are ignorant and either badly influenced or not influenced at all. They draw a thick line between what belongs, historically, to the past and what belongs to the present : people perceive more and more clearly that nothing is permanent, that everything is only adapted for the moment ; why, then, is so much importance attached to money making ? Their perception fails them here as it failed Cervantes' well-known fool.

A grey Sunday—yesterday evening we retired to the house at eight o'clock. I slept badly ; it is not cheerful in Italy.

Look upon this as a diary, to-morrow I will write something beautiful in it . . . (I am better.)

Anzoletti read the sketch for Arlecchino and he liked it. Anfossi said to him à propos of the Sonatina seconda that I did not know what I was doing (—" believe me ").

BOLOGNA, 2 *October* 1913.

Sunshine, stillness, monastery courtyard, fountain, someone hums a song in the next house ; then clouds again which veil the sun, no one visible. Near me, in the next room, stands Rossini's Napoleonic bed, slumbers his wig—whose hair might it be ? The porter's old wife, fat, good-natured, whitehaired, moustached, greeted me with uplifted arms : " Welcome, Mr. Director, you who are beloved by all."

The porter, a handsome man, still vigorous, knew me as a boy : " I knew you as a boy and now you have become so famous ! " . . .

Very busy yesterday. Calls, administration, concert programme. For a week I have been eating figs every day. (To be enjoyed, they should be eaten straight from the tree.)

The pianos are put up. Perhaps I can live here in the house.

It is said that Foscolo once wrote " Everything that can be obtained with money is not worth so much as the money itself, but more valuable than money is that which one cannot have for money." This should be engraved on the base of the statue of Liberty, New York, N.Y., U.S.A.

Am very distracted. Still no composure. Many too many men ; no women at all. . . .

The people are coming back to the town gradually from the country . . . I see from the calendar that to-morrow and the day after to-morrow are holidays. Here, instead of the date, one says the name of the Saint. To-morrow, (pardon, the day after to-morrow) is not the 4th of October but " San Petronio " . . .

I visited the mayor yesterday in the pompous town hall. Shallow steps lead up to the entrance of it, up which they used to *ride* in former days. It's like going to court.

In order to avoid the people I have found a way through quite an alarming side street, which goes across from the hotel to the Liceo. It is curious, old, narrow and twisted ; in the windowless entrances to unspeakable houses, one sees women (prostitutes) crouching together like goats in a stable.

In the dialect of the people the street is called " The road to hell."

I am learning Bolognese.

Forgive the chronicle-style.

How beautiful it is that you are in the world, dear Gerda. . . .


BOLOGNA, 3 *October* 1913.

A town without water and without trees would be almost unique ; if the neighbouring towns (up to Modena) were not made from the same " pattern." By contrast, the effect produced by the landscape is all the more beautiful. What lines ! Richness in forms ! Abundance of Life !

The two Anzolettis and I went for a motor drive yesterday and drove in a roundabout way up to S. Vittore. Such a beautiful drive ! Up and down hill (it undulates like the sea) and down roads so overgrown with grass that the chauffeur looked round enquiringly at us.

We passed big country houses, two of which bear the old aristocratic name, Mazzacorati, which comes from Amazza-Curati and means *Priest-murderer*.

" Yes, they murdered and stole " ; (" but no one is perfect," as Heine sings) . . .

The evenings here are bad and I have yet to find a suitable way of filling in the time. If one retires to the house about 11 o'clock (when everything seems extinct) then—in bed—one is surprised and disturbed by the amount of noise going on.

I believe just because of the great quietness one hears every single sound.

*Three* orchestral concerts are fixed : the invitations to Serato and Petri and the performance of the " Faust-Symphony " almost decided upon. The latter is as little known here as Brahms' violin Concerto. I think the last programme may be :

> Freischütz Overture
> Franck, Les Djinns
> Liszt, Spanish Rhapsody
> Liszt, Faust Symphony

All new for Bologna.

I still continue to do nothing, although I write five to six letters daily, have conferences, make plans.

There is nothing special going on here for which I should feel you must come. Mais, nous verrons !

Thank you for your beautiful letter. I think of you on every pleasant occasion and at other times too. . . .

BOLOGNA, 4 *October* 1913.

Your letters are refreshing, real and vivid, like your whole nature. I know that what I write is sometimes rather abstract and discursive ; but I must tell you everything that comes into my head and I reflect a great deal. " Professional things " I load on to Egon sometimes. However you know (you, best of all) that I have feeling. That is so, is it not, dear Gerda ?

Your card from Weimar has just arrived ; it gives me ease of mind to know that you are undertaking something without me. It is a good distance even to Wartburg from Weimar. Here I miss those warm autumn landscapes . . . I wonder if it is not too late to transplant myself back again ? I see things too clearly and have to force myself to do some things against my feeling . . .

I was told that the old Queen (Margherita) had expressed herself very enthusiastically about my art.

I expect these lines will find you at home again ? Be happy. I love you. (Benni now understands you much better.)

That queer fellow Augusto has helped me a lot . . .
unfortunately he has to go to his island in a few days.


BOLOGNA, 5 *October* 1913.

. . . I still do not see how to divide my work and finish it,
but I shall find a way.  It is impossible to work here in the
evening and I have given up the idea of sleeping in the Liceo.
For there is no light and the whole storey is uninhabited.  " With
the exception of some rats, mice, and a couple of owls I rightly
think ; no living being." [1]  I should be obliged to walk through
the big hall and the enormous corridor with a candle and then
live surrounded by all this empty darkness.  The walls are hung
with portraits of old gentlemen and the appearance of some of
them does not invite intimate acquaintanceship.  There is a dwarf
especially who, to me, is odious.  I imagined he came into the
room with Rossini's wig on and presented me with his roll of
music to play through.  And close by is the library, wrapped
in silence and clinging to its old, useless and boring books, all
classified.

There is a spinet in the library—supposing it were to begin to
tinkle ? . . .

A glass of wine too much before going to bed and in one night
I could lose every hair on my head.

But Italy has no ghosts, the ghost here is almost as profane
and ridiculous as the one in Wilde's book.  (I believe that it is
even incorrect when Mereschkowsky lets an Italian witch ride up
the chimney ; that custom belongs to witches of Germanic
origin.)

No, the Italians are " matter of fact," they see the stars stark-
clear and rayless ; if they murdered they had no fear of " spirits
coming back."  Murder was safe business if one wished to have
*Rest*.  With it the disagreeableness stopped.  Whilst in German
murder stories the unpleasantness only begins properly when the
person has been killed.  They seem to fear the living more than
the dead here.  Yes, each one fears the other . . .

Augusto holds the theory that the best people do not show
themselves simply because they are too wise to do so.

Your card came from Eisenach to-day ; I hope (and believe
from what you write) that you have had a little pleasure. . . .

[1] Quotation from the Brautwahl.

240

Yesterday evening with Anzoletti was extremely stimulating ; talked about poetry, languages, medicine and many other things. What a wonderful intelligence ! . . .


BOLOGNA, 7 *October* 1913.
. . . Frau Jella arrived in " good spirits " ; I showed her Santo Stefano and was extraordinarily moved myself by the austere mysticism and form of this interior, in which the altar stands as if it were in a casket.  This altar, which in one line unites altar, pulpit, and two flights of stairs, is like a musical composition ; strong and yet gracious, of beautiful material, and sensuous colour, a symbol of its aim and unique in form ; perhaps only Bach, in one of his best moments, had anything similar in music.

Faith—unaffectedness—perfect suitability of the form to the aim—for us these moments are lost !


*Afternoon.*
Three hundred years ago, or more, the following event took place in Bologna : A young Bolognese had a quarrel with a young stranger and was killed by him in a duel on the spot.  A door yielding to his pressure, the stranger fled into a house.  He mounted the stairs and at the top found himself in front of a noble lady.  He fell on his knees and begged for protection (he confessed what he had done) and the lady accorded him a safe hiding-place in one of the inner rooms of her house, at the same time swearing that she would help him to save his life.  A short time afterwards the patrol was announced, asked for the fugitive and searched the house, but they received no answer nor did they find the man for whom they searched.  Then the Captain said aloud : " This lady cannot know that the man who is hiding is her son's murderer."  But after a short heroic decision the lady lied still further, dismissed the administrators of the law and betook herself to the stranger.  She said : " You have taken my son from me ; now you shall be my son in his place."  In memory of this deed the street was afterwards named Strada Pia, the street of compassion.  I find this chronicle simple and beautiful.  More beautiful than the usual three-cornered drama

with the deceived husband.  A good one-act play could be made out of it.

. . . Marinetti is " manifesting " the importance of Variété as that of the true theatre of the future.

I find :  that Variété is simply the old annual fair, with this difference ;  at the fair the performances were given at *different* places at the *same time*, and in Variété they are given in *one* place in *succession*.

This journal will, I fear, pine away for lack of material—— But I have still one good memorandum to enter to-day.

Yesterday I saw a villa which pleased me very much . . .  Outside the Porta Maggiore is the street which leads on to the suburb in a straight line . . .  If one steps through the door of No. 55 one finds on the other side of the wall, garden and country, broad and free, as far as the furthest hills.  It is just like the situation in Wells's story of " The Door in the Wall."  It is surprisingly beautiful !  The house is not a " Villino " nor a castle, but a country manor-house.  It would please you and it is to be had. If the inside of the house is good too, I shall take it.  Then, for the present, I should have the following plan.  To pass the spring and autumn here, to travel in the winter and to be in Berlin for a short time (at Christmas and in January).  It is impossible to be here during July and August.  (The gardener said that too.) Therefore I should like to keep my summer work in Berlin very much.  I should like to enjoy this happiness which, to me, is such a necessity before I am an old man.  It keeps me young ; otherwise I should go to pieces prematurely.  So there must be a flat in Berlin.  I believe it is possible to do all this and I should like to hear your opinion.  Perhaps it may yet be very nice and according to your wishes too.

So we will look forward to it, dear Gerda, you and your

FERRUCCIO.


BOLOGNA, 11 *October* 1913.

Yesterday I had a visit from the newly appointed *Capo Banda* (he conducts the band which dispenses military music here) ; he is a young Neapolitan, lively, cheerful and friendly.  A pleasant contrast to these dusty Bolognese, who are as old as their own institutions.

He seemed to come from another world. There is a great deal of ineffective solemnity here ; he struck me as quite " modern " in the good sense of the word . . .

BOLOGNA, 15 October 1913.

There have just been a number of people here about various concerns. Although so much is left in my hands it is very difficult to get anything done.

(It is as if someone made me a present of an island and took away the ship in which to get there.)

(1) The Direction of the School of Music.

(2) The Concerts of the Società del Quartetto.

(3) A new musical paper which has been placed at my disposal.

(4) A seat on the Committee for performances at the theatre.

The last is the most hopeless of all, for everyone trembles before Ricordi and he is in command.

It is suddenly cold and sunny after a week of sirocco, which is a danger to the stomach.

All blessings till we meet again.

BOLOGNA, 21 October 1913.

. . . Bologna is not very different from Trieste ; what one knows about other countries only happens to come by chance from abroad, and one mistakes Sudermann for Ibsen. In addition, everything remains as it has been for the last 30 years ; they still act and speak in the same way and, as I have been saying until it is almost a proverb, San Petronio is still unfinished ; Marconi, who is a Bolognese, was here to-day. He lost an eye in a motor-car accident.

Should not " seeing without eyes " be a possible discovery ? I believe in everything so long as nothing has been proved to the contrary ! Hearing without ears is really there in music (by reading it)—— It occurred to me that I never *smoke* or *drink* when I dream. The mechanism of dreams has never yet been fully explained. I began to study it and found one thing : if one dreams something " endless " it is only because one had had no new thoughts.   If I think I am driving, this drive goes on until I have another idea.   But in 5 seconds one can think of any length of distance ! . . .

Goodbye, dear Gerda.

Isadora Duncan, after a telegraphic announcement from Viareggio, received me yesterday at 5 o'clock.

You know that six months ago she had the most inconceivable misfortune : both her children were drowned together.   That is infinitely hard and severe and she is bound to suffer very much. In spite of that, when she told me that now she was only spirit, and how a month before the catastrophe she constantly saw three black birds fluttering in the room, and that these birds in olden times were thought to be harbingers of death—when she said all that and other things, it reminded me of d'Annunzio, who in a smilingly self-satisfied way protested that he was infinitely un-happy.   She could " dance properly " no more but she would like to symbolize something religious and dance some movements to some choruses by Palestrina—My God !—

In Isadora's opinion the genius of the future will be a godlike dancer, and a composer too, who will thus fill up the chasm, as it now exists, between music and dancing.   Her son, who was only three years old, had shown natural tendencies towards becoming this genius.   I had scarcely left her when she wrote a letter to me. . . .

I had an invitation to the Borgattis' for the same evening. Renata did me good, after the other one.   The house is rich, light, new, cold and inartistic.   At the end, Borgatti sang two scenes from Parsifal excellently.   Renata accompanied like a young mare, but she does get through everything and controls it all.   Respighi was there too—— He is witty.   They spoke of an operation where a missing finger had been replaced by one of the same person's toes.   Respighi said : " If he gives anyone a box on the ear now, it will be a kick."   He is going to be married.   I said : " Life is short, marriage is long."   In Bologna the days slip by but not the hours.

I visited a church which is used as a *gymnasium*.   With a few alterations one can imagine it as a concert hall, which is badly needed.   I already have the plan ready and written down.   The gymnastic teacher, " Professor," greeted me with the words, " he *had already had the pleasure of bothering me.*"

The church, unimportant as such, would be exceptional as a concert hall. One sees by this on what a high level church architecture must stand. . . .

Da Motta wrote a good, warm letter, which really delighted me.


BOLOGNA, 26 October 1913.

. . . On Friday evening an (election) candidate made a speech from a platform in the public square, before the Town Hall, to many thousands of men. It made a beautiful old-world picture. The Elections have caused unrest in the town during the last week, and one saw still more men than usual.

The whole week at the Liceo has been taken up with examinations. It struck me that the girls who have studied singing perform much better and more attractively than the pianists. They are freer, and I think the " natural " instrument must be the cause of this. The teachers for string players are excellent here.

Have you seen the puppets in Berlin play Faust ? If it is still being given, do go and see it for me. . . . Fregoli [1] has been giving performances here, " one laughs."

I thank you with all my heart for your good, dear letters which are full of understanding. The days which brought them were always more beautiful.

I shall see you soon and kiss you . . .


BOLOGNA, 28 October 1913.

I shall be obliged to stop here until the end of this week, though I don't know how I shall have finished with everything even then : I am quite fidgety.

And, please, be prepared to come to Russia with me, or else I shall feel quite homeless ; this is not a command, of course, but I think it is what you wish also. . . . .

[1] A transformation artist.

# 1 9 1 4

Tours, 30 January 1914.

I travelled from Nantes to Tours in order to catch the Paris-Bordeaux Express and had two hours to wait . . .

Architecture and landscape very charming and very alive—spring weather—and a " model " hotel, which is the reason for my stopping the night in Tours . . .

It is astonishingly beautiful here ; the whole neighbourhood full of castles ; on the way I passed Angers, Saumur—and those Cathedrals !

I was very happy for some hours . . .

Heidelberg, 8 April 1914.

My thoughts were clearer when I woke in Heidelberg to-day, and my mood more cheerful ; but to counterbalance that, I shall have to continue the journey without a break. I read the story of a jewel robbery and I saw more clearly than I have ever done that " Property " is an empty, senseless idea.

Well-known gems, with a name and a history, are inherited, given away, stolen, worn, or stowed away in a cupboard—and the only way in which they can be possessed at all is by accepting the responsibility and danger imposed on one by them. But generations die out and the gems are indestructible ; they never get lost, they only *visit* people by turns.

" Owning " land and castles is just the same ; the people *walk about* on their land and go in and out of their castles, but they are *obliged* to leave them behind ; land and castle continue to exist.

As gems pay visits to people, so land and houses *receive* the so-called owners. In Hauptmann's play, " Schluck und Jan," he tries to make this thought clear . . .

It is imagination for Dr. von Hase to think that he possesses the firm of Breitkopf & Härtel.  The firm possesses him *completely* ; he is its prisoner.

A possessor only has the negative right of being able to destroy, and then only if *he alone* is affected by the consequences.

Taking into consideration everything, now is the best time of my life.  I look into the future firmly and happily and am glad that you take part in it all.

I am expecting a new edition of " Le nouveau monde " from the " Atlantic " (A bookshop). . . . According to the prospectus, the book refers to America, and not, (as one might expect from V(illiers)) to an ideal world . . .  (Am curious to know who will write a new " Aida " for the opening of the Panama Canal.)

HOTEL BAGLIONI, BOLOGNA, 13 *June* 1914.

I decided, yesterday at five o'clock, " without a moment's hesitation," and moved to this place.

To remain in the villa *alone* was impossible, or at least very difficult to put up with.  I felt it was harming me morally, and that had a bad effect on me physically.  It required strength of mind to return there every evening, for it gets lonelier and darker all the way back . . .

How gladly I went to bed last night, and how cheerfully I woke up this morning !

I almost feel as if I were on the way home . . .

Four short pieces, which Bach calls Duette, gave me great pleasure when I was preparing the Bach edition.  I shall play them in public, for they are as mature and on as high a level as the last Bagatelles by Beethoven.

One is always discovering new things in Bach . . .  I have changed the way in which I am going to produce the " Bach Edition," and Part II of the Wohltemperiertes Clavier will be very remarkable, if I am able to carry it out.  However, the later I begin it, the more valuable and full of experience my work for it may be.

There was a strike for three days ; all shops were closed, no newspapers, post not delivered, telegraph wires were cut, railway lines taken up ; amongst other things, there were fights, and even fatal incidents.—Mon Dieu !—The man from the Francesca struck too, but when he was asked, he did not know why, himself ! . . .

Dr. Augusto took his so-called holidays.  But he suffers from the interruption to his usual routine of work more than he is able to enjoy the freedom. (I understand this from my own experience). . . .

BOLOGNA, 15 *June* 1914.

In the meanwhile, I got your good letter, and the envelope with the newspapers. Richard Strauss was too much "for them" at first, but now his compositions are esteemed, "they" demand more of them in an almost threatening way . . .

By the way, only this morning, I found the story of the "Miracle" recounted again in the "Nouveaux Contes Cruels." [1] Quite different from Gottfried Keller's "Legend"; more aristocratic, shorter and stronger ; only seven pages . . .

As I have told nobody that I am living in the Baglioni, *nobody finds me.* I am as well hidden as the openly displayed letter in Poe's tale. Thank God, I am better. Staying in the hotel has given me a feeling of being on my way home and the last week begins to-day.

In a story by Villiers de L'Isle-Adams, a diabolical priest discloses "the secret of the church." "*There is,*" he says, "*no purgatory !*" Dear Gerda, I know *differently.*

Just as in America no one has heard me play as I can play (because the country makes it impossible), *nobody has heard me here either* . . . because in this circle I cannot think, speak or behave as I am able to in my own circle. There is continual misunderstanding . . . Enough.

I must make a plan for my life again, and for that I must be at home. I am waiting for the moment already, and I *am curious* to know how the consultation with myself will turn out, how it will go on, and to what place the new "step" will lead me . . .

BOLOGNA, 17 *June* 1914.

. . . When I am a long time from home and in one place, I feel as if I were far away from myself and had to come back to myself. In the end, the only thing left of me in the foreign place is my body, and that I drag round with difficulty.

Only a few days now ! But the feeling of waiting *just for the days to pass* is demoralizing too . . .

In other respects, I am in a state of happy expectation.

[1] By Villiers de L'Isle-Adam.

Is it to-day that summer begins ?   It does for me, for to-day
is the last day of the school.   To-morrow, I shall start . . .

Vollmoeller was with me yesterday for half-an-hour between
trains.   I was another person during that half-hour.   One could
talk about things without first explaining what the things were.
One could see the bird's-eye view without first having to climb
the hill !   For instance the theatre here is an important thing in
most people's lives.   Yet I have never met anybody who knew
what a permanent theatre in Germany is, or could understand the
meaning of it.   Once or twice I have tried to explain and saw in
front of me open mouths and eyes falling out, but no compre-
hension and no wish to make further enquiries into the question.
(That is only one example.)   They remain too much in their own
country.   They weaken each other mutually with discussions
about their own conditions.   Everything is personal, and culmin-
ates in discussing where they can get help from personal influence.
Vollmoeller was three months in America and came back very
refreshed and invigorated.   (He did not play the piano there !)
You know, I should like to go to America, and have no tour, just
once, to try . . .

I shall break the journey for two days, and arrive on Thursday
or Friday . . .

Another chapter ended.

I look forward to our beautiful meeting. . . .

# 1 9 1 5

(*Addressed to New York*)

CHICAGO, 27 *March* 1915.

I am here already, and with pleasant feelings—relatively.

I consider it necessary to be alone for the next few days in order to get some composure.

Kansas City, in spite of its size, is a town which is quite in its infancy, built entirely without plan, and unfinished everywhere. They have not thought yet about how things look. Although the revolver has been laid aside, it is genuinely Wild West in tone and customs. But the impression one gets is that the people there are a human society, still free from social presumption and that they all have a common aim, which is to lay a firm foundation and not trouble about anything else for the present . . .

I feel that our whole system of life is difficult and false, and this feeling is confirmed by Wells in an excellent book called "In the Days of the Comet," which I brought with me. He sketches a masterly picture of the absurdities of our conditions as seen by someone in the future, after the Comet has grazed the earth and purified the air chemically. As the result of this purification, which kills all poisonous matter, people become clear in their ideas and think rightly. In this book, written in 1906, he writes prophetically of the present war, condemning it unconditionally . . . And now he is a war fanatic !

Italy will join in *yet*. I have always felt this and there will be no end to the War.

Oh, Gerda dear, I never used to complain about " bad times." I thought all times were alike. But this is worse than anything has been before. Everybody has to struggle *with himself* (too little importance is attached to this), and every country has enough to do and to sacrifice just to keep itself morally clean. And the madness over machinery is just as unprogressive, just as destructive, and promotes as much unhappiness as war. There is no difference between the big employer, sacrificing the existence of a hundred thousand people for his own satisfaction, and the maker of wars. If one looks into the heart of England's industrial district, the picture is just as infernal as that of a battle-field. Workers and soldiers have a similar lot; an identical situation. And the artificial kind of places, which the wealthy people build as health resorts, and think they look beautiful, look miserable, and produce an overwhelming feeling of melancholy.

And the system to-day for " dispensing " Art is altogether distorted and unhealthy. The wonderful thing about art is that in spite of everything it is still alive and creative. Really, everything has been done to stifle it.

Apart from these reflections, which are always with me, the state of my mood is fairly well balanced. In thought I have resigned myself to the fact that I shall be unable to work for some time; but that cannot be otherwise . . . One must make a " reason " for oneself, and wait; and use the time of waiting in the best possible way.

I hope to get your letter, and I embrace you and the boys . . .


(*Addressed to New York*)

CHICAGO, 28 *March* 1915.

There was a concert yesterday evening. I went to it out of politeness. How it happened that everyone knew I was here already, I don't know.

1. Schumann, Symphony in C major. With the exception of two or three exciting moments, and when something begins which arouses expectation, it is a weak piece and full of deficiencies.

2. Bach's Chaconne, arranged by Middelschulte for string orchestra and organ . . . There are so many possibilities if once one begins making variations with this piece, that it is difficult for a contrapuntalist to show why he has chosen one possibility rather than another. Whenever they came to a well-known passage, the violinists played in the style of a David or Joachim, which was always disturbing!

3. The first Cellist played a violoncello concerto by Molique.

4. Tschaikowsky's " Hamlet." Imagine, please, Hamlet and Tschaikowsky. A beautiful combination. Everything sounds old-fashioned and without talent. Even Stock admitted this.

Altogether the programme was like an animal with a pig's tail, dog's head and donkey's back . . .

After the concert, I played Beethoven's Bagatelles to myself (it was very late, so I played softly).

I saw that the Chaconne would not do for a big apparatus. It loses in bigness. It always sounds best transcribed for the piano . . .


(*Addressed to New York*)

CHICAGO, 30 *March* 1915.

. . . I am occupied the whole day, read, think, play, eat, occasionally go out, but come home almost at once, write, drink tea, smoke.

I was carried away by Wells's book, but it feels as one closes it as if one were awaking from a beautiful dream to bitter reality.

I am looking forward very much to the concert here.

To-day is the 30th March. This year has been horrible.

" Lift up your hearts, ye everlasting doors."

Greetings from the bottom of the heart of

Your FERRUCCIO.


(*Addressed to New York*)

CHICAGO, 31 *March* 1915.

I have received your letter with gratitude and joy. I have two external reasons for the ending I have thought of for my composition.[1]

1. I am following the tradition of the Marionettes.

2. It makes a striking picture.

And if I obey the inner logic, this ending is inevitable. This man is wise enough to be able to make his own laws, but he has not used his wisdom well, for he is guilty of several murders and really no good deed can be put down to his credit.

Then, as a nightwatchman, the devil, no longer connected with evil, is brought into everyday human affairs, so that the situation is hardly symbolic any longer.

Finally, Faust himself says,

" If life is only an illusion,
What else can death be ? "

---

[1] Dr. Faust.

252

So that a doubt is raised as to the reality of the idea of the devil, which therefore lessens its importance.

What has the last Act got to do with the devil ? A man, ill, disappointed, tormented by his conscience, dies of heart failure and is found by the nightwatchman. The last word, too, is " a victim " (and not " condemned," or anything like it).

What brought me to this conclusion was that I cannot feel it in any other way, and I was led straight to this point in the same strange state of somnambulism in which the whole seems to have been dictated to me.

This morning I woke up as the sun came out of the water like a ball, just opposite to my bed. It looked uncanny and pre-historic . . .


(*Addressed to New York*)

CHICAGO, 1 *April* 1915.

The orchestra greeted me with a " noisy flourish " at the rehearsal to-day.[1]

The prices of the seats are raised for the concert to-morrow and the hall will be sold out. I had a pleasant lunch with Stock, Middelschulte and Gunn.

The piano people have answered in the same strain as before and so I have " finished " with the concert at St. Louis . . . Then there will be some calm, and we must take counsel together . . .


(*Addressed to New York*)

CHICAGO, 3 *April* 1915.

It seems almost uncanny that to-day should be the 3rd April. But my time in Chicago has not been quite lost. Middelschulte and I discussed many contrapuntal questions which will benefit the Wohltemperiertes Clavier. I have been getting on with my Rondo Harlequinesque, and I had a beautiful concert yesterday . . .

The great industries of Chicago, which carry on a fabulous export business with Europe, believe that they can make an estimate of the state of European finances by the orders and

[1] It was Busoni's 49th birthday.

payments they receive. They think that the War *must* be over in August at latest on account of money conditions.

Good and bad. Such an end to the War would satisfy nobody, no-one would be the victor, and hatred would not be extinguished. Peace without superiority on one side and without reconciliation is a very uncertain peace . . .

I have thought a good deal more about the puppet show and cannot help thinking that the last scene is good just as it is. The idea of reconciliation would be possible in only *one* form, namely : that the Students should find the corpse on their return and that the nightwatchman should come too late. In this way, Wagner, the Famulus, would triumph. That is not strong enough and not simple enough . . .

A young American pianist (Reuter) is going to play my two Sonatinas to me to-day. People are beginning to laugh rather indulgently at Debussy and there is a reaction (again almost unjust) against Wagner.

In ten years' time he will stand in his right place and nobody will discuss the matter further. Such is history ! . . .

(*Addressed to New York*)

ST. LOUIS, 5 *April* 1915.

Your letter, and this indescribably sunny morning (by the river !) make a beautiful welcome to St. Louis . . . My windows are open and the sun floods over everything, penetrates everywhere and makes a radiant picture, even out of this monstrous heap of human misery . . . The morning looks as though it heralded a new and more perfect epoch.

People had a wonderful opportunity to create something beautiful in this part of the globe, which was discovered so late. And how unskilful they have shown themselves to be. I believe it is as impossible to construct a country as it is a language . . .

I can't work my way through Björnson's tales ; but I read his plays with pleasure. Heroic dramas with old Nordic content were what he began with too, then he went over to the conversation play (where the people all talk so " naturally " !) and ended with symbolizing an abstraction. Anyhow, that shows the important personality of the man.

Has it ever occurred to you that Ibsen (with the exception of a few poems) never wrote anything but pure drama ? I at least know nothing of his which contains any of his opinions or theories. (Perhaps in his letters?) He never seems to have tried story-telling. There is a remarkable unity and singleness of purpose in this man, whereas Björnson must have had the arrogant intention of being a Goethe of the north . . .

# 1917

(*Addressed to Zürich*)

BERN, 6 *September* 1917.

The impression made by Bern just now is not a very sympathetic one, and it is full of people of various types : Diplomats of every description, the younger ones dressed in sports clothes, with very reserved expressions . . . Some people with faces like policemen, people suffering from spinal complaints, and Frenchmen looking like baritones in the old operas. Amongst them all some matter-of-fact Swiss women who might be sisters of the legionary soldiers ; Austrian Jews with Virginia cigars peeping out of their waistcoat pockets ; rich types of prostitutes (belles femmes with evil expressions) ; flappers, and youths looking like the youth of Bismarck's time. And all these are crowded into a small space not 500 yards long.

At 2.55 I start for Geneva again— Why ?

Heaven knows . . .

(*Addressed to Geneva*)

ZÜRICH, 29 *September* 1917.

This very moment—just after the mid-day meal—I have written the last bar of the 1st scene of my fourth opera [Dr. Faust]. Now I can turn my mind to something else, which is very necessary for me at the moment.

(*Addressed to Geneva*)

ZÜRICH, 30 *September* 1917.

. . . I am satisfied with the result of my summer work. I have looked through the new part of this score as objectively as possible to-day, and I came to the conclusion that it contains

256

some of the best work I have done.    With this score to do I shall be in harness again for some time. . . .    There is still some work to do on the end of the libretto.    I must wait for a happy inspiration.

# 1918

(*Addressed to Degersheim*)

ZÜRICH, 6 *August* 1918.

Strolled about nearly all day yesterday, half-unsatisfied. Staying at home to-day. At midnight was still writing a new chapter of Arlecchino, " *the geese of the Capitol* " (good, I think) . . .

Sketched the idea for a 5th sonatina using a Bach theme ; also the appearance of Gretchen's brother at the end. Wrote several letters. (Anyhow, something done) . . .

(*Addressed to Degersheim*)

ZÜRICH, 13 *August* 1918.

Yesterday I constructed and transcribed a *concert suite* from " *Idomeneo,*" and it makes an attractive little work . . .

To-day I wrote down a large page of the score, the first part of a number of pages (almost finished in my head) . . .

Considering how much I miss you, the time passes surprisingly quickly ; but this feeling is only connected with my work . . .

(*Addressed to Degersheim*)

ZÜRICH, 18 *August* 1918.

. . . I don't know what to do about the publishing of the libretto of Faust. Shall I simply have it printed in its original form, without regard to the changes which will have to be made because of the music, or shall I wait ? . . . I have made a small, separate piece out of the part for the 6 spirits ; like a set of variations. (I have thought of doing this for a long time.)

At the *fifth* the chorus joins in ; at the *sixth* there is an outburst of evil mockery, to intimidate Faust. It is stopped by Faust's great cry, " Be silent." Now that joins on organically to

> " A single one remains. I hesitate
> To destroy the last hope."

You see what a lot has to be changed. That is why a composer must be *a poet too*. . . .

*(Addressed to Degersheim)*

ZÜRICH, 20 *August* 1918.

. . . Yesterday and the day before I composed a short sonatina on 3 bars of Bach, with which I am very satisfied . . .

*(Addressed to Degersheim)*

ZÜRICH, 21 *August* 1918.

. . . Dear Derdi, I only work till 4 o'clock. After that there are still 8 hours to waste, loitering about in the most despicable way.

Mozart and Bach must have been quite different ; they must have slaved at their work. I must live like this. I love " dawdling " then and it does me no harm . . .

I am expecting Jarnach, to whom I have dedicated the new sonatina. . . .

No news—have worked well.

*Late afternoon.*

I gave Jarnach the sonatina, which pleased him very much. I showed him the introduction to the *last scene* of " Faust " ; he took it in extraordinarily well. After that, in retrospect, he sketched a picture of my development as a composer, which gave evidence of his possessing exceptional sagacity and good instinct. He quite moved me. There is a great deal in this man . . .

The score progresses well ; there will be still more fruit ripe to-morrow. I rejoice now at every forward step . . .

ZÜRICH, 23 *August* 1918.

Yesterday afternoon we had a " housefull " here ; to-day I won't see anyone ! . . . the last was X—— —with his silly, idle talk going round in circles, and in the end I had rather to snub him. With his " If I can only touch the money " and

" Well, what *do* you want ? "—his passport and railway privileges, his exemptions and his bulging pocket-book—" if you only have a pull in the right quarter,"—he infuriated me. " Here's a roaring lions' den," says he. However, he borrowed something to read on the journey, and even wanted to go off with a paper knife ! . . .

(*Addressed to Degersheim*)

ZÜRICH, 25 *August* 1918.

I am already in a state of happy expectation. I hope that this " strenuous cure " has not been too much for your nerves. The beautiful weather, unfortunately, is over suddenly. Yesterday evening there was a warning of autumn in the air. What will autumn bring ? The first half of the Faust score, for certain, and that is something ; then I believe I shall be forced to make a decision. Perhaps the autumn will bring our Benni, and that would be one point cleared up.

In any case I look at everything with deliberate calm, and beg you to arm yourself with cheerfulness (I don't say liveliness) and to practise your loving patience still further.

News. None. But lots of things will turn out well . . .

(*Addressed to Degersheim*)

ZÜRICH, 26 *August* 1918.

So Martin Krause, too, is no more ; he was 65. When I saw him last I did not take him for a sexagenarian. He was a very good friend to me for many years. Requiescat.

Lello is going to have an exhibition of pen and ink drawings at Tanner's in September. He is a talented boy and honest, too. I have had some long talks with him . . .

Why one should always throw Bach's music into the same consecrated pot with the services of the Protestant Church is just as difficult to understand as are many other things to your loving

FERROMANN.

Busoni, 1918

# 1 9 1 9

*(Addressed to Ascona)*

ZÜRICH, 15 *April* 1919.

. . . I have looked through my score of Faust and I am satisfied with it ; I am hoping for a new inspiration to take me a good deal further. Some passages are dated 1917 ! But it must be made as perfect as possible. By the time a work is finished the author has made so much progress that, taking his continual development for granted, the work itself is behindhand.

This forces one to begin a new work, and in this way progress is always being made without everything having been said. (This has been proved in the cases of Michelangelo, Goethe, Verdi) . . .

Just think, in Paris, on the 50th anniversary of Berlioz' death, they wanted to give a festival of his compositions, but could not do so because there were no more copies to be bought at the French publishers. They were so little in demand that they were out of print. And they did not want to apply to Breitkopf & Härtel !

There is a revolution going on in the Vienna School of Music and Bopp has gone. But " Director " Loewe is there in his place . . .

*(Addressed to Ascona)*

ZÜRICH, 17 *April* 1919.

Schoek's opera, Ranudo, yesterday was quite delightful ; some very good moments, and the performance satisfying from a spectacular and musical point of view. . . .

Herr Avenarius has taken the 2nd part of Goethe's Faust and *rewritten* it " in the light of modern research." This is the secret republic of letters. Two long articles in the Zürcher Zeitung give an account of it—without a sign of indignation—and call this piece of simple folly " the ripe fruits of the war " or something of the sort . . .

(*Addressed to Ascona*)

ZÜRICH, *Saturday*, 19 *April* 1919.
. . . Feeling a little downcast at having to pass Easter Sunday without you. I received an Easter Egg from Ascona, with little parcels which I shall open to-morrow at lunch time. I am well, thank God. Yesterday I went to Lochbrunner's doctor in order to be reassured. He sounded me very carefully and decided there is *nothing* wrong with me. That is a pleasant Easter present for you, and I am glad ! But I need some kind of recreation. The question is what kind ?

Great fuss in the paper about Schoek's opera. Everybody, to-day, must belong definitely to some country. Liszt and I are left alone.

Wolfrum sent me his preface to Liszt's church music (for the collected edition). Nobody wanted to have anything to do with him. Not even the Catholics of Regensburg . . .

We must not be idle and we must go on hoping.

Your very loving
F. M.

(*Addressed to Rovio*)

ZÜRICH, 23 *July* 1919.
. . . I have skimmed through " La porte étroite " by Gide ; it seems to be completely without character.

A letter from London announces that my first concert will be in Liverpool on 2nd October . . . I appear with Mme Melba— What miserable buffoonery ! I shall demand a double fee . . .

(*Addressed to Rovio*)

ZÜRICH, 24 *July* 1919.
. . . Everybody wishes they were going away ; " peace psychology " is shown by a desire to see the world, striking out into new plans and changing centres . . .

Yesterday, after a long interval, I went to the Bellevue again. It seems so long ago that I was a frequent visitor there, on account of the opera, that I might have been away in between . . .

(*Addressed to Rovio*)

ZÜRICH, 25 *July* 1919.
. . . The gathering here in the afternoon was *British* this time . . . Milner said, " English people have good taste." I said, " They *avoid* the bad taste, I think that is all." (Milner agreed at once.) My aphorism about B. Shaw was a great success : He is a minister disguised as a clown.

There has been a *Zilcher* week in Munich !

What a pity that this feeling of good will is lacking in Italy. " O, Jerusalem, Jerusalem, thou that killest the prophets and stonest them which are sent unto thee ! " It seems to me that the " Prophet " is working well . . .

(*Addressed to St. Moritz*)

ZÜRICH, 16 *August* 1919.
. . . Bösendorfer left some last instructions : the news of his death was not to be made public until he had been buried. The coffin was to be driven to the churchyard by his own workmen in the piano van.

His wishes were carried out.

He remained the same up to the end, and kept his original simplicity and his simple originality. A delightful figure, not to be forgotten.

The Brautwahl has occupied me for 2 days. There is so much in it. It is much too sincere. It will be performed again ; if I am able to change it to a certain extent . . .

(*With the exception of the letters on the 15th and 16th October all the following letters in 1919 are addressed to Zürich.*)

PARIS, 21 *September* 1919.
Yesterday I was on the Boulevard Magenta, the Champs-Elysées and Place Malesherbes, but not on the " left side of the river." I walked to the Porte St. Martin and then in the opposite direction up to the Place de la Madeleine as far as to where Philipp lives. The Grand Boulevard looks horribly like the East Fourteenth Street in New York now ; it looks ignoble, glaring and dirty. The Faubourgs do not seem to have changed, from what I have seen of them ; the little bourgeois people,

always preoccupied and anxious, buying the necessities of life for exaggerated prices. The uselessness of everything is so obvious ; and Paris sad—it has not the allure of a victorious city . . .

The taxis are perpetually on the move and always engaged ; none of them are ever stationary and one catches them on the wing. I paid 1 franc 80 cts. from my hotel to the Boulevard Magenta, and in Zürich that would have cost 18 frs. . . .

One sees many American soldiers, with indifferent, insolent-looking faces ; and even officers of my age with cheap prostitutes, who have raised their prices for the occasion. They walk by their sides without gaiety and without speaking, simply because they believe it is the right thing to do in Paris. They call themselves the " Knights of Columbus." They are not liked . . .

All this is neither gay, fitting, nor moral ; it makes me think of the last chapter in Dr. Moreau, where the beasts fall down on all fours and behave according to their original nature . . .

I paid Philipp a long visit. To-day we are going to lunch together and recapitulate our conversation of yesterday. His one idea is that my place, from henceforth, is in Italy. He even recommends me to return to—Bologna ! . . .

People have violent ideas about Zürich here. I do not quite understand it. Philipp certainly likes me and had the highest opinion of me. He begins to look like a " kindly Clemenceau." He has suffered horribly from the war ; whilst telling me about it he cried many times. I am glad that I avoided the countries which were at war. Who knows what point I should have reached in my development by now ?

I am eager for London, provided there is no new disillusionment. We must always hope and try to direct hope to the path of realization . . .

I feel that you think of me. I love you and embrace you, my three dear ones . . . I think of Giotto [1] and feel moved whenever I see a dog.

LONDON, 24 *September* 1919.

It was very nice to find a letter from home on the very first day. Kiss Benni for me and tell him I hope he will feel well and will like the little town which has given us so many good things . . .

I hoped to get a feeling of liberation from London and the

---

[1] Busoni's Newfoundland dog.

264

first impressions have been very beautiful. The town has not changed, but I am another person.

I notice that I expect nothing *from outside* and formerly I expected everything. This does not make me unhappy, but quieter and more alone.

" Nothing comes back again as it was," A. France says in a book which I brought with me from Paris. It is called " La Vie Littéraire " in 4 volumes (it is a collection of articles). " That makes the charm of the past." " The change makes us sad and amuses us at the same time." England, which up to the time of the war was the most democratic of all countries, is now—unchanged—the most aristocratic of them all. How attentive and considerate the people are individually, in spite of all the hurry and competition ! . . .

I was travelling for 19 hours from Paris to London ! . . . The country round Southampton is enchanting. What lovely meadows and old trees ! . . .

I was received like a relation by Powell, at Monico's . . .

Philipp told me he had been present when Debussy heard Liszt's " Les Jeux d'Eaux " for the first time, and how dumbfounded Debussy was by it ! Yes, Liszt in his last period was prophetic . . .

LONDON, 26 *September* 1919.

Up to the present I have not discovered how to resume connections with my old outside world : that, too, is not quite the same as it was, for the social conditions seem to be quite threatening. This is obvious in Paris too, and is shown quite brazenly.

I think of you all every morning and evening. About Benni's plans and of Giotto too, who, it is to be hoped, understands who Benni is . . . If I can be with you all again at Christmas, like Arlecchino, I shall be able to say :

" The three minutes are ended " . . .

Send me the photos of Giotto.

LONDON, 28 *September* 1919.

. . . I take everything with calm and deliberation, am less nervous than I was in Zürich. Reading Anatole France's " gentle philosophy " has fortified me very much . . . But

265

things do not look well in the world ; even the gentlest philosopher must admit that ! . . .

" Atlantide "[1] has disappointed me very much, and finally I decided it was " rubbish." Fundamentally, all these novels originate from Poe's " Gordon Pym." J. Verne was more kindly and instructive. As the representation of a super-woman Atlantide, who is really only a Parisian, misses fire altogether. In order to make her extraordinary power comprehensible the author should have endowed her with extraordinary gifts. It is impossible to decide her age and one is led to suppose that, to her, a hundred years are like twenty years to other people. To every man she ought to appear as his ideal seen in dreams ; every man should see her differently, too, and how she looks in reality should remain a secret. Riddles like this are thought out and solved in a more magnificent way in the 1001 Nights.

Reading this book is like going to a fair, a " Luna Park," and Anatole France's causerie, which is so quiet, good and clear, is like enjoying the peace of home afterwards. He is only malicious once, and that is over a book by George Ohnet. He writes sharply and without consideration about Zola too.

It is strange how I have always avoided Ohnet instinctively, although at one time he was in everybody's hands . . .

There are three articles dedicated to marionettes, written very sympathetically. . . .

LONDON, 30 *September* 1919.

. . . As far as the strike is concerned, it is serious . . . They have funds to keep the strike going for *three weeks*. That will mean general disaster. At present only the railways and mines have ceased working ; but they say the omnibuses are going to join the strike too. That is disturbing and dangerous. People do not seem to be able to recover from their momentary troubles and difficulties and so no good work can be done and no good idea put into practice. We are still in a stupor and we shall go

[1] By Pierre Benoit.

on being in it. The Idealists are like beautiful blossoms of poisonous plants ; they bloom and blossom in vain, and then fall off. Perhaps, with age, the poison in the plants will decrease (such a thing has been known), but epochs must pass before this can take place and the plants will never be altogether harmless.


*In the afternoon.*

At Steinways' everything is dormant, and one looks round for cobwebs. They have three old grands, fit for a museum, and nothing more . . .

Dear Caufall has gone ; I hoped to find him here still . . .

In Zürich I was still able to " educate " people musically but here—where can one begin ?

An Englishman who admits Wagner is very enlightened and with this admission he has made the greatest possible effort for the progress of genuine music. Besides, at bottom, nobody is interested in music. No, all that is worse than I feared.

I am still reserving my judgment and collecting impressions and observations, and my decisions will be directed by what comes out of them all. A little patience is still necessary.

I like the " Embankment " best this time in London. The river with its bridges, Westminster, St. Paul's, the Tower, wharves, ships, and the wonderfully rich façade of Buckingham Palace. One can see some of it from the windows at the back of the hotel ; it is equally beautiful in sunshine or fog.

I look less at the people than I usually do, for I dislike the expression in their faces profoundly.

I should describe the architecture of London as " cautious." It is like someone playing a piece very correctly, with taste, and not without understanding, but playing it too slowly and not so loudly as it ought to be played. I remember what I used to say, that an Englishman can be tasteful without being artistic. Even in architecture they are anxious not to be " out of the ordinary " (and woe betide them if they try !) It is beautiful how architecture (and this is an old thought) quietly keeps its position as the solid background for moving history ; that is what I call strength and victory.

Waterloo Bridge is good. Between each of the arches, which

are very powerful, there is a Doric double column, of primitive simplicity, with the abacus jutting out exaggeratedly and without a socle ; but this is repeated without swing or rhythm for the whole length of the bridge.

All my little old bookshops have been swallowed up by the War. . . .

LONDON, 1 *October* 1919.

To-day, October 1st, is the *fourteenth* day since I started : have experienced much movement and noise during these two weeks, and " summa summarum " nothing has happened, and I have done nothing which connects at all with what happened last ! I have never noticed so much movement with so little result before ; and that, it seems to me, is one of the bad characteristics of the moment.

My passivity is almost pathological and as I look on I am neither amused nor annoyed. But indirectly I suffer. For the result of this quite confused activity is that the people have no attention or interest left to give to other things . . .

LONDON, 2 *October* 1919.

. . . If I am not to have come to England for nothing, I shall be obliged to take a car to Manchester to-morrow . . . Yesterday I wrote one page of music. I have been lifted quite out of the saddle ; the English air is not very good for creative work. Nothing more from outside. From inside, I have considered whether I could get a one-act libretto from Bernard Shaw's pen. Who knows ! If Arlecchino should be given in two parts, I shall want another piece for the Turandot evening. Anyhow, it is an exciting thought . . .

LONDON, 4 *October* 1919.

. . . These morning hours are charming, the sight of old trees is consoling . . . I see a garden once more, which it gives me pleasure to look at . . .

To-day, for the first time since I have been in London, I am morally better and quieter. The first week was really not good. The strike continues and the first two concerts have had to be given up.  For this reason I am giving my own recital at the Wigmore Hall on the 15th ; and in November *Wood* will give a programme, which I shall choose.  Philipp, who is always taking trouble for me, wrote yesterday to tell me that there would be a concert of my compositions.  This March in Paris promises many pleasant things.  There is almost half a year till then.  The world is bound to look a little different by then, but which direction will the bias take ?  It seemed to me that in Paris especially, everything was working up for an explosion . . .

It is evening now and the post has brought nothing from you, and to-morrow is Sunday.  I suffer very much from having nobody to talk to.  The people understand nothing, not even that a man can be used up after six years and a war . . . I am in fact convinced that they think I am not worth so much as I was before the war . . .

You will not be able to complain of this letter being instructive.  Here one forgets what one has learnt.  Nobody listens . . .

LONDON, 5 *October* 1919.

. . . I know that Zürich is not a kingdom of dreams, but consequently not one of nightmares either—as the big cities are now.  With the exception of the glorious trees in Regent's Park (which, however, I only enjoy in the *morning* and not, like Walt Whitman, in the evening too), I have really experienced nothing beautiful here.  One Saturday evening, the red sky lighted by the sunset, with an endless perspective of bright yellow lights from the lamps, made a very beautiful effect.  The workpeople were driving home, standing in lorries which were packed.  Then there are still the inexhaustible book-shops.  Smoking and drinking is made very difficult and is bad.  Elegance in the streets has almost disappeared.  One sees only shabby people.  The atmosphere is uncertain, everybody anxious and unquiet, the whole tone of society is coarsened.  Here in " West Wing," certainly, everything looks quite idealistic—even if uneventful and lonely ; but to make up for that, a great number of men, blinded in the war, are lodged in the next building ; a stimulating sight for those who, unfortunately, can see.  All this does not look like victory and peace, nor like a country that has made a very good transaction.  The strike oppresses everyone and interferes with all communications. For me, personally, it is a satisfaction to know that at last, in England, someone is " protesting," but I would rather it were already over, or that it had begun later.

A strange discordant time ! Still in the middle ages and the future that has been striven for is still not here. A twilight ; and one does not know whether it precedes morning or night. Interesting ? Oh yes. But not excessively so. It is astonishing, how undistinguished, conventional, and of secondary importance the musical life is here.

About new books, too, I can hear of nothing which attracts my attention . . .

I am starving for the companionship of a man like Jarnach, for instance. Van Dieren is in Holland, unfortunately.

So I am very isolated and wait for something to happen ; an idea, or an experience.

But on the whole, I feel that concert tours are unworthy and only lead to new and endless misunderstandings . . .

LONDON, 6 *October* 1919.

It was thought yesterday evening that the strike would be called off this morning. *The Times* confirms this news to-day, so this incubus is lifted ! Deo gratia ! The train service will be normal to-morrow. What next ? One has to ask oneself that these days. I am curious to see what it will look like in the streets to-day. It was said that there were 250,000 volunteer helpers during the strike who drove the trains in order to provide for the food in the towns.

Yesterday afternoon I walked from here to Piccadilly Circus. It took me almost an hour. I have to get used to the proportions again ; I miscalculate the distances. But on a Sunday, this walk was bitterly dismal, such an inhospitable road ; on the way not a single bench on which to sit, not a single place to turn into and have a rest, everything locked up in front of one's nose, as if walks on a Sunday were a crime and would be punished. Because of this, there is hardly anybody out of doors . . .

The whole of Regent's Park is full of barracks which still serve for post-military purposes ; filled with wounded soldiers who are led about by affectionate " nurses " ; but they are often the soldiers' wives, who come—sometimes even singing—to visit " our " blind.

LONDON, 7 October 1919.

. . . The strike delayed the distribution of the post. To-day, everything is working again. (But the same thing will recur. Everything always comes again ; unreasonable, but alarming.)

Meanwhile, the beloved " great Wagner night " runs its usual course at the Queen's Hall ; conducted by Wood, with his usual " devotion."

When I think that I have passed the best years of my life in foreign places, waiting for a concert to take place (as now again), I don't value my sense of discernment very highly ! Thank God, the autumn is so very beautiful ! (I am waiting for the next post) . . . The old trees are touchingly beautiful, with all their leaves on still, and still almost green. Sometimes my heart overflows when I look at them . . .

To-day, I woke up—contented. I thought over my life work and of what I still hope to bring to completion . . .

I have been looking through " Crime and Punishment " again. What a distressing book ! How big and how childish at the same time ! In short : how Russian ! I am reading it in English, and that does not harmonize with the content of the book.

England terrorizes the world at large, without guns, but not less than others do with them . . . A remarkable, indefatigable kind of policy to take for oneself and forbid others to do the same ! (All the same, things are not going at all well for them here).

To-morrow it will be three weeks since I left you : nothing done ! . . .

LONDON, 9 October 1919.

. . . Have just come back from Bradford, a place which I know well, the audience similar to one in Western America. " Old Melba " (she is over sixty) is doing what Patti did. Although she is old and very rich, she cannot give up singing in public. It is a great strain for her now, but the production of the voice in her clarinet style is exemplary in its own way and enjoyable even now. Only, I can no longer understand this form of " art for art's sake " which makes the mastery of the instrument with the cheapest possible effect its sole aim. And this form is the only one which the great English audience expects and demands and by which it is charmed. To prove that this is not just an antiquated idea, a young tenor appeared who had the same ambition ; I should describe him as something between Caruso and a head waiter. There was nothing much more in the whole affair than could be done by trained animals . . .

10 a.m.

. . . To-day I begin to be active again. I shall begin to prepare for the London Recital (Goldberg Variations, " 106," Liszt Group) ; then I have promised Philipp Cadenzas for Mozart's C Major Concerto, which I must do soon . . . Thank God there are things to be done. For me, this condition is as necessary as health . . .

LONDON, 13 October 1919.

Your letters are always a warm consolation to me . . .

The programme advertised is in horrible taste. I almost regret that my compositions are in it. It is like a fair ! Here, they never seem to get away from the idea of a Variety programme in its most ordinary sense. The problem is, are concerts there for people, or are the public there for musicians ? It becomes so confused that one would like to be able to sweep them both out of the world . . .

I sent Philipp one of the promised Cadenzas for Mozart's C major Concerto. The finale bit has still to be done . . .

(Addressed to Geneva)

LONDON, 15 October 1919.

. . . To-day I give my London recital, which makes me a little tense. For this reason, I am not in a state to undertake anything particular in writing. An evening, as it will be to-night, makes the " moment " worth while.

In other respects it has actually been a characteristic weakness of mine to let the moment pass by in imagining a future one of more importance, whilst the " clever " people take advantage of the " moment " as of something real and present. Who is right ? Probably we all deceive ourselves, each according to his temperament and grade of intelligence. . . .

(*Addressed to Geneva*)

LONDON, 16 *October* 1919.

Although I feel " done up " this morning, I must quickly write a few words to you ; for I am taking a *holiday* and going out for lunch.

The crowded hall in Wigmore Street welcomed me warmly yesterday evening ! I was obliged to get up from my seat three times before I could begin. I was really touched. I played with great intensity and with success throughout the concert ; the piano was obedient. The clamour at the end was such as had not been heard at a London concert for years ; so the people told me.

All the people who spoke German formerly speak English now, and if they risk a sentence in German, they whisper it, as if they were going to tell an indecent story. Stupid world, weak people ! ! . . .

EDINBURGH, 19 *October* 1919.

It is Sunday, and a beautiful morning in Edinburgh . . .

Yesterday was full of little annoyances. I had to wait many hours for a room and when I got it finally—about eleven o'clock —was surprised by the news that the concert was in the afternoon instead of in the evening. I had brought no clothes for an afternoon concert, so played in street clothes, because in this inflexible country this after all was considered more correct than dress clothes.

As I was half asleep and half frozen, you can imagine how beautiful the concert was ! I comforted myself with a nice meal afterwards. Before I started, I finished the missing Cadenza and sent it off to Philipp . . .

Dr. Milner is my escort. Through him, I was able to have a fire in my room, which in hotels now can only be had by showing " a Doctor's certificate." Milner was clever enough, therefore, to bring forward his " Dr.," and enforce the fire. These are uninteresting details, but I have nothing important to relate. To-morrow evening in Glasgow—always with Melba—and then the most unpleasant part is over . . .

It means that with patience I have to pass two days here. On Tuesday morning, I hope to be in Regent's Park. Edinburgh is just as beautiful as ever, but this time the surprise is missing, for during previous visits I have often examined the town in detail. Thank God, in spite of making efforts, and being frozen, I am comparatively well. I am looking forward, like a child, to finding letters in London.

Still another month, which perhaps may still produce something pleasant ; but one is safer if one expects nothing.

Scotland remained fairly untouched by the war. It is, so it seems, a very contented country : but quite out of the world (Perhaps on this account, more contented) . . .

EDINBURGH, 20 *October* 1919.

Yesterday, Sunday, a day of senseless doing nothing, also came to an end. I feel freer to-day. In an hour I start for Glasgow, and back to *London* in the evening . . .

Milner took endless trouble to lighten the Sunday for me ; the good fellow . . .

I got a volume of Villiers de L'Isle-Adam in which are a couple of things unknown to me. I had the confidence to read the others again (for the details). There is not one unnecessary word here, nor is the *choice* of them ever accidental : the details, incidental remarks and reflections, are all thought and felt. But—the sum total of every piece is simply an aphorism ; an aphorism with decorations, so to speak. But the " style " has some connecting link with my last compositions—in so far as such a comparison is permissible.

Even the unsuspecting " Scotsman " writes to-day that the frame in which I appeared was not big enough for me. . . .

It is interesting to notice how every so-called Impresario awakens in me " exactly the same kind of antipathy and suspicion " ; whether Jew, Christian, Englishman, or anything else. I mean a definite kind and a definite degree of antipathy, which is not to be confused with other antipathies. Perhaps in about the same way that a dog arouses a definite *nuance* of sympathy in me. I felt that again when I

274

saw a bulldog yesterday ; indescribably ugly and wonderfully benevolent.

And now I am going to start . . . The world is bearable to-day . . .


LONDON, 21 October 1919.

From Villiers de L'Isle-Adam :

A poet with two friends was celebrating his birthday in an attic ; they heard groans from the next room as if someone were dying. The poet said an old king in exile was lying there, sceptre in hand, dreaming of his treasures. The other two thought that was a beautiful picture but that one ought to go and see what was happening. Do go : said the poet, and settle the matter. But I warn you, if you go, *you will never have any imagination.*

Dear Gerda, how extraordinarily true and simple this is ! (Of course it is amplified much more).


LONDON, 22 October 1919.

Yesterday and to-day letters came from you ; they have done me so much good. The tale which Rilke [1] told you is fine and worthy of consideration. What I feel to be necessary at this moment, to counterbalance Dr. Faust, is something short and amusing. Something that could be given on the same evening as Turandot, if Arlecchino parts 1 *and* 2 take up an evening to themselves.


LONDON, 22 October 1919.

During the afternoon, when I was occupied with music, an excellent letter from Philipp arrived. First of all, he writes the following, word for word, which, of course, has cheered me very much :

" The oftener I read your Arlecchino, the more I like it. It is a hundred years away from Rossini, it is a work of genius. What invention, what rhythm, what life there is in it all ! I believe that they would understand your work here."

[1] Rilke had related the tale of a little mystical story to Mrs. Busoni in Geneva.

LONDON, 23 *October* 1919.

Herewith : this very beautiful plan for March in Paris :

*From the 5th to the 23rd March, Paris*

Two concerts in the Conservatoire of the Société
des Concerts :
  I.  E flat major Concerto, Beethoven.
      Concerto, Saint-Saëns.
  II. Mozart Concerto.
      Indian Fantasie.
Two recitals in the Salle Erard.
Two concerts for the Association of Old Pupils.
  I.  My compositions with orchestra, including
      *concerto with chorus.*
  II. Liszt Recital.

That is really worthy and festive, but it means a lot of work for me ! Philipp begged me to dedicate the Cadenzas to his old favourite Mlle Marcelle Herrenschmidt. I knew her before, I saw her again the other day in Paris ; she is extremely sympathetic. I received a pretty letter of thanks from her to-day, full of happiness . . .

If one looks out of the window, one is aware of the trees only because one knows they are there—everything all round is hidden by such a thick fog . . .

Benni has not grasped yet that we have to thank others for the chief part of our means of existence and therefore we dare not repulse people, but we have to hold out our hands to one another. The right to turn others aside will necessarily be achieved with difficulty, for to do that, it is necessary to surpass others in something ; and that is a thing which always remains relative . . .

I have too little to do here, really ; I try to occupy myself with something of my own. It always requires strength of mind to go out—from here—it generally means disarrangement of many things. You know, one cannot get home so easily in London . . . London was never the town for harmless adventures (for which, too, I have little inclination)—so books and my own little reflections are the only things left with which to fill up the days. I see remarkably few people.

Now I have been chatting a little . . .

Do you hear from Berlin ?

276

BOURNEMOUTH, 25 *October* 1919.

Whilst waiting for the time when my concert begins (at three o'clock) I am thinking of you, and send you a greeting. A nice, quiet place, you know, lots of old ladies in rocking chairs. The concert grand is ten years old . . . Yesterday I revised the Rondo of that Mozart Concerto, which I am going to play in Zürich. It is full of places *which are not worked out*, obviously written quickly, easily and brilliantly. I believe it will be splendid now. That occupied me from early morning till 5.30 p.m. Last night, I thought over the necessity for recomposing the music for the third and fourth spirits in Dr. Faust—and the seventh (Mephistopheles) is still on the lap of the gods . . .


LONDON, 28 *October* 1919.

. . . They are making plans for a permanent Shakespeare theatre here and Bernard Shaw was called upon to make a public speech about it. He began something like this : " This is a highly ' national ' affair which concerns every Englishman. The subscription list is opened. So far, there has been only one subscriber, and he is a German, and he has sent £25,000." (Isn't that amusing ?) I have not seen him yet. You may be quite right in what you think . . .

My newest friend is an old tom-cat belonging to the house. He seems to love me—sits next to me on my chair at table. He is old, should be quite white, but is of an uncertain grey colour. An old dog called " Beauty " resides here too, he is toothless and holds growling conversations with himself. He, on the other hand, is quite black . . .

It is very delightful to observe how well Milner is developing here. He has made marked progress in his thought, and what he says is often quite right and sensible. At the same time he is always affectionate and true, but he is (one might almost say, unfortunately) no longer so unsuspecting as he was in Zürich.

Da Motta wrote me a second remarkably beautiful letter. He will have me in Portugal " at any price " (meant literally) . . .

I think of you so very much, even more than before. That is beautiful but almost painful, for I cannot always see the way yet, and feel that it is hard for you to bear. Everything might have been so good at this moment ; put up with it patiently, meanwhile, with my love, till the better things come (and I believe they will come) . . .

. . . The streets of London are changed, it seems to me, although I could not say precisely how much of this impression is due to my own way of looking at things.   In any case it is certainly true that the people are uglier and that elegance has almost disappeared.   Many in uniforms (it is distressing to see *women* in uniform), many cripples too : perhaps it is a comfort, on the whole, to gain respect through wearing a uniform ; rationing and closed bars add their note to the picture ! a defiant manner amongst those who serve, and in consequence of all these things, a deterioration in taste.

It is not good ;  and it seems as if the houses, and even daylight itself, no longer exercised their magic ;  for democratic rule treads on holy ground with heavy boots.

. . . Now I am sitting at lunch, and to-day is the last day of the month of October, which to me has seemed a very long one ; for outwardly it contained many more experiences than we are accustomed to in Zürich.   For my inner self this does not signify much gain ;  the only thing it has done is to put me in contact again with bigger conditions.   The revision of Mozart's E flat Concerto (completed yesterday) is the only work I have done during this time.   (Also the little Cadenzas to the C. Major one) . . .

Milner is having good luck, for he is singing " Iago " at Covent Garden on Monday.   I studied this with him once.   (In England, he is considered a very versatile actor) . . .

The Beecham Opera Company is giving no less than *five* Russian Operas, together with the Russian ballet.   I saw the piano score of the " famous " Prince Igor, by Borodin.   It is utterly weak.   Altogether, there is much Russian music given, even in concerts.   The condition of everything is quite lamentable !   In the showrooms which were formerly Bechstein's, there are twenty to twenty-five beautiful pianos standing in a row, like books—and one is not allowed to play on them !   Is it not mad ? We must thank God for our little bit of clear sight. I am quite well, to-day especially so . . .

LONDON, 1 *November* 1919.

Yesterday afternoon, G. B. Shaw came to tea (which he did not drink). He is now 63, very tall, and in appearance he might be a brother of old Hase, a wittier, more lively, and sharper brother. He talks too much and he cannot cloak his vanity. He began at once by shooting off one of his witty little darts. Maudi was saying that she had just come out of a nursing home. " I wonder that you are still alive," said G.B.S., " for in a hospital they throw you out into the street before you are half cured, but in a nursing home they don't let you out until you are dead." (" There is a remedy for that," I said. " You can stop paying.")

During tea he spoke chiefly about music, and evidently wished to display his knowledge. He loves Mozart with understanding. " Mozart was my master, I learnt from him how to say important things, and yet remain light and conversational." " How do you make that tally," I asked, " with your admiration for Wagner ? "

" Oh, there is room for many different things in the world. And it was necessary at that time to protest against senseless misunderstandings. But I confess, much as I love Tristan, I could wish that Tristan might die a little sooner."

" Why," I asked, " have you never *written* that ? "

But he did not know how to answer that.

Then he began to praise Elgar, and his intimate knowledge of the orchestra.

" He showed me," (said S.), " how one could make a place in Leonora, which never sounds well, acceptable." He described how Elgar corrects it, which is bad.

" Excuse me," (I said again), " but I should do so and so, as one can see it done in Mozart's compositions." (And I explained my example.)

" I had not thought of that," he said, somewhat abashed.

He does not seem to have considered *the nature* of opera. " He couldn't write a libretto, he would write just as he always wrote." I said, " It would attract me to try and write music for the scene in hell in ' Man and Superman.' "

" That would be waste of work," (said S.), " because it could bring in no profit."

" That is not what attracts me," I said.

" Oh, but you *must* reckon with that, everybody has to reckon with it. Of course, I am now a famous artist, (he added, half jokingly), I can allow myself to ride hobby horses " (or something similar).

Now that was not very nice, and still less tactful.

He talks so much and so quickly that the result is very unequal ; he often says things like an impudent youth, things which are not weighed or proved, and not wise ; and for his age, not dignified. As a musician, he is still an amateur ; of course, such an intelligent amateur is incomparably better than professionals like the conductors, C. or K. But what stamps the amateur is joy in his own discoveries and pleasure in different things which do not belong to one another . . .

His tone was almost unbearably inconsiderate (softened by humour and liveliness), but I (without agreeing with everything) spoke respectfully and quietly . . .

He is coming to Wood's concert on the 22nd. Then he will begin to know me . . .

LONDON, 2 *November* 1919.

. . . Yesterday, I wrote a detailed account of G.B.S. (In England, it is a sign of the greatest popularity to be spoken of by your initials) ; I mean about George Bernard Shaw. I omitted to say that he is a shade like the Danish Georg Brandes ; especially in his excessive talkativeness and the accompanying self-satisfaction.

He is writing—so he says—a big play, divided into four performances, with the title " Back to Methuselah," in which he demonstrates that the things of the world have become so extensive and complicated that life is too short to see them all, and manage them. For this reason, modern man develops long life and endeavours to reach the age of Methuselah—300 years. During the piece people achieve this.

The first part is in Paradise, before people knew that they had to die, and death appears on the earth for the first time.

The second part is played in the present time. Lloyd George and Asquith bring a bill into Parliament for settling the age of man at 300 years.

The third part is played some hundreds of years later, when people have, in fact, reached that age. (Meanwhile, an American had discovered a means for breathing under water, which was much advertised.)

In these new times, the situations are still more complicated and absurd.

He does not himself know yet what he will do with the fourth part. It will take place several thousand years later, and he (Shaw) has not yet been able to think out for himself what the world would be like at this stage.

He begins a piece without any plan and relies on an idea for its continuation. (Yes, one feels that too.) Oh, respected Shaw! what realism, what a machinery for making people happy!

Shaw loves the people *theoretically* (his telegraphic address is " Socialist," London). He is certainly a great egoist himself. Now he is training himself to become a second Methuselah, and plays at being a " lively youth."

It is settled that my last date in England will be the 6th December. Still one month and four days! I am not suffering, I am even enjoying some things. But yet, the time seems to me to be wrongly employed. I have got accustomed to the conditions. (They seem less big to me than they were before.) It is easier for me now, with more mature eyes, to survey everything. The masses stream past and there are new faces to be seen every day, with every step; but the existence of each one is small, wretched and uninteresting. The faces one sees in the streets look strikingly unimportant. Greatness does not lie in quantity. But here the quality is perhaps lower than elsewhere.

LONDON, 6 *November* 1919.

. . . There is still one more " Melba-Concert," in the Albert Hall, next Sunday, and then I have finished with " this kind " of concert. It is one of the saddest things imaginable to see how people have learnt absolutely nothing from this last convulsion of the world! Only this morning, I received a letter asking me if I would not play Chopin's Fantasie Impromptu at my next concert. This well-known piece, a shallow salon study, will never be criticized badly, in the way Liszt's compositions are so frequently criticized.

Robert Newman lost a son in the war, he saw him die; he

has a paralysed eye, and is white and old. He thinks, however, that it is of the utmost importance that I should play the Chappell pianos ! He called on purpose to see me about this . . .

Rosamond has hunted out a copy of Carlyle's Frederick the Great for me in Cambridge. I said jokingly, " Having got that, the aim of my journey is accomplished ! Now I can go home." . . . I have collected 50 volumes again here. Don't know how I shall bring them home . . .

LONDON, 9 *November* 1919.

To my dismay, I see it is Sunday again ! . . . Time moves quickly, and yet it crawls. I still have to stop here another four weeks exactly from to-day and that seems an endless time to me. Schopenhauer's comparison of looking the wrong way through opera glasses suits the case perfectly again.

Philipp, who at first found the Cadenzas " charming," says now : " I have looked more closely at your Cadenzas for the concerto in C. They are two little master-pieces full of spirit and subtlety. How the composer of the ' Sonatina in diem Nativitatis ' is able to write the fine embroideries of these Cadenzas, is the secret of genius." Da Motta writes about the Sonatina, " To me it is like Gothic sculpture both in its firmness of line and in its ethereal serenity."

The evening post yesterday brought your letter with the description of the concert. It amused me very much . . . Between the comfortable-going Swiss school of music and some uncomfortable " Futurists " of this country, lies the golden throne of what is genuine, beautiful, and exalted . . .

The piano pieces by X and XX, which are beginning to be popular here, are " beautiful " too. They have neither imagination, nor feeling, nor form, it is only an attempt to produce sound, but that is distressing. It surely cannot be that I have remained stationary ! These pieces are demonstrably bad. (I should like to put this down to the war, which seems to have brought everything to stagnation or intoxication.) Mr. G. has written a piece, in A major for the right hand and A flat major for the left hand. Those are old jokes that we used to make at Kämps Hotel after the " *coffee with avec* " ! This piece is quite a commonplace (and boring) waltz, merely with the harmonies displaced . . .

I do not want to end this letter with dissonances, but make it ring with the pure union of our hearts . . .

LONDON, 10 *November* 1919.

The concert yesterday was rather more respectable than those in the provinces. The Albert Hall was full ! One must first imagine between eight and ten thousand people, and then think what the quality of such a mass can be, on a Sunday . . . The artists' room was full of Australians. Melba, her accompanist, Clutsam and his wife. These Australians are different from Americans. They have not the flagrant self-consciousness and do not " advertise " their country as their older cousins do . . .

I made myself a little " fine " for the concert and Maudi was charmed ; she thought I looked as I did twenty years ago . . . I play now with great deliberation, without effort and without any nervousness. So it gives me pleasure. I am looking forward a little to the 22nd with Wood. I have helped the drunken programme on to its legs a bit ; everything that concerns me is now to be played in the *first part*, before the interval. We shall see how that works. I shall conduct my own compositions . . . I am quite well, although the day looks like " Autumn multiplied by London " . . .

LONDON, 10 *November* 1919.

I have just had two charming experiences ; I have made the acquaintance of one of Mozart's smaller concertos (F major) that begins playfully and becomes more and more complicated ; everything gracious and lively : and I have received a parcel by post, containing Frederick II, by Carlyle ; a present from Rosamond . . .

Tak-tak-tak goes on under my window. Those are the blind, tapping with their sticks on the railings in order to find their way . . .

LONDON, 13 *November* 1919.

Reproaches are useless in this case and it is of no help to see the matter clearly. The case is as follows : As soon as I make the aim of anything a *profitable* one, from the moment it begins to be a practical advantage to do it, something in me begins to bleed, a kind of disablement overtakes me, and it is only with pain and effort that I can carry through what otherwise I could achieve easily, happily, and better. (You know that I *can* be industrious and energetic.) A similar feeling comes over me when I see others behaving and thinking in a purely utilitarian manner in matters connected with art (and outside art too); a nausea against it sets in. If I play only because of the fee, I always play badly, worse than the average pianist. Besides this, I am always *ashamed* whilst I am playing and afterwards too, and that is distressing . . . I think there is a similar vein in Benni, which has become excessively potent . . . He is a purely distilled anti-utilitarian and for this side of him I have extraordinary sympathy; it is the perfection of what I am myself. But unfortunately he has only this one side, for the æsthetically egoistic energy, the merciless development of his own talents, which is what should be in the other side of the scales, is hardly present at all. Or perhaps he has an instinctive philosophy which tells him that even the best and most beautiful things are illusory and of no purpose.

Fundamentally this is true of them as it is of fame and money. Isn't Giotto beautiful and likeable just *for himself* and not because he wins a prize or wears an expensive collar or is shown as a pedigree dog at dog shows? This is the only way in which one should value people, too, but exactly the contrary happens; and even the people who know better are forced to adjust themselves to this wrong valuation, if they are afraid of not being rightly esteemed or of being considered inferior. So we only need money, because we are required by others, who cannot see our true value, to prove it by means of money. And fame, about which, unfortunately, the artist is more sensitive, plays a similar part in the world, for the lesser artists have put it up on a false pedestal.

I read this simple, strong definition of genius in Carlyle. " A man of genius (Frederick II), that is, a man of originality and veracity: capable of seeing with his eyes and incapable of not believing what he sees."

What a letter! Where have I got to! Enough ruminating!

Yesterday, I had the pleasure of seeing a charming young Indian woman. Her nose is absolutely straight, the underlip a thought projecting, the dull complexion quite smooth, and besides that, eyes like deep black velvet. (The whole a little under life-size.)  When one sees a living person like that, one begins to understand Indian miniatures . . .

LONDON, 14 November 1919.

· There are some things to tell you about again.  (After all, that is the point of one's being in London.)  Yesterday evening for the first time, I saw the inside of *Covent Garden.*  I thought it lovely.  (Obviously made from an Italian model, or perhaps built by an Italian.)  It is well proportioned, not so enormous as I feared, but with comfortable proportions.  Milner had got a seat for me in my favourite place, immediately behind the conductor ;  so that I was in contact with the orchestra, (who probably knew me), and I kept up my little correspondence with the players, as I used to in Zürich.   I heard and saw Verdi's " Otello," with the " demoniacal " Milner ;  also a solid, excellent tenor (who resembled the late violinist, Halir) ;  some scenery, partly from the Russian ballet, and partly from Liberty's shop ;  a good orchestra, and rather a vain young conductor, who neither felt nor understood the work.   An unequal composition and it brought back my first impressions of it . . .[1]

Much of it is too long and not quick enough compared with the concise and thrilling moments of genius which flash like lightning in between . . .   The subject, according to my feeling, is thoroughly opposed to music, which in the coarse climaxes becomes brutal noise . . .

The first of my three rehearsals took place to-day.  A warm reception by the Queen's Hall orchestra.  Applause at the end of the rehearsal.  Sir Henry Wood was very kind ;  he said, " A wonderful impression and completely original.  We will play the pieces in Manchester too."  That takes place on November 29th.

It was a pleasant morning ;  there was a light fog, but it was dry.  As I went into the hall, I heard sounds of Berlioz' " Queen Mab."  This piece is a little miracle . . .

LONDON, 15 November 1919.

. . . The work for the gramophone records begins on Monday. That is also one of the things that I am half-hearted about ;  the

---

[1] In the year 1887, Busoni, at that time in Leipzig, wrote a review of the opera, from the piano score.

285

result of this discord in me about business things is that they only half come off. I won't quite spoil the business and I won't quite lie—so it is impossible for anything to succeed. (I know that I have faults ; I am continually working to improve them.) I took a quiet day again to-day, thinking quietly about many things . . . These kind of days, in their, way, are often quite productive.

LONDON, 17 *November* 1919.
. . . Dent paid us a visit yesterday. He had this little show, the same evening, to which he invited me and to which I went. Far in the south-west, in the evening, Sunday, and raining. A small theatre—people smoked pipes. The harpsichord player, a lady of about 65, played on a pretty old instrument like a little witch. The scenery and costumes quite in the style of Hogarth. One could almost think one was looking at one of his etchings.

The tone of Dent's speech suspiciously under the influence of B. Shaw. " He (Pergolesi) died of consumption, of course not before he had written a Stabat Mater, which church music is written in the style of a comic opera." (When will people understand that music is only " music " and that the idea of " church," " theatre " and so on only comes through the words !)

On the whole, though, quite an interesting little experience ; getting home was complicated (Underground—on foot—by taxi). It was not unromantic, the remote quarter, London by night and in the rain ! Anywhere else it would *only* have been uncomfortable, here there was something else beside . . .

Imagine, dear Gerda, I have an almost painful longing for Giotto ; he would have had such a good time here and I should have had him with me . . .

LONDON, 18 *November* 1919.
. . . Please read through the Manchester programme ! It would not be passed even in the Café des Banques. Look at the rubbish from Milan too ! Toscanini as a candidate for the election ! It is high time that I began my political career. To-day I had my first sitting for the gramophone records. This too : a via crucis. Senseless. There is no hope of anything better ! Why strive ? Because one cannot do otherwise. Such a man is

Your loving Husband.

LONDON, 20 *November* 1919.

. . . My suffering over the toil of making gramophone records came to an end yesterday, after playing for 3½ hours ! I feel rather battered to-day, but it is over. Since the first day, I have been as depressed as if I were expecting to have an operation. To do it is stupid and a strain. Here is an example of what happens. They wanted the Faust waltz (which lasts a good ten minutes) *but it was only to take four minutes* ! That meant quickly cutting, patching and improvising, so that there should still be some sense left in it ; watching the pedal (because it sounds bad) ; thinking of certain notes which had to be stronger or weaker in order to please this devilish machine : not letting oneself go for fear of inaccuracies and being conscious the whole time that every note was going to be there for eternity ; how can there be any question of inspiration, freedom, swing, or poetry ? Enough that yesterday for 9 pieces of 4 minutes each (half an hour in all) I worked for three and a half hours ! Two of these pieces I played four or five times. Having to think so quickly at the same time was a severe effort. In the end, I felt the effects in my arms ; after that, I had to sit for a photograph, and sign the discs.—At last it was finished ! . . .


LONDON, 23 *November* 1919.

Yesterday (most of my letters begin with " yesterday ") every-thing went well. The people with understanding were delighted with the Mozart Concerto, and I was too, and both my com-positions [1] were excellently played and there were three recalls. I was pleased with my good music, in which there are no dead places, and no patches. The only paper I have read to-day passes over it lightly and without any understanding ; as they do over the Cadenzas too, which " leap over quite a hundred years " because they know that I wrote them. You often say that I do very little for my own things. I assure you I really regret having done what little I have done. However, we will wait for all the opinions. It made a great impression on all my intimate friends (Dent included). Wood was enthusiastic, or behaved as if he were ; said to Maudi, " He is now *so* great," and lifted his arms . . .

Delius has come back from Frankfurt, full of enthusiasm. He

[1] Sarabande and Cortège from " Dr. Faust."

287

is the first to bring good news from Germany. His " Niels
Lyhne " was performed there at great expense and with much
care . . . It was a relief to hear something good about Germany
for once . . .

It is a very sympathetic trait in A. to wish for money *in order
to give it away*. The fault lies with those who wish to make
money for the sake of money, in order to make more money out
of it—not to mention those who make a standard out of it for
measuring the *value of people*. And to think that really—it does
not exist ! For wealth and possession (also only an idea) are
only the *soil* and *work*. But no " essay " to-day . . .
I thoroughly dislike the business-like ways of S. Between the
quiet artist and the obvious charlatan stands the *career-maker*
the commonest type. But why in our " practical " times do
we not have the courage to go a step further and make undis-
guised use of advertisement ? That would be a sensible pro-
position. One would read in the tram, for instance," N.N.'s
songs are the most beautiful " or " A song by N.N. is recom-
mended in every musical family before going to bed " . . . or
" No compositions are more original and startling than mine ;
Wassili Dreksky provides you with an exciting quarter of an
hour " . . .
Have just read " The Times." It has made me sad. Therefore I shall not write any more and I embrace you as my only
friend . . .

Yours and Andreae's impressions of Stravinsky are alike. He
no longer excites interest except in so far as he gives the thoughtless
public and the critics without any judgment a *false* picture of what
should be progressive in music. What is new in music will be
judged by this example. I have suffered from it again here.
The " Daily Telegraph " was more sensible than the other papers
and took the trouble to " listen." (" They hear what they
believe and do not believe what they hear.") An interesting
piece is boring, a boring one is interesting, according to the

attitude they have chosen to adopt beforehand in relation to what they will hear and what they wish to hear . . .

You will know from my letter yesterday what I feel about my own " Propaganda." Nevertheless, one could think over *Geneva*. (Really, I have a horror of it.)

I met Delius and his wife in the street yesterday. At his wish, we arranged to meet for dinner. As he was going, he turned round again, as if he had forgotten some form of politeness. " I like the Sarabande best," he said in a consoling voice. I turned my back on him. And in the taxi, I let myself go : I was obliged to cry.

To-day, I am better . . .

London makes much less impression on me this time, I see only individual and commonplace things and I no longer look upon a " mass " of anything as a mysterious power—as I used to feel when I was young.

But there is always something remarkable to see in London. Yesterday, in the middle of big bus traffic, down the middle of Shaftesbury Avenue, trotted my dear, heaven-sent donkey,[1] peaceful and innocent. All the cars had to swerve past him, for he went more slowly than they did. That went to my stupid heart . . .

Kaikhusru Sorabji turns out to be an Indian, quite young. I gave him a letter of introduction for which he asked me. A fine, unusual person, in spite of his ugly music. A primeval forest with many weeds and briars, but strange and voluptuous . . .

LONDON, 28 *November* 1919.

I received a letter from B. Shaw this morning. I should think it would be impossible for him to express himself more warmly and it rejoiced me to get it. What a good sentence this is, and how true : " But you should compose under an assumed name. It is incredible that one man could do more than one thing well ; and when I heard you play, I said, ' It is impossible that he should compose : there is not room enough in a single life for more than one supreme excellence.' You seem to be a virtuoso of the first order in handling instruments : in fact, your danger is an excessive sensitiveness to shades of tone and delicacies of harmonies " . . .

[1] There is a donkey in Busoni's Arlecchino.

Your letter to-day was really wonderful, so uplifting and strengthening, I cannot thank you enough for it !

Meanwhile some good reviews have appeared. After Shaw's letter there was a beautiful article by Dent in the " Athenæum," " Busoni as a Composer," and it makes me realize that, at the bottom, Dent loves me very much. I took the whole thing a little too much to heart this time ; it was not exactly *this* thing, but the well-known " drops " which overflowed. As a physical result of this, I had pimples all over my body ; a nervous outbreak, accompanied by a little fever . . .

Lamond has proved himself to be a very dear friend who always comes to hear me and expresses himself very warmly. I am very tired to-day (but not unwell) and a little exhausted in my head . . .

LONDON, 3 *December* 1919.

Everything looked better to-day, when I woke from a wonderful sleep—unbroken until broad daylight. And now (about 12), your dear letter has come . . .

I rejoice with all my heart to hear that M. Klinger is still alive.[1] A pity he mixed himself up with music so much and only made " discoveries " honestly and comfortably within the limits of his country and his epoch. He wanted to break his chains, and only clanked about with them.

Beethoven as Zeus, with a background of pre-Raphaelite heads of angels, and the Crucifixion—what a confused summary of everything that Germany honoured with so much gravity from 1875–95 (with all respect for the seriousness of the idea and the artistic effort). But I am glad that he is living. Perhaps he will see and admit to many other things now . . .

War and money—money and war—God the Father need not have planted the tree of knowledge in Paradise for that. It is called in Italian *l'albero del bene e del male*, which almost looks as if the first men had the *choice* between good and evil—and God washed his hands in the oceans and said, It is not my fault —which happened again with his son and Pilate. Revenge ! Whereupon M. Klinger stirs the broth with—Beethoven . . .

. . . Not only concert programmes, but everything else too has gone downhill here. They fear competition from Germany,

[1] His death had been reported.

and—don't work ! Not on Saturday or Sunday, not on Thursday afternoon ; and work is over at six o'clock every day. The licensing hours have been very restricted, 12–2, 6–10, because. the people who came back from the war did nothing but drink all day. That, of course, brings disorder, poverty and crime in its train. About midnight London was a drunken Carnival. Manners are looser (in the wrong sense) and the novelists write openly about questions of sex. Literature is perhaps in a worse state than anything. What a desert ! I received Shaw's last volume yesterday, which I have not read yet.

Now I must prepare for the journey. My passport is already in order, on Tuesday, perhaps, I shall start for Paris, where I shall remain for as short a time as possible.

And then, dear Gerda, how beautiful it will be ! . . .

LONDON, 7 December 1919.

. . . It is Sunday morning once more, a soft winter sunshine over the Park, a fire in the grate and—peace. The latter, in me, is relative only, and urges me to work, after three wasted months . . .

I am very tired to-day. The programme looked more harmless on paper than it proved to be in performance. The standard of the recital was as high as that of the first one ; quite successful and perfect, the hall sold out, the best kind of audience that it is possible to get here. It was again something which had my entire interest and consequently I have expended very much strength both mentally and physically.

When I had changed (what heat and perspiration !) I held a *petite cour* in the artists' room, and finally there was a small intimate dinner at Dorothy's (I now like her very much) with Sybil and Maudi . . .

If we draw up the net result of my visit, there have been only three important occasions, the London ones, and Mr. Powell has had nothing to do with them, for I arranged them myself. Whereas everything which Mr. Powell thought out, undertook and carried through, was done tradesman fashion, and was unworthy, painful and even harmful. Counting the records for the Gramophone Company, I have made 15 appearances.

The best things yesterday were the Waldstein Sonata, and the fourth Chopin Ballade. In that atmosphere they sound extremely

serious pieces and they seemed monumental. The " Caprice
über die Abreise " was a small gem in the programme. Many
people came from outside London, between 200 and 300 people
had to be turned away because there were no seats for them. The
Hall Manager was proud. " It is a record," he said. It is
eighteen years since the hall was opened by me, and many of the
virtuosi, whose portraits hang on the walls in the artists' room,
are no longer alive. Others, such as Galston and Ysaye, are in
the shade now. (Ysaye's faithful friend, Ortmans, said, " He
can play no more.")

It is not easy to keep one's position. Above all, the people
always want to be aroused and impressed afresh and events are
constantly taking place which cause everything to be forgotten
again. New powers and new movements arise and in order to
make a fresh impression one has to overcome distaste and un-
willingness in oneself. This is easier for me now, thank God,
but it is still not quite effortless and good strength is valuable, and
should be used only for good things.

That is why I think that this will be the *last* " Tour " of this
type . . .

LONDON, 9 *December* 1919.
This 44th letter will be my last one from England before I
leave. I have settled to go the day after to-morrow (Thursday
the 11th). This time I can go by the short route to Paris (Folke-
stone–Boulogne). The recital made quite a stir. On Sunday
many people called : Lamond, Dent, Major Trevor (" Daily
Express " critic), a charming and understanding man. Lamond
was extraordinarily kind and friendly, even affectionate. I was
very touched by it.

Milner sang some of Arlecchino . . . It was pleasant at
breakfast this morning to receive a few lines from Benni : the
little letter was charming ; I believe we can rejoice very much
indeed over our boys ; they are fine persons . . .

It rains engagements here . . .

LONDON, 10 *December* 1919.
The 45th after all ; because I must tell you that I experienced
the great pleasure yesterday of receiving a quite unexpected

letter from—Galsworthy! I do not know him, but (as you know) I have a very high esteem for him.

My playing, he writes, " is a lesson in the long task, which confronts us all, of expressing the utmost of emotion in forms perfect and *controlled*—the only indestructible art. One goes to one's work refreshed and inspirited." I was told that Galsworthy went to Spain yesterday morning. That he wanted to write a letter to me the evening before he started makes me very happy . . .

# 1920

LUGANO, 31 *January* 1920.

. . . Arriving in Lugano gave me the impression of a dream and that encouraged me to remain here for some days. My room in the hotel overlooks a terrace and all the rooms in my row lead out on to it. Old black trees, moonlight, bubbling springs below, and behind that, the lake : it was (as I said) like the 500½th night.

Now, of course, with my damned conscientiousness, I am thinking that I really ought to go to Milan this evening. But it wouldn't be very much good, because I should not be in a very fresh condition to try the piano . . .

I am well known here, more so than I expected ! Even at the station I was greeted *by name*, and the same thing happened here in the Hotel.

In the small Gasthof Croce Rossa in Chiasso I sat at the same table with Italians, evidently men of the world, who had a young Swedish woman with them whom they were showing round ; and a gentleman from Padua. They had all been in Germany and Austria lately ; were of the opinion that things did not look well. But they all thought that Germany would soon come up again . . .

Best birthday wishes to Lello ! I love him dearly . . . Wish him a beautiful day and numberless ones, just as beautiful, to follow.

I feel I have come to a very good understanding with Benni. He has joined on again, and with his excellent thinking powers he will develop quickly now . . .

I embrace you all with my whole heart . . .

*(Addressed to Paris)*

ZÜRICH, 10 *June* 1920.

. . . I am at last on the track of the shape my Mephistopheles must take ; for even a devil must have a shape. Couldn't practise. Was in a nervous state because of your going away . . .

I made every effort to hide my disquietude from you ; in the end I felt my brain galloping ; perhaps the journey will be good for that . . .

*(Addressed to Paris)*

LONDON, 5 *July* 1920.

. . . Your card this morning rejoiced me ; now you are on the go and are roaming through Paris. May God preserve your freshness. Discuss things a little with Philipp. It is so hard for me to say yes, and still harder to say no. The young man Walton (who was at the Spanish Restaurant) sent me some manuscript music. He has a little gift for counterpoint. In other respects, they all write according to a formula : notes, notes, notes, all "hither and yon", without imagination or feeling. Taste in connection with the conception of *beauty* is certainly changeable. Wagner's music, for instance, is often "beautiful" ; he knew very well that this too belongs to the craft. Talent is really at the root of the matter and is the deciding factor.

Dear Gerda, be happy ; think a little too, about

Your loving FERRUCCIO.

*(Addressed to Paris)*

LONDON, 8 *July* 1920.

. . . These days have been very " enervating " and I feel that I must stop doing this kind of work as soon as possible. I have already given it two weeks longer than I calculated. Sybil and Dent got the Faust.[1] Sybil was " away " ; Dent used the word " meraviglioso." (I believe for the first time.) I am glad about both the successes . . . Everything else (there is

---

[1] The libretto.

not much) I will tell you when we meet. I feel so *liberated* to-day. (What a pity one can't " dawdle " round for a bit.) . . .

(*Addressed to Zürich*)
BERLIN, 11 *September* 1920.
I have been scarcely two hours in Berlin and must write to you without delay . . .
It was a pleasure to arrive at the German frontier and find the Customs officials friendly and human . . .
It is touching to see how bashfully proud the South Germans are about " having everything." The cultivation of the country in Swabia looked splendid. Compared with the Swiss towns, Stuttgart made an imposing and fantastic effect seen from above. One sees the town from above first of all and then one travels downwards in a long spiral, so that the town alternately disappears and comes into sight again, nearer each time. There was confusion at the station! The sleeping-car arrangements were normal and the train arrived punctually. I have only seen Berlin between 8–9 in the morning as yet, in beautiful weather . . . The porter at our house welcomed me like a father. The flat is astonishingly well kept and looks so rich and beautiful . . .
I must collect myself a little . . .

*Afternoon.*
There is a strange contrast between the modest, often poor clothing one sees, and the high prices which are taken as a matter of course . . . On the whole, I am still not able to judge . . .
This letter is quite disjointed, at which you will not be surprised ; for I am not quite clear, and a little excited. But the flat is beautiful. Everything is radiant. A little beaming, too, is
Your F.

(*Addressed to Zürich*)
BERLIN, 12 *September* 1920.
I sit in my library—" la cité des livres," says A. France—where every book (as far as I can see) is in its place ; paper, ink, pen and everything for writing is all ready ! I was timid about

entering this room, and only decided to do so this morning.[1] It is Sunday and it is raining, so I shall remain comfortably at home.

. . . Here, inside it is glorious. Unfortunately, outside it is not so. It is once more a fight to keep one's standard high. After America and Zürich—now Berlin. But I can say nothing definite to-day. You will see how things are. If this does not do, we must make another choice. But I am still convinced that it will have to be tried. We must take over the house in order to decide what is best ; in order to *know* everything . . .

I think I shall do much work. I shall concentrate. I miss Giotto quite lamentably. Yes, I am looking forward to work, even to experimenting at the piano again.

The first night was passable . . .

Buddha looks as if he were made of flesh and blood, and as if he might move. I often think he does move. And that is all for to-day. I will write again to-morrow . . .

Yesterday, I met Hans Herrmann (Berlin king of lieder singing). " Well, Busoni, it is good to meet you. I want you to sign a fan for a lady." Is such a thing possible ? ! !


(*Addressed to Zürich*)

BERLIN, 14 *September* 1920.

. . . Everybody was very cordial, altogether the tone in Berlin is human and pleasant. I have scarcely been out of the house. (I have so much to occupy me and take pleasure in it) . . . It is like a dream to think this is already the fourth day since I came here.

I await your arrival with impatience. Your short but very dear letter made my heart throb, I was so rejoiced to get it. Thank you. I will write more to-morrow. I kiss you three dear people, you, Benni and Lello . . .


(*Addressed to Zürich*)

BERLIN, 16 *September* 1920.

To-day—at last—I have finished the Toccata, really finished it, with date and signature . . .

[1] Busoni had anxiously guarded the key of his library for more than five years, and always carried it with him.

I feel I could work if they would only leave me in peace! At home it is, of course, really inspiring . . . Letters are raining in.

After finishing the Toccata I am feeling rather like a holiday, and also tired . . .

*(Addressed to Zürich)*

BERLIN, 19 *September* 1920.

It is already the second Sunday!

To-day, at my invitation, the master-bookbinder, Schmid, came. I thought I would establish a little atmosphere in my library.

I have been busy; am very contented with the Toccata; to-day, for a " joke," I wrote a—Tanzwalzer . . .

And when are you coming? I am waiting impatiently for you. Poor Gerda, who knows how tired you are! You ought really to enjoy a holiday now in Switzerland. Please, do just what you like best. I can get on here quite well for the present, although I wish for you. I kiss you lovingly and gratefully . . .

*(Addressed to Zürich)*

BERLIN, 21 *September* 1920.

. . . I am working pleasantly, have " re-Toccata-ed " the Toccata and am scoring the Tanzwalzer . . .

. . . To-day the X's came. Have I gone forward, or have they gone back? I try to keep my door barred, but something always trickles through. I am in a strange situation, but as " officially " I am still incognito, I cannot know how it will all develop . . .

These weeks have been the hardest of my life, on the whole; I am surprised that I have preserved quite a lot of harmony and am glad to be able to tell you this. I rest in my own way, am occupied in my library and go out in the streets a little in the later afternoon . . . I have drawn up the concert plan with piano recitals and three orchestral concerts of my own compositions. I should not like more for the present . . . Milner's programme is *all right*. I once made a good transcription of

the " An den Wassern zu Babel " for Clark, which I have mislaid
or lost . . .

I kiss you, and should like you to enjoy yourself a little longer
there still . . . I also had a delightful card from Jarnach and
friends . . .


(*Addressed to Zürich*)

BERLIN, 24 *September* 1920.

My beloved Gerda, I do not know if this letter will reach you.
But I cannot leave you without news, in case you might still
be in Zürich. It is true I have nothing important to report.
Have done more to the scoring of the Tanzwalzer ; I settled
the composition concerts and reviewed the so-called *Busoni
Number* of the " Anbruch." I should like it to be a good issue.
The prospect seems very hopeful at present. Otherwise, I
shut myself in and live for myself. It is very calming and
attractive . . .

Many things here are stunted, but not unbearably so ; and
one can watch them improving . . .

I am so glad about you. Hope for a letter to-morrow . . .


LONDON, 6 *October* 1920.

I did not see much of Edinburgh this time, because the concert
was in the middle of the day. I was only able to go for a walk
at seven in the evening and then I walked for two hours (how
thankful I was for the chance of doing it). It was Saturday, the
shops were closed and the principal streets were thronged with
the " populace." The " plebs " in Edinburgh and Glasgow
belong to the lowest and rawest of their kind that I have ever
seen. By comparison, the West American is something " genteel." On Saturday evening they are let loose and make a
vicious tumult . . .

The " Todtentanz " by Strindberg is a strange, almost demoniacal piece. At the first glance it seems to be the description
of a bad marriage : but afterwards one sees that the whole
thing turns round the character of the man. That the woman
who is with him most frequently and for the longest time should
come in for the strongest reactions is natural, but yet it is not

principally the story of a marriage . . . The play appealed to me strongly and is fearfully suggestive ; it gets one down (as they say). All the same, I do not count it a work of art, and am not sure whether it was right to choose the dramatic form. And on the other hand, the rôle of the " Captain " makes one want to become an actor at once in order to play the part. I can say nothing about the language (the translation is not very good) but in any case it is not poetical ; it keeps the technique of naturalness and Ibsen ; that is to say, everyday things are said in an everyday form. Only here and there it is lighted up by a philosophical thought, a sentence of real experience, an aphorism . . . An individual technique, all the same. The laconic style and the tempo are often full of virtuosity and effect. Only what is absolutely necessary is said, but it hits the nail on the head.

From Strindberg to Friend Backhaus is a leap, but quite a wholesome one.

Here is a tale he related : Rubinstein had advertised a *Beethoven recital* and a *Chopin recital* in Liverpool. The Beethoven recital was *empty* and Rubinstein went off without waiting for the second recital. (" I will not play again in this village.")

When Backhaus had got as far as this with the story, he shook his head in a dissatisfied way and remarked, " I believe that was a mistake." " What do you mean ? " I asked, extremely amused and a little nonplussed. " The Chopin recital was sold out," he concluded in a resigned voice.

It is Sunday morning, rather wintry. I have just come back from Edinburgh ; have a day's rest, which I need badly.

The week was as follows :

Monday, arrived.

Tuesday, 5 hours to Leeds, evening concert, 6 hours' night journey back again.

Wednesday, arrived 6 a.m. Worked.

Thursday, $3\frac{1}{2}$ hours to Cheltenham, $3\frac{1}{2}$ hours back, and in between, a concert.

Friday, $4\frac{1}{2}$ hours to Liverpool, rehearsal with Kreisler, concert ; at night to Glasgow.

Saturday, from Glasgow to Edinburgh, concert ; at night, back to London—arrived

Sunday, *To-day*, 6th October, *free*.

My own recitals were sold out, the concerts with Kreisler less good. Kreisler plays very well, very carefully, has some little violin specialities. Is a dear fellow at heart, and his manner with me is admirable. We got on very well together this time . . .

# 1 9 2 1

HAMBURG, 15 *January* 1921.

It was a magical, sunny winter morning when I woke up to-day. As a " precaution," Brecher was ready by nine o'clock. The orchestra is morally and artistically in ruins . . .

I have made the painful discovery that nobody *loves* and *feels* music. Some practise it as a trade, some as time-beaters, and some from vanity. (I was quite angry at the rehearsal. Of course, the people in the audience thought I was behaving like a " star," although they did not listen to my playing.) After all, the " time-beaters " are the ones most worthy of respect, even if they are as far away from music as the others . . .

I arrived yesterday at midnight. The journey was cold . . .

I think of you as the only woman . . .


(*Addressed to Grosz-Gmain bei Salzburg*)

BERLIN, 20 *July* 1921.

. . . The scoring goes on by itself ; it pulls me along, instead of my leading it—like Giotto ! (I am working at this scene with the greatest pleasure and it promises to be some of my best work) . . .


(*Addressed to Grosz-Gmain*)

BERLIN, 23 *July* 1921.

This very moment I have finished scoring the students' scene ; it is, perhaps, technically the most perfect piece I have done in an opera. (At the same time very lively.)

. . . So far, I have had only a card from you and—in spite of your not being here—the week is suddenly at an end (to-day is Saturday) . . .

My mind is in the best state possible, thank God, touch wood, and I am looking forward to my next assault on the libretto . . .

(*Addressed to Grosz-Gmain*)

BERLIN, 30 *July* 1921.

. . . I rejoice over the good impression you have of Salzburg, which unfortunately I do not know ; although they stuffed me enough with the " beauties of Austria " in the " lovely days of Youth." That was the time when many illustrated luxury editions were published and they appeared in numbers " in order to make it possible even for the less well-to-do to possess the treasury." I must tell you about Frau B. sending me a volume like this to look at. It was a volume of Goethe's dramas ; Faust is made to look like Dr. Wilhelm Kienzl, always sitting in old German wine shops, on " Luther chairs," with bottle-glass window panes as a background. I returned the volume with thanks, with the remark that it was not according to my taste . . .

The young men [1] come on Mondays and Thursdays, but I can send them away after an hour or an hour and a half. I work regularly and have got on a good deal ; in thought still more than on paper, but on paper too it is already well advanced.

I am expecting you with impatience . . .

[1] His composition pupils.

303

# 1 9 2 2

LONDON, 20 *January* 1922.

On the assumption that the letter will arrive before your departure I write to announce my safe landing after a normal crossing. The passport officials were charming. " How long will you stay *this* time in England, Mr. Busoni ? Are you going to play soon ? " And the customs officials chalked my things without asking any questions. Two Dutchmen who travelled with me took me for a diplomat travelling to England on a mission for the Government. The first "half" of genuine Heidsieck in the Dutch restaurant car was quite a little experience. When he was asked if he would take German money, the waiter said, Yes, and he reckoned up 650 marks for the half bottle. " And how much do you reckon it to be in English money ? " He said, " Thirteen shillings." So I paid him in English money, because optically and acoustically it gives one an easier conscience. One is still so dependent on " numbers." I have *thought* of nothing the whole day, this I consider is an impossible condition to be in. And how boring it is ! ! . . . Unfortunately, nobody met me at the station. And now I am looking forward to your arrival . . .

(*Addressed to Paris*)

LONDON, 20 *February* 1922.

A deaf and dumb emptiness seems to surround me since you left the hotel. I send these lines hurrying after you to keep us in touch. It is terrifying to feel what a stranger one always remains in this country ; how the people here automatically accept everything without giving anything in exchange, except in their own " circle."

The two or three who are unselfishly loyal cannot alter this national feature.—What power there is in this defensive attitude. But it breaks in time, and the time has begun. India and Ireland are rising, and inside the island the ugly demon of industrial unrest is raising its head. It was these clever fools themselves who invented the " strike " !

I am longing for my workroom (and for a city of refuge on the Mediterranean). I have a lot of work to do in Paris . . .


(*Addressed to Paris*)

LONDON, 21 *February* 1922.

Yesterday evening I ordered a fire to be lighted at eight o'clock this morning and spent the morning in front of the fireplace at my " Workroom " [1] as I usually do when I am alone . . . Prince Fürstenburg has again invited me to take part in the next music festival.

Yesterday, I wrote a good letter about Berlioz to Ernest Newman ; last Sunday he called him " an *opera composer manqué.*" (But with regard to Berlioz, the French have much on their conscience.)

I must be here next Monday, in order to get this absurd gramophone business out of my life ! . . .


(*Addressed to Paris*)

MANCHESTER, 24 *February* 1922.

. . . I shall probably come to Paris on the 1st March—a day earlier, if I can. To-morrow, Saturday, I shall hear Egon's recital in London ; then I must pack the books which he is taking with him.

Sunday, prepare gramophone programme.

Monday, " Recording."

Therefore, I think I must draw a breath on Tuesday.

Wednesday is the 1st March.

I don't see clearly how I can have the five programmes ready for Paris. My own compositions I hardly know at all yet.

Yesterday Wagner's " Faust " Overture was played. Almost everything that he did later is in it : Holländer, Tristan, Parsifal.

---

[1] Consisting of " table " and chair. Busoni made the table himself by placing his little suitcase on a chair. That is how he worked in hotels.

F.B.                                     305                                     U

But stiff, ungifted and even badly scored ! And why is Wagner's composition called " Faust " ? Puzzle.

I have still to thank you for your dear letter. I had already discovered the grey dress next to the two thermos flasks. It was touching to look at this forsaken still-life . . .

HAMBURG, 25 *March* 1922.

This sheet of paper should lie on the breakfast table on Monday as a morning greeting . . .

Werner Wolff is a very respectable musician and conductor who manages everything creditably, and with taste. The Sarabande and Cortège were better played here to-day than in Paris ; in spite of the humbler orchestra. Fiat justitia.

The pieces again quite pleased me. This gives me still more courage to complete the work . . .

The town from outside looks well ordered and busy. It made a grand picture as we came into it. But in the evening, directly after the shops close, everything is dark and empty . . . Hamburg really is quite separate from the realm of Germany, almost like an island. " A pocket edition of England."

HAMBURG, 26 *March* 1922.

That was really dear of you to write, and what you write is correct. I played very well at the rehearsal yesterday, in spite of not having touched the piano in between. The Hall was sold out, the audience very warm (about my compositions too) ; Pfohl was very pleased.

The performances were not quite so good as at the first rehearsal ; for that reason it will go better again to-morrow. All kinds of proposals were raining in to the artists' room. Next season with Pollack ; if possible, even a recital this April ; Rahter's successor wanted to order a " suite " ; and finally, a man from New York was there, with big plans. Piano-playing pleases me better again ; I should still like to acquire yet another side to it ; and I almost think that I shall do it ! . . .

# 1 9 2 3

BERLIN, 28 *July* 1923.

. . . In the new number of the Anbruch, Bekker passes over entirely to the side of youth. . . . Is he afraid of getting old ? But it is inconsistent that he should admit Stravinsky's " Soldier " and not pay any attention at all to the idea of " oneness " in music . . .

Ask Jarnach some time what he thinks of Bekker's case. Greet him, and remember me to the Prince and Princess, Burkard, and other friends.

I hope so much that you will not like it less there than you did the first time.

A little diversion, and surroundings other than you are accustomed to, were very necessary for you. For that reason, I wish you as much pleasure as possible, embrace you warmly and expect you again with a peal of bells.

Your FERRUCCIO.

# INDEX

Liszt, Franz, 23, 24, 25, 27, 28, 33, 34, 39, 41, 47, 51, 52, 60, 66, 71, 74, 75, 76, 100, 111, 115, 116, 117, 118–120, 122, 123, 126, 128, 129, 139, 145, 151, 166, 170, 178, 183, 184, 186, 196, 200, 209, 214, 221, 227, 229, 233, 239, 262, 265, 272, 276, 281, 287
Lloyd George, David, 280
Lochbrunner, Ernest (pianist in Zürich), 39, 262
Loeffler, Charles Martin (composer in Boston), 72
Loewe, Ferdinand (conductor in Vienna), 261
Lori, see Schrotzberg
Louis XI, King of France, 90
Louis XIV, King of France, 90

Machiavelli, Niccolò, 139, 149, 187
Mälzel, Johann Nepomuk, 40
Maeterlinck, Maurice, 51
Mahler, Gustav, 31, 67, 68, 155, 161, 162, 167, 182, 183, 194, 217
Mahler, Frau Alma, 162
Mannstädt, Franz (conductor), 21
Marconi, Gulielmo, 73, 219, 243
Marga, see Weigert
Margherita, Queen of Italy, 239
Marinetti, Filippo Tommaso (author and founder of the " Futurists "), 223
Marteau, Henri, 41
Mascagni, Pietro, 133, 177
Massenet, Jules, 171
Matesdorf, Frau Clarita, 31, 85
Matesdorf, Dorothy, 291
Matesdorf, Sybil, 291, 295
Matesdorf, Theodor (merchant in London), 32, 33
Maudi, see Allan
Mayer, Max (pianist in Manchester), 34
Mazzacorati (Italian nobility), 238
Melba, Nellie [ = Helen Porter Mitchell] (soprano), 32, 209, 262, 271, 274, 281, 283
Mendelssohn Bartholdy, Felix, 74, 116, 231
Mengelberg, Willem, 19, 43, 44, 87
Mercadante, Saverio, 179
Mereschkowsky, Dmitri, 137, 138, 240
Messel, Alfred (architect), 149

Meurice (hotel in Paris), 206
Meyer, Lilly, 230
Meyerbeer, Giacomo, 133, 186, 226, 231
Meyrinck, Gustav, 131
Michelangelo Buonarroti, 149, 261
Middelschulte, Wilhelm (German composer and organist in Chicago), 154, 166, 251, 253
Milner, Augustus (baritone in London), 263, 273, 274, 277, 278, 285, 292, 298
Molière (Poquelin),Jean Baptiste,73
Molina, Tirso de [ = Gabriel Tellez], 104
Molique, Bernhard, 251
Monico (restaurant in London), 85, 201, 265
Monteverdi, Claudio, 149
da Motta, José Vianna (pianist and composer), 245, 277, 382
Mottl, Felix, 75
Mozart, Wolfgang Amadeus, 54, 89, 103, 116, 129, 131, 132, 133, 136, 142, 161, 189, 196, 258, 259, 272, 276, 277, 278, 279, 282, 283, 287
Muck, Carl, 32
Muck, Frau, 32
Musset, Alfred de, 234

Nansen, Fridtjof, 15
Napoleon, 94, 100, 102, 105, 114, 149, 223, 233, 237
Nedbal, Oskar (viola player in the Bohemian string quartet, conductor and composer), 16
Newman, Ernest (writer on musical subjects and critic in London), 305
Newman, Robert (concert agent in London), 50, 53, 281, 282
Niehaus, Charles Henry (American sculptor), 79
Nikisch, Arthur, 56, 57, 214

Obrist, Aloys (conductor in Weimar), 116
Oehlenschläger, Adam, 54, 58
Ohnet, Georges, 266
Oppenheimer, Frau Jella, 241
Ortmans (violinist in London), 292

Pachmann, Vladimir v., 96
Paderewski, Ignaz Josef, 23

317

318

Verdi, Giuseppe, 102, 103, 129–
131, 144, 247, 261, 278, 285
Verne, Jules, 41, 266
Vernet, Horace, 234
Verrocchio, Andrea del, 149, 171
Villiers de l'Isle-Adam, Auguste
Count v., 202, 204, 247, 248, 274,
275
Vogeler, Heinrich (painter and
black and white artist), 58
Vollmoeller, Karl (author), 204,
206–208, 249

Wagner, Cosima, 139
Wagner, Richard, 75, 76, 83, 115,
117, 133, 136, 137, 146, 177, 188,
189, 202, 207, 217, 218, 221, 231,
244, 254, 267, 271, 279, 295, 305
Walter (American acquaintance of
Busoni's), 187, 191
Walton, William Turner (English
composer), 295
Wassermann, Jakob, 219, 220
Weber, Carl Maria v., 29, 52, 73,
96, 177, 239
Wedekind, Frank, 203, 204
Weigert, Marga (pupil of Busoni's),
67
Weingartner, Felix v., 56, 62, 177
Weiss, Giuseppe (Busoni's grand-
father in Triest), 95
Wells, Herbert George, 185–187,
190, 191, 194, 234, 242, 250, 252,
264
Wersbilowitsch, Alexander (violon-
cellist in St. Petersburg), 214
Wertheimstein, Frau v. (in
Vienna), 115
Wetzler, Hermann Hans (composer
and conductor), 211

Whistler, McNeill, 64, 72, 76
Whitman, Walt, 269
Wichert, Fritz (art historian), 221
Widemann, Wilhelm (sculptor in
Berlin), 113
Widor, Charles Marie, 206
Wijsman, Johan (pianist), 56
Wilde, Oscar, 226, 240
Wildenbruch, Ernest v., 225
Wilhelm II, German Emperor, 59
Witek, Anton (violinist), 181
Wolff, Johannes (violinist in Lon-
don), 32
Wolff, Werner (conductor), 306
Wolff & Sachs (concert agents in
Berlin), 112
Wolfrum, Philipp, 262
Wood, Sir Henry (conductor in
London), 29, 269, 271, 280, 283,
285, 287
Wrede (in Helsingfors), 211
Wright, Wilbur and Orville (avia-
tors), 148
Wüllner, Ludwig, 175

Young, Edward, 234
Ysaye, Eugène, 32, 41, 50, 51, 53,
56, 89, 106, 134, 209, 292

Zemlinsky, Alexander v. (con-
ductor and composer), 231
Ziehn, Bernhard (German music
theorist in Chicago), 154
Zilcher, Hermann, 263
Zille, Heinrich, 191
Zimmermann, Julius Heinrich
(music publisher), 181
Zimmermann, jr., 181
Zola, Émile, 64, 266